Patrick White's Theatre

SYDNEY STUDIES IN AUSTRALIAN LITERATURE

Robert Dixon, Series Editor

The **Sydney Studies in Australian Literature** series publishes original, peer-reviewed research in the field of Australian literary studies. It offers engagingly written evaluations of the nature and importance of Australian literature, and aims to reinvigorate its study both locally and internationally.

Alex Miller: The Ruin of Time
Robert Dixon

Australian Books and Authors in the American Marketplace 1840s–1940s
David Carter and Roger Osborne

Christina Stead and the Matter of America
Fiona Morrison

Colonial Australian Fiction: Character Types, Social Formations and the Colonial Economy
Ken Gelder and Rachael Weaver

Contemporary Australian Literature: A World Not Yet Dead
Nicholas Birns

Eliza Hamilton Dunlop: Writing from the Colonial Frontier
Ed. Anna Johnston and Elizabeth Webby

Elizabeth Harrower: Critical Essays
Ed. Elizabeth McMahon and Brigitta Olubas

Fallen Among Reformers: Miles Franklin, Modernity, and the New Woman
Janet Lee

The Fiction of Tim Winton: Earthed and Sacred
Lyn McCredden

Gail Jones: Word, Image, Ethics
Tanya Dalziell

Gerald Murnane: Another World in This One
Ed. Anthony Uhlmann

Patrick White's Theatre: Australian Modernism on Stage, 1960–2018
Denise Varney

Richard Flanagan: Critical Essays
Ed. Robert Dixon

Shirley Hazzard: New Critical Essays
Ed. Brigitta Olubas

Patrick White's Theatre

Australian Modernism on Stage, 1960–2018

Denise Varney

SYDNEY UNIVERSITY PRESS

First published by Sydney University Press
© Denise Varney 2021
© Sydney University Press 2021

Reproduction and communication for other purposes

Except as permitted under the Act, no part of this edition may be reproduced, stored in a retrieval system, or communicated in any form or by any means without prior written permission. All requests for reproduction or communication should be made to Sydney University Press at the address below:

Sydney University Press
Fisher Library F03
University of Sydney NSW 2006
Australia
sup.info@sydney.edu.au
sydneyuniversitypress.com.au

A catalogue record for this book is available from the National Library of Australia.

ISBN 9781743327555 paperback
ISBN 9781743327562 epub
ISBN 9781743327616 mobi
ISBN 9781743327609 pdf

Cover image: Geoff Revell and Jacquy Phillips as the Two Ladies in Patrick White's *The Ham Funeral*, directed by Adam Cook. Adelaide Festival of Arts, State Theatre Company of South Australia, 2012. Photo: Shane Reid. Cover design by Miguel Yamin

The Ham Funeral was famously rejected for the 1962 Adelaide Festival and first staged by the University of Adelaide instead in 1961. Fifty years later the 2012 Adelaide Festival coincided with Patrick White's centennial. Festival Director Paul Grabowsky made a special point of 'atoning' for the rejection in 1962 with this exuberant new production. Denise Varney saw it in Adelaide and it inspired the study that has led to this book.

Contents

List of Figures vii
Acknowledgements ix

Introduction 1
1 Reading the Early Plays: A Critical Reflection 21
2 Reading the Later Plays: Anticipating Revival 49
3 Expressionist Theatricality: *The Ham Funeral* 1961–2017 75
4 Staging Suburbia: *The Season at Sarsaparilla* 97
5 Performing Militant Virtue and Loneliness: *A Cheery Soul* 117
6 Country Retreat: *Night on Bald Mountain* and *Netherwood* 137
7 Sydney, Sexuality and Uranium: *Big Toys* and *Signal Driver* 159
8 Enchantment and Critique: *Shepherd on the Rocks* 175
Conclusion 185

Works Cited 189
Index 199

List of Figures

Figure 3.1 Dan Spielman, Lucy Taylor and Julie Forsyth as the Young Man, Anima/Girl and Alma Lusty in Patrick White's *The Ham Funeral*, directed by Michael Kantor, Malthouse Theatre, Melbourne, 2005. Photo: Lisa Tomasetti. — 87

Figure 3.2 Amanda Muggleton as Alma Lusty in Patrick White's *The Ham Funeral*, directed by Adam Cook. Adelaide Festival of Arts, State Theatre Company of South Australia, 2012. Photo: Shane Reid. — 91

Figure 3.3 Jacquy Phillips, Geoff Revell, Jonathan Mill and Jonathan Elsom as the Relatives in Patrick White's *The Ham Funeral*, directed by Adam Cook. Adelaide Festival of Arts, State Theatre Company of South Australia, 2012. Photo: Shane Reid. — 92

Figure 4.1 Emily Russell as Mavis, Peter Carroll as Girlie and Pamela Rabe as Nola in Patrick White's *The Season at Sarsaparilla*, directed by Benedict Andrews, Sydney Theatre Company, 2007. Photo: Tania Kelley © Tania Kelley/Copyright Agency, 2020. — 113

Figure 5.1 Robyn Nevin as Miss Docker in Patrick White's *A Cheery Soul*, directed by Neil Armfield, Sydney Theatre Company, 2000. Photo: Heidrun Lohr. — 131

Figure 5.2 Sarah Peirse as Miss Docker in Patrick White's *A Cheery Soul*, directed by Kip Williams, Sydney Theatre Company, 2018. Photo: Daniel Boud. — 136

Figure 6.1 Dale Ferguson's set for Patrick White's *Night on Bald Mountain*, directed by Matthew Lutton, Malthouse Theatre, Melbourne, 2014. Photo: Pia Johnson. — 147

Figure 6.2 Julie Forsyth as the Goat Keeper and Melita Jurisic as Miriam in Patrick White's *Night on Bald Mountain*, directed by Matthew Lutton, Malthouse Theatre, Melbourne, 2014. Photo: Pia Johnson. — 149

Acknowledgements

This book owes its existence to those who took part in the adventure of the making of modern Australian theatre. My thanks in particular are to the artists who made it happen. I never met Patrick White, whose theatre is the subject of this book, and first encountered his work through reading *Voss* at university. I went on to read and enjoy many of his novels, unaware that he wrote eight plays, and that they represented a corpus of work largely unknown to Australians. Benedict Andrews' remarkable revival of *The Season at Sarsaparilla* for the Sydney Theatre Company in 2007 opened my eyes. Here I acknowledge the vision and creative audacity of all who were involved in the production, which was the inspiration for this book.

Research for the book was made possible through the Australian Research Council Discovery Grant Scheme, which provided the essential funding to visit the archives – in libraries and theatre companies – across Australia. These textual, visual and media archives have provided the information on which this book has developed its historical and analytical study of Patrick White's theatre. I am deeply indebted to Dr Sandra D'Urso, who joined the project as a research assistant but quickly became a collaborator and co-author of articles and a book, *Governing Culture: Patrick White and the Adelaide Festival of Arts* published in 2018. Sandra contributed to sourcing and managing the mountains of archival material that we accumulated, the permissions and protocols, the theory and the analysis. She conducted many of the remarkable interviews with theatre directors, designers and performers, whose insights are the backbone of this study. Thank you to Sandra and those she interviewed especially Neil Armfield, Kate Fitzpatrick, Kate Gaul, Michael Kantor, David Marr, Jim Sharman, Brian Thomson and William Yang for your thoughts and recollections.

I am also deeply appreciative of colleagues, students and friends in English and Theatre Studies at the University of Melbourne, and in theatre departments across Australia, who encouraged the idea of a research project on Patrick White's theatre. I especially acknowledge and thank Peta Tait, Peter Eckersall, Rachel Fensham, Ken Gelder, Julian Meyrick, Ian Maxwell, Laura Ginters and Andrew Fuhrmann.

I am especially grateful to the many archivists and library staff, who have been unfailingly helpful and have generously provided invaluable assistance with the research. Here I make special mention of staff at the Barr Smith Library at the University of South Australia, and to the foresight of Beryl Sheasby of the Union Theatre, now retired, whose donated collection of archival materials is a national treasure. Thank you also to librarians at the National Library of Australia that holds the Patrick White Papers, the State Library of South Australia (State Records Section), the Adelaide Festival, and the Baillieu Library at the University of Melbourne.

Special thanks go to the specialist archivists and staff at the major theatre companies, who provided access to video and digital recordings and essential production materials and ephemera including photographs and programs. I want to give very special mention to Ms Judith Seeff at the Sydney Theatre Company, with whom I have worked for many years over several publications for this and other projects. A brilliant and meticulous archivist, Judith is dedicated to looking after and making available a precious collection of materials for Australian theatre researchers. She is also very kind to researchers. Many days after I had returned to Melbourne after a visit, Judith miraculously rescued a gold ring that had slipped off my finger and lodged itself in the white glove that I had worn in the archive. Thank you, Judith. Mark Pritchard at the Malthouse Theatre Melbourne is another hero who cares about the vital access to knowledge that researchers gain from sitting in front of a screen stopping and starting performance recordings and taking notes. Thank you, Mark, for your support and encouragement.

Thank you to the production photographers – Pia Johnson, Daniel Boud, Tania Kelley, Heidrun Lohr, Shane Reid, Lisa Tomasetti – who have generously given permission for the use of their photographs and to the many performers who gave their permission to publish their images. It was lovely to speak to Jacquy Phillips (*Netherwood, The Ham Funeral*) about the book.

I especially thank Robert Dixon and Susan Murray at Sydney University Press for their continuing support and understanding as the date for publication was extended several times. I would also like to thank the team at SUP, especially Denise O'Dea and Nathan Grice. To Haydie Gooder, thank you, for your impeccable editing during the COVID-19 lockdown in challenging working from home conditions. At the University of Melbourne, this publication was greatly assisted by the Faculty of Arts Internal Grant Scheme and a School of Culture and Communication Publication Subsidy, for which I am grateful.

Finally, I thank my colleagues in the Australia Centre at the University of Melbourne, particularly Ken Gelder, Alexis Wright and Amanda Morris for their support and encouragement. And to my family and friends.

Introduction

This book is a critical study of Patrick White's plays and their theatrical productions between 1961 and 2018. Recent revivals of the 1960s plays – *The Ham Funeral*, *A Cheery Soul*, *The Season at Sarsaparilla* and *Night on Bald Mountain* – indicate that artists, critics and spectators find White's play texts open to contemporary interpretation. These reinterpretations capture White's theatrical imagination and social commentary as never before, taking advantage of developments in theatre technology and performance practice. The 1970s and '80s plays – *Big Toys*, *Signal Driver*, *Netherwood* and *Shepherd on the Rocks* – are, however, long overdue for revival in a theatrical landscape now better suited to their experimental vision.

Over sixty years of productions of White's plays, an archive of photographs, letters and other contemporaneous documents (such as newspaper reviews) offer unprecedented opportunities to track the historical trajectory of White's theatre and its once controversial and rejected images of modern Australia. The book's focus is therefore the theatrical productions of White's eight plays over a sixty-year period, rather than a genealogy of the playwright's influences, although these are referred to when instructive. It is principally a study of the theatrical practices motivated by a body of work that is primarily concerned with Australian society and culture. This focus will drive the analysis of the textual and thematic, but also the scenographic and aural elements of White's theatre, in other words, how Australian modernism looks and sounds on stage.

The historical span of the productions also allows for a simultaneous tracking of the major shifts in theatre practice over time, for example, from text and playwright-driven drama to contemporary collaborative, multimodal performance. The concept of the performed text and the understanding that plays must be performed to be fully experienced is now well accepted in Theatre Studies. As this book argues, the syncretic complexity of linguistic, aural, corporeal, visual and scenic systems, evident in the extent and detail of White's extra-dialogic commentary, contributes to the unique theatricality of his theatre. The later plays in particular accorded a higher status to theatricality than to narrative and plot, much to the exasperation of plot-centred critics. Theatricality is therefore central for renewed recognition of Patrick White's contribution to Australian theatre.

In offering a critical study of White's theatre, the book will nevertheless deal with the narrative of White the playwright. One of the earliest narratives was that White was a novelist who merely dabbled in playwriting – lured into, and distracted from, important literary work by the call of theatre. As David Marr notes, friends, acquaintances and literary figures, such as White's New York publisher Ben Huebsch, tried to save him from "wasting" his talents in "other fields".[1] Critics such as Harry Kippax offered a version of this narrative: in his review of the publication of the first four plays, he refers to White "The novelist as dramatist".[2] Yet Marr, and those who worked with White in the theatre, especially Jim Sharman and Neil Armfield, speak of White's lifelong experiments with playwriting beginning at school.[3] We might speak therefore of the playwright who turned to the novel and returned to theatre.

Another early narrative about White the playwright was that he was something of a local oddity. Australian theatre was hardly welcoming of a playwright whose plays had none of the sentiment and charm of Ray Lawler's work. The *Summer of the Seventeenth Doll*, for example – first staged to immediate acclaim in 1955, and said to have launched a new school of Australian playwriting styled "backyard realism" – featured the lives of the urban poor through a conventional three-act dramatic structure.[4] Other notable proponents of "the *Doll* school"[5] included Richard Beynon's drama about immigrant workers in *The Shifting Heart*, first performed in 1957, and Alan Seymour's critique of military nationalism in *The One Day of the Year*, first performed in an amateur production in Adelaide in 1960.

White's early plays stood outside the *Doll* school in so far as they took an anti-realist approach to plot and character, and featured non-naturalist staging in heightened, often satirical, representations of Australian place, language, and social class. They challenged public taste with grotesque funerals, a foetus in a rubbish bin, bitches in season, meddling do-gooders, and bucking goats. Referring to a minor scene in *The Ham Funeral*, Australian Elizabethan Theatre Trust (the Trust) Executive Director Neil Hutchison (taking White's bait) declared: "As for the abortion in the dust bin … Really, words fail me".[6] The context for reception of Australian drama in the early 1960s was a complex mix of desire to advance Australian playwriting (with subsidies from the Trust) and caution about the form

---

1 David Marr, *Patrick White: A Life* (Milsons Point: Vintage Books,1992), 406.
2 Harry Kippax, "The Novelist as Dramatist", *Sydney Morning Herald*, 23 October 1965, 19.
3 Marr, David. "White's London". In *Patrick White Beyond the Grave*, ed Ian Henderson and Anouk Lang. (London: Anthem Press, 2015), 69.
4 John McCallum, *Belonging: Australian Playwriting in the Twentieth Century* (Sydney: Currency Press, 2009), 83.
5 McCallum, *Belonging*.
6 Neil Hutchison to Charles Wicks, 15 April 1961, State Records of South Australia 1962, Adelaide Festival Correspondence 1959–62, GRG 153/36/1.

it would take and the Australia it would represent. Patrick White's plays upped the ante on that anxiety by refusing to conform to the *Doll* school. Two decades later, Brian Kiernan reflected that White's early plays "constituted a watershed between the conventionally realistic structures of *The Summer of the Seventeenth Doll* and its many successors and the experiments of the *new* wave of playwrights seeking their own appropriate, and absurdist, forms in the later 1960s, or early 1970s".[7] A key element in understanding the tenor of White's theatre was that in avoiding the *Doll* school, he was a singular playwright, whereas the new wave writers formed a collective that was part of the social and cultural currents that gave it momentum.[8] As Julian Meyrick puts it, White's four 1960s plays constituted, "an abruptly appearing modernist *oeuvre*"[9] that stood out as odd and strange. Although championed by a small cohort of literary and cultural figures, among them Geoffrey Dutton, Max Harris and Harry Medlin, the prevailing view was that White's plays were unsuitable for public performance culminating in the infamous rejection of *The Ham Funeral* and *Night on Bald Mountain* for the 1962 and 1964 Adelaide Festivals. The governors of the Adelaide Festival flinched at White's apparent disregard for good taste as well as his rejection of the conventions of realism and naturalism.[10] London producers doubted their commercial viability. It was not until directors Jim Sharman and Neil Armfield, designers such as Brian Thomson and Wendy Dickson and performers such as Robyn Nevin embraced White's theatre that it began to play an important part in a modern Australian theatre community. The point here is not to argue that the early plays should have had a better reception, but that rejection went too far.

In the 1960s, the premieres of the early plays took place at either the Theatre Guild at the University of Adelaide or the Union Theatre Repertory Company at the University of Melbourne. Imported theatrical modernism had made its appearance at small, leftist and university theatres from the 1940s,[11] but as Meyrick points out, university audiences were not uncritical of White's new plays. Audiences were critical of *A Cheery Soul* and *Night on Bald Mountain* with both running at a loss.[12] As this book shows, the early plays went on to meet far more receptive audiences in the coming decades, as theatre artists unmoored themselves from naturalism and realism.

---

7   Brian Kiernan, "From The Ham Funeral to Signal Driver: Patrick White on Stage", *Sydney Morning Herald*, 6 March 1982, 46.
8   Denise Varney, *Radical Visions 1968–2008: The Impact of the Sixties on Australian Drama* (Amsterdam & New York: Rodopi, 2011), 270.
9   Julian Meyrick, "Modernist Drama Decried: Patrick White, Spoiled Identity", *Australasian Drama Studies* 71 (October 2017): 44.
10 Denise Varney and Sandra D'Urso. *Australian Theatre, Modernism and Patrick White: Governing Culture.* (London: Anthem Books, 2018), 51–54.
11 AusStage data base lists productions or readings of plays by Samuel Beckett, Bertolt Brecht, George Bernard Shaw, Thornton Wilder and Tennessee Williams, and later Eugene Ionesco, Arthur Miller and Harold Pinter. https://www.ausstage.edu.au/pages/browse/
12 Meyrick, "Modernist Drama Decried".

The turning point occurred in the 1970s with revivals of *The Season at Sarsaparilla* and *A Cheery Soul* directed to great acclaim by Jim Sharman. Even then, the conservative tabloid press mounted a campaign asking of the characters in these plays: "could this really be us?"[13] The volume and quality of the subsequent revivals and adaptations indicates that White should not to be considered for his novels alone, or as a novelist dabbling in the *demi-monde* of theatre, but a creative force who brought about change in the possibilities for theatre artists. They attracted new theatre audiences to see a distinctive mode of representing Australian culture and society. The question of the distinctiveness is explored in the chapters that follow.

Critical Literature and Patrick White's Drama

Academic essays on Patrick White's theatre appeared as early as 1964 when the four early plays were published in a volume by Eyre and Spottiswoode, London (later republished by Currency Press in 1985).[14] Keith Macartney and Robert Brissenden both published early pieces in the literary magazine *Meanjin Quarterly*. The essays begin by acknowledging White's unquestionable reputation as contemporary Australia's most distinguished novelist with Macartney suggesting theatre audiences would find much to admire in White's plays, especially his "acute ear for the tone and idioms of Australian lower-middle class speech". The plays also presented a microcosm of something larger with "more enduring and universal implications".[15] But taking *A Cheery Soul* as his example, Macartney conceded the potential for a "humorously edged drama" but finds limitations in the episodic structure and the playwright's ambivalence towards Miss Docker, the anti-heroine.[16] The four plays are anti-naturalist (which Macartney is prepared to accept), but "marred" by stylisation, chorus-like commentary, too many scenic changes and lapses in authenticity. These flaws are attributed to those of a "novelist turned dramatist" rather than, for instance, the struggle to represent the social, emotional, and philosophical complexities of Australian culture beyond backyard realism.[17]

From a 1960s vantage point, Robert Brissenden predicted that White would prove to be Australia's first substantial playwright who "had to develop new ways" to represent the nation as theatre.[18] For the moment he finds the early plays "awkwardly constructed and theatrically unconvincing" while conceding they are

---

13 Institutional resistance to Patrick White's non-realist theatre included the Adelaide Festival of Arts, the Australian Elizabethan Theatre Trust, and the Drama Department of the Australian Broadcasting Commission. See Varney and D'Urso, *Australian Theatre*. See also Meyrick, "Modernist Drama Decried". The quote is from Norman Kessel, "Could this really be Us", *The Sun*, 15 May 1963.
14 Patrick White, *Four Plays*. (London: Eyre and Spottiswoode, 1965).
15 Keith Macartney, "Patrick White's Four Plays", *Meanjin Quarterly* 24, no. 4 (December 1965): 528.
16 Keith Macartney, "Patrick White's 'A Cheery Soul'", *Meanjin Quarterly* 23, no. 3 (March 1964): 93.
17 Macartney, "Patrick White's Four Plays", 530.

"difficult, uncomfortable pieces of work in some ways, both in subject matter and technique".[19] He qualifies his critique by stating that these difficulties might be signs of "vitality" while noting the success of productions of *The Ham Funeral* and *The Season at Sarsaparilla*.

Another essay appearing at the time was by musician and critic Roger Covell, who expressed a sense of "pure elation" to discover that Patrick White, the novelist, was a playwright after all, noting the historically unprecedented scale of production of a single Australian playwright over a condensed four-year period.[20] He noted that, "The principal reason his plays disconcert many people is that they are not orderly structures but mix their conversation as freely as if they were a variety bill".[21] Covell foresaw that the mixture of vaudevillian review sketches and expressionism, combined with a modernism displayed by writers such as Auden, Isherwood and Brecht, would have greater acceptance over time. Recognition of the historic importance of White's plays in the 1960s speaks to the absence up to that point of a modern Australian playwright of the stature of T.S. Eliot, George Bernard Shaw, Samuel Beckett, Arthur Miller or Tennessee Williams.

The first monograph on Patrick White's theatre appeared in the early 1970s, ten years after these initial reviews, in which Jessie Dyce addressed the first four plays. Fourteen years on May-Brit Akerholt's book followed and included White's later plays with a short appendix on *Shepherd on the Rocks*.[22] Dyce argues that the expressionist and symbolist elements of the written texts add anti-mimetic elements that "dispense with the illusion that the theatrical use of time, place, and action bears a constant relationship with everyday reality".[23] Elinor Fuchs would later refer to this practice as one in which theatricalist texts mix ontological worlds such as the everyday with "commensurate" worlds of magic, dreams, the supernatural and the metaphysical, to create complex effects.[24] The modernist playwright, according to Dyce, wants the "freedom to transcend" the proscenium arch and delve into themes to do with the spirit, the soul and the psyche.[25] Where Dyce is interested in understanding the composition of theatricalist dramaturgy, Peter Fitzpatrick is more in agreement with Brissenden. In *After 'The Doll': Australian Drama Since 1955*, he recognises White's special contribution to Australian theatre describing it as "distinctive, both in its eclecticism and its idiosyncrasy" but finds the anti-realist aesthetic incoherent and born of a "disregard

---

18   R.F. Brissenden, "The Plays of Patrick White", *Meanjin Quarterly* 23, no. 3 (September 1964): 244.
19   Brissenden, "The Plays of Patrick White", 243.
20   Roger Covell, "Patrick White's Plays", *Quadrant* 8, no. 1 (April–May 1964): 7.
21   Covell, "Patrick White's Plays".
22   J.R. Dyce, *Patrick White as Playwright* (St Lucia: University of Queensland Press, 1974); May-Brit Akerholt, *Patrick White* (Amsterdam: Rodopi Press, 1988).
23   Dyce, *Patrick White*, 5.
24   Elinor Fuchs, "Clown Shows: Anti-Theatricalist Theatricalism in Four Twentieth-Century Plays", *Modern Drama* 44, no. 3 (Fall 2001): 338.
25   Dyce, *Patrick White*, 6.

for consistency of form" and of audience expectations.[26] A decade later, Akerholt describes White's technique as innovative in terms of fostering "new trends in the development of contemporary theatre" towards a greater focus on the inner world of "the Australian consciousness and psyche".[27] Akerholt's implicit recognition of White's consciously modernist rejection of stage naturalism also finds the use of irony and satire as an expression of an ambivalent love–hate representation of Australia and Australians.

White's Formative Period

Patrick White was born in London in 1912 to wealthy Australian parents of British descent. The family lived in houses and properties in London, Sydney and New South Wales. White was educated in the English boarding school tradition and later at Kings College Cambridge, where he studied modern languages. After graduating in 1935 he lived in London, served with the British Army in Egypt, stayed on in Cairo with his partner Manoly Lascaris, before returning to London and then Australia in 1948. While in Europe, he kept in touch with Australia for school holidays, as a jackaroo on a New South Wales property and through lengthy visits to Sydney as an adult. This dual national background was formative of White's cultural education and experience, and his identity. In an interview in Sydney in 1973, having been awarded the Nobel Prize for Literature, White admitted to David Marr: "I feel what I am, I don't feel particularly Australian. I live here and work here. A Londoner is what I think I am at heart but my blood is Australian and that's what gets me going".[28] The apparent separation of heart and blood seems affected, but if heart means love and blood a life force then it makes sense. As a Londoner, White went to the theatre and as Marr records, "began to write plays",[29] but with the exception of *The Ham Funeral*, all his later plays are written and set in Australia, where he "got going".

The question of White's early theatre influences resides in the interwar years in London where he wrote an unknown number of plays, most of which are lost. Marr records that "Miracle", set in the East End, "was perhaps his first" play and was followed by titles such as "Marriages are Made in Hell" and "It is a Pity She is Blind", among others.[30] Other early plays include: *Bread and Butter Women*, a comedy written while at Cambridge in the early 1930s, *School for Friends*, a one-act social satire entered anonymously in a competition in Sydney in 1937, and *Return to Abyssinia*, a three-act play about the Spanish Civil War, which was staged at

---

26   Peter Fitzpatrick, *After 'The Doll': Australian Drama Since 1955* (Melbourne: Edward Arnold, 1979), 49–50.
27   Akerholt, *Patrick White*, 3.
28   Marr, "White's London", 67.
29   Marr, "White's London", 69.
30   Marr, "White's London", 70.

Introduction

Bolton's Theatre Club in London in 1947 to good reviews.[31] Another play, *Peter Plover's Party*, was a sketch based on White's London neighbour, journalist Godfrey Winn.[32] Marr along with White's later theatre directors including Jim Sharman attest to White's taste for comedy review and satire, of which there was plenty to see in London.[33] White's early plays, based on people, situations, events and places known to the playwright, and whose social dimensions and pretences he exaggerated for theatrical purposes, bear out practices that continued throughout his later career. Characters such as Alma Lusty, Girlie Pogson, and Miss Docker, and situations satirised in *Netherwood* and *Shepherd on the Rocks*, drew on people and events White had met or observed. Elements such as social commentary, the performativity of the everyday and physicalised representations of social status would characterise the theatre that White went on to create. The early plays indicate a lifelong interest in dramatic writing and the theatre, and rehearsed themes and styles for the plays that followed. He was not a novelist dabbling in theatre but a playwright who developed his craft over many formative years.

The influence of English literary drama in the interwar years was also important in terms of language and style. The period was dominated by figures such as Christopher Isherwood, W.H. Auden, T.S. Eliot and Bernard Shaw. According to Marr, White also saw examples of European theatrical modernism in productions of Strindberg and Wedekind's expressionist plays.[34] Reflecting on theatre in the London metropole in the 1930s, Claire Warden's essay on a relatively unknown play by Ewan MacColl offers an indicative view of the circulation of expressionist influences that may have influenced *The Ham Funeral*.[35] MacColl's *The Other Animals* (1948) offers an English adaptation of expressionist interest in the dual psyche of a prominent single character, who drives the dramatic narrative. Other minor characters represent the social positions and attitudes with which the main character wrestles. The play features the character Hanau/Robert, played by two actors, in which Robert is the alter ego, the locus of consciousness and the rebellious other of Hanau. The similarity with *The Ham Funeral* is striking. In White's play, the divided subjectivity of the Young Man and the Girl concentrate attention on the formation of the modern artist as a subject who expresses a particular vision of the world and who is attentive to its metaphysics. It is not known if White saw MacColl's play, but the example suggests the circulation of expressionist tropes in English theatre at the time that may have been influential when he attempted a three-act play about an artist in the early postwar years in London.

---

31 Marr, *Patrick White: A Life*, 249. See also Fitzpatrick, *After 'The Doll'*, 49.
32 For fragments of information on *Bread and Butter Woman* see Marr, *Patrick White: A Life*, n. 667. See also Laura Ginters, "Before the Ham Funeral: 'The Young Man Appears' – John Tasker Returns Home", *Australasian Drama Studies* 71 (October 2017): 15.
33 Marr, "White's London", 70. Jim Sharman, Interview with Sandra D'Urso, 2017.
34 Marr, "White's London", 70.
35 Claire Altree Warden, "The Shadows and the Rush of Light: Ewan MacColl and Expressionist Drama" *New Theatre Quarterly* 23, no. 4, (2007): 317–25.

Towards Australian Theatrical Modernism

To locate Patrick White's theatre within an emergent Australian theatrical modernism is not to impose an imported regime of aesthetics and periodisation on the plays themselves or on the nation's theatre and drama. The key historical interest, explained in more detail over the next few pages, is to understand White's *theatricalisation* of local, regional and provincial modernism as it assembles and reveals itself in relation to the national landscape, while drawing on and adapting theatrical models circulating within "global" and "planetary" modernisms.[36] The modernist framework is used throughout this book to explore the emergence of local, experimental, socially critical, non-naturalist theatre in Australia. The link between artistic experimentation and social critique relates to debates about aesthetics and politics staged by Brecht, Benjamin and Adorno in the first half of the twentieth century, a period in which Cambridge-educated, German language student Patrick White, spent time in the cultural flows of intellectual and theatrical Europe. Whether he was aware of these debates or not, White's theatre evokes aesthetics and politics – not in a party-political way, although that became increasingly important in his later years. Rather, the politics appear as an ideological stance on capitalist materialism and postwar industrialisation for its effects on human relationships and aspirations. As already indicated, with the exception of *The Ham Funeral*, which was written in London in 1947 and set in the East End after the Great War, White's seven later plays are located within and respond to the conditions of industrial, economic and technological modernity in the Australia context. The connection between modernist theatre and modernity is crucial here. If modernity is industrialisation and capitalism, and is promiscuous about its affiliations with liberal democracy and authoritarianism, modernist drama, or as Elin Diamond puts it "modernity's drama", exposes its effects on human subjects and the environment.[37]

Moreover, White's theatre is concerned with character types in different urban and rural spaces that can be viewed on stage as "containers of the present", to borrow Elinor Fuchs and Una Chaudhuri's phrase for the way modern drama represents everyday habitats that are rich in information about human life in developed economies.[38] In the Sarsaparilla plays, for example, Sarsaparilla is a local place in which provincial life is being overtaken by suburbia, itself influenced by the consumerism of global modernity. Characters embody dialogic positions; the stage is a container for the conflicts that run through and animate Australian life in the second half of the

---

36   Susan Stanford Friedman, *Planetary Modernisms: Provocations of Modernity Across Time* (New York: Columbia Press, 2015).
37   Elin Diamond, "Modern Drama/Modernity's Drama", *Modern Drama* 44, no. 1 (Spring 2001): 3–15.
38   Elinor Fuchs and Una Chaudhuri, eds., *Land/Scape/Theater* (Ann Arbor: University of Michigan Press, 2002), 13–14.

twentieth century. The presence of conflict and contradiction marks White's modernist theatre as political before they became increasingly anti-development.

The nexus between aesthetics and social critique continues into new productions of White's plays for the twenty-first century where revivals extend the plays' aesthetic and critical relationship (this same nexus of aesthetics and critique) to Australian modernity up to the present. As Fredric Jameson argues, aesthetic modernism can describe a "corpus" of texts; here I would add theatrical productions, for elaborating and reconstructing the "various ideologies of modernity".[39]

There are precedents in the history of Australian theatre for the links between experimentation with form and historical or political events to be understood within a modernist framework. A small number of socially progressive, semi-professional and amateur ensembles such as Louis and Hilda Esson's Pioneer Players, as well as the New Theatre movement, were nationalist and socialist respectively, while experimenting with modernism as a style, and modern drama as a literary genre. Veronica Kelly's research on the Dutch-Australian World War One veteran, Sydney Tomholt, identifies the playwright as a forerunner for Patrick White. She argues that Tomholt is a significant Australian modernist playwright, whose "heightened and poetic non-naturalism" was overwhelmed by the dominance of naturalism in Australian theatre in the 1930s.[40] Of interest is her account of how Tomholt's anti- naturalism was driven by the imperative to memorialise the emotional impact of the Great War on the Australian psyche. The unassimilable loss of life, and its effects on Australian culture, seemed to call for something other than the repetition of the unity and coherence of given forms of realism and naturalism. The parallel with Patrick White is arresting. Where Tomholt responds to the Australian experience of the Great War, Patrick White, who had returned to London in 1947 after serving in Egypt in the war, sits down to write a play. There is a bomb site next door, and *The Ham Funeral* emerges, in White's words, amidst "the despair and confusion" of the early years after World War Two.[41] In this view, the play's grotesque mordant humour, from the foetus in the dust bin to the conduct of the ham funeral, expresses something of the callous disregard for life that is war. Once again, realism as a form was considered inadequate to the task of expressing the effects on consciousness of historical and epoch-changing events.

Where realism as a form can be an effective mirror of social life and expose the workings of class, gender and race, the expression of interiority, inarticulate states of consciousness as well as deep emotion, call for more poetic forms of expression. Martin Esslin, among others, linked the horror of World War Two to the emergence

---

39 Fredric Jameson, *A Singular Modernity* (London: Verso, 2002), 212.
40 Veronica Kelly, "Spatialialising the Ghosts of Anzac in the Plays of Sydney Tomholt: The Absent Soldier and the War Memorial", *Australian Literary Studies* 23, no. 1 (2007): 19.
41 Patrick White, "Author's Note on THE HAM FUNERAL", World Premiere Season at Union Hall (Adelaide University Theatre Guild, 15–25 November 1961), theatre program, Patrick White Collection, Series 1477, Barr Smith Library, University of Adelaide.

of the Theatre of the Absurd. In a Samuel Beckett or Eugène Ionesco play, he wrote, it is "unclear whether the action is meant to represent a dream world of nightmares or real happenings". But this ontological uncertainty was expressive of "the erosion" of a "fixed and self-evident framework of generally accepted values".[42] For *The Ham Funeral*, White writes a tragi-farce in two acts with expressionist, surrealist and vaudeville elements remixed for the postwar period. It is unclear if characters are "real" world or embodiments of the dreams of a young poet, fearful of engaging with the world. Kelly understood modernist form entwined with historical event was critical to the analysis of Tomholt's modernist plays including *The Last Post* in the 1936. The critical neglect of Tomholt's pioneering modernist theatre, and the later rejections of Patrick White's early plays are not related to their lack of aesthetic worth but to the untimely position they occupied in cultures of denial about the erosion of fixed and abiding values.

Modernism also encompasses the feminist critique of patriarchy. Rachel Fensham's work on writer and director Jenny Kemp argues that Kemp represents a feminist modernism, amidst the overall neglect within Australian theatre history of the contribution of women playwrights to modern interpretations of female lives, and feminist perspectives on modern society. Referring to the broader field of Australian theatre and the cultural dominance of realist drama, she notes it is as if "the intellectual and creative ferment of the early twentieth century modern era in Europe and America passed Australian theatre".[43] Female playwrights and directors such as Jenny Kemp, are prominent in developing an "implicit critique" of realism by utilising "a modernist aesthetics of 'formally self-conscious, experimental, anti-mimetic features'".[44] For Richard Murphet, late modernism describes a category for distinguishing artists who became active under the influence of the Cold War and the politics of the 1960s that took the form of an ethos and sensibility that resisted literary drama and realism in favour of formal experimentation.[45] Murphet applies the category to a small cohort of avant-garde artists, including Kemp, whose writing and directing develop over two decades from the late 1960s into the twenty-first century.

In the last decade, John McCallum's reflections on Patrick White's theatre locate his corpus within a modernist framework of innovation and experimentation but also one that acknowledges the importance of the immaterial and the spiritual despite the overriding secular logic of modernity. White's theatricalist stagings of the "transcendent" resonate with literary accounts of White's metaphysics in which the sacred or the sublime elude language but are articulated as presence or experience.[46] Arguably, White's tendency towards the spiritual and the imaginary

---

42 Martin Esslin, "The Theatre of the Absurd", *The Tulane Drama Review* 4, no. 4 (May 1960): 6.
43 Rachel Fensham, "Modernity and the White Imaginary in Australian Feminist Theatre", *Hecate* 29, no. 1 (2003): 8.
44 Fensham, "Modernity and the White Imaginary", 8.
45 Richard Murphet, *Acts of Resistance in Late Modernist Theatre: Writing and Directing in Contemporary Theatre Practice* (Amsterdam: Brill, 2019).

participates in an anti-secular, anti-rational modernist impulse akin to the Artaudian idea of alchemical theatre and is to be found especially in *Night on Bald Mountain*, inspired by Modest Mussorgsky's composition of the same name, and in *Signal Driver* and *Shepherd on the Rocks*. Although Artaud wrote in and for a different cultural and stylistic context, this book will draw on the concept of theatre and alchemy to understand White's linking of uranium mining, for example, with cosmic chaos.[47]

The modernist aesthetics of White's later plays are immersed in the historical shift from the playwright to the director and demonstrate a greater emphasis on theatricality and performativity. Yet it is also the case, as the analysis will show, that these elements are present in White's plays from the beginning. This is evident in the volume of "extra-dialogic" commentary in the texts through which White gives expression to the imagery and environments that contribute to the overall theatrical world.[48] Dialogue and extra-dialogical effects work together, without being co-dependently restrictive on future interpretations. Modernist theatricality refines the excesses of tragedy, baroque artifice and melodrama without submitting to realism's straightjacket or the rule of strict plausibility about plot. Where Roland Barthes refers to theatricality in the formulation "theatre-minus-text", indicating the "density of signs and sensations" including gesture, tone, distance, substance and light "which submerges the text beneath the profusion of its external language", there is scope to consider White's modernist theatricality as theatre-plus-text.[49]

Reflecting on the recent scholarly recognition of White as a theatrical modernist, David O'Donnell notes that his work paved the way for "a broad acceptance" of later modernists beginning with the New Wave in the late 1960s.[50] Several further essays on White's theatrical modernism appear in a recent Special Issue of *Australasian Drama Studies* 2017.[51]

Having aligned Patrick White's modernist theatre with contemporary, experimental and critically engaged Australian theatre, and traced its roots to twentieth-century Europe, the colonial legacy of Australian modernity to which it is attached, comes into view. Postcolonial resistance to the colonial era introduction of

---

46 McCallum, *Belonging*, 147.
47 Antonin Artaud, *The Theatre and Its Double*, trans. Mary Caroline Richards (New York: Grove Press, 1958), 51–52.
48 Elaine Aston and George Savona, *Theatre as a Sign-System* (London: Routledge, 1991), 125.
49 Roland Barthes, *Critical Essays*, trans. Richard Howard (Evanston, IL: Northwestern University Press, 1972), 26.
50 David O'Donnell, "Staging Modernity in the 'New Oceania': Modernism in Australian, New Zealand and Pacific Islands Theatre", in *The Modernist World*, eds. Allana Lindgren and Stephen Ross (London: Routledge, 2015), 283–84. The New Wave refers to the period from the late 1960s through to 1970s in which "a new generation of practitioners" experimented with form and style to lay the foundations of Australian drama. See Katharine Brisbane, *Not Wrong – Just Different: Observations on the Rise of Contemporary Australian Theatre*, (Sydney: Currency Press, 2005), 29.
51 *Australasian Drama Studies* "Special Issue, Patrick White and Australian Theatrical Modernism" 71, no. 2 (2017).

European theatre and drama in Asia and Australia, Africa and the Latin Americas has been the focus of late twentieth-century studies of the cultural impact of colonialism on Indigenous cultures. Helen Gilbert and Joanne Tompkins argued in a ground-breaking study over twenty-five years ago that theatre could act as a strategy of resistance to colonial erasure of Indigenous culture by attending to "the reclamation of, for example, pre-contact forms of performance, ritual, song, music, language, history".[52] They continue: "story-telling facilitates the foregrounding of indigenous cultures in spite of imperial attempts to eradicate that which was not European and ostensibly civilised and controllable".[53] Patrick White's theatre is broadly postcolonial in so far as it responds to or resists aspects of Australian culture that are the product of British imperialism. The character Hugo Sword, the English literature professor in *Night on Bald Mountain* is a critical representation of the imperialist type – self-regarding, entitled and cruel. On the other hand, White's theatre does not engage with the regeneration of traditional practices or interrogate the hegemony of white Australia, which it reproduces. There is a militant localism in his theatre's representation of a distinctively critical view of Australian life but it arguably continues the project of European modernism in its local and provincial setting.

White's modernism is local in a "modern globalised world".[54] It belongs to that which Douglas Mao and Rebecca L. Walkowitz articulate as a three-way expansion of the temporal, spatial and social boundaries of European modernism. On this model, Asia and Australia, for instance, come into view as sites that reveal "modernism as a global practice".[55] The effect is that the older vertical distinction between high modernism, as an aesthetic movement by and for social elites, as opposed to popular or low culture, practised by the masses, has been disrupted by the greater diversity of late twentieth-century writers and the postmodern levelling of cultural hierarchies. Stephen Ross' and Allana Lindgren's edited volume on the modernist world surveys the broad field of performing and visual arts and calls for a rethinking of existing conceptual frameworks to think about "plural modernisms globally" in "planetary terms".[56] For Julian Murphet the plural form, modernisms, is marked by an "unevenness" expressed in uneven global distributions of technological and market advance, which is then mirrored through other forms of geographic inequality.[57]

Reflecting on the expanded use of modernism as a critical framework in Theatre Studies, Penny Farfan writes that "attention to modernism's local, material,

---

52 Helen Gilbert and Joanne Tompkins, *Post-Colonial Drama: Theory, Practice, Politics* (London: Routledge, 1996), 294.
53 Gilbert and Tompkins, *Post-Colonial Drama*, 294.
54 Friedman, *Planetary Modernisms*, 38.
55 Douglas Mao and Rebecca L. Walkowitz, "The New Modernist Studies", *PMLA* 123, no. 3 (2008): 738.
56 Stephen Ross and Allana Lindgren, "Introduction", in *The Modernist World*, eds. Allana Lindgren and Stephen Ross (London: Routledge, 2015), 2, 12.
57 Julian Murphet, "Introduction: On the Market and Uneven Development", *Affirmations of the Modern* 1, no. 1 (2013): 12.

corporeal, lexical, and interactive dimensions in performance" helps us understand the critical relationship between "theatre and modernity".[58] Applied to Australia, modernism offers a broad framework for understanding White's plays in terms of their critical engagement with Australian modernity. The modernist frame helps to identify what was new and innovative about White's plays and how they synthesised and reflected Australian culture and society in the throes of modernity. Theatrical modernism, like other modernisms, is suspended between a formal aesthetic movement and a response to particular social, cultural, political and technological changes. This book is interested in what White's formal innovation, disruption of convention, rejection of tradition, boundary breaking and remaking help us say, do, feel and reflect when considering Australian modernity. It hopes to complement New Wave, postcolonial, intercultural, Indigenous, and postmodern studies of Australian theatre to make the case that White's theatre can be examined in terms of the unresolved issues confronting the nation's history and present.

Close Readings of Dramatic Texts

Close readings of dramatic texts are greatly enhanced by theatre and performance theory, especially around the concept of dramaturgy derived from the Greek concepts of *dramatourgia* (to write a text in dramatic form), and *dramatopoia*, (dramatic composition).[59] Contemporary understandings of the term have moved beyond text-based drama and its theatrical performance to account for postdramatic theatre, a theatre that Hans-Thies Lehmann originally theorised as "a theatre that feels bound to operate beyond drama, as a time 'after' the authority of the dramatic paradigm in theatre."[60] Leaving aside the debate about whether dramatic theatre is "weakened and exhausted"[61] (it clearly is not), dramaturgy is adaptable to offering accounts of dramatic and postdramatic theatre including forms such as dance, media, chorus, performance art and so on. Dramaturgy can describe how text- and non-text-based performances address, critique and disrupt social and cultural identities, states of being and belonging, and affects such as hate and shame.[62] Describing textual interpretations of the concept, Mary Luckhurst writes,

> One of the two common senses of *dramaturgy* relates to the internal structures of a play-text and is concerned with the arrangement of formal elements by the

---

58 Penny Farfan, "Editorial Comment: 'Modernism'", *Theatre Journal* 65, no. 4 (December 2013): xiii.
59 Mary Luckhurst, *Dramaturgy: A Revolution* (Cambridge: Cambridge University Press, 2005), 5.
60 Hans-Thies Lehmann, *Postdramatic Theatre*, trans. Karen Jürs-Munby (London: Routledge, 2006), 27.
61 Lehmann, *Postdramatic Theatre*, 27.
62 See Peter Eckersall, Helena Grehan and Edward Scheer, *New Media Dramaturgy: Performance, Media and New Materialism* (London: Palgrave Macmillan, 2017).

playwright – plot, construction of narrative, character, time frame and stage action. Conversely, dramaturgy can also refer to external elements relating to staging, the overall artistic concept behind the staging, the politics of performance, and the calculated manipulation of audience response (hence the associations with deceit).[63]

Dramaturgy in contemporary usage includes the idea of making, doing, presenting or choreographing the elements of performance including bodies, movement, space, sound and multimedia. In this book, dramaturgy is used in the modernist sense to refer to the playwright's structuring of the text, use of form and convention and how these elements combine to present their overall subject, Australia, in a certain light.

Dramaturgy is also described as metatheatrical or theatricalist. Here I draw on Elinor Fuchs' description of drama that is self-reflexive and self-referential.[64] This description suits Patrick White's compositional style, which makes use of non-human figurations including anima figures, the dead, celestial voices and imaginary animals as well as astral phenomena, illuminated objects and apocalyptic light as found in *The Ham Funeral, A Cheery Soul, Signal Driver* and *Shepherd on the Rocks*. These elements unsettle the secular rationality of realism as described by Raymond Williams, but were never intended to replace character, time frames and stage action, pointing instead to other possible worlds co-signalled in the text and potentially given material form in the theatre.[65] These worlds exceed the purely textual construction of a play. As Fuchs writes:

> theatricalist plays multiply dramatic complexity by bringing different places of reality into the same structure. Conflict in these structures is played out more between levels of representation than by individual figures, and is resolved by victory or defeat for a contending ontological principle (or perhaps a cheerful truce).[66]

If dramatic conflict is between different realities rather than individualised characters then theatricalist texts play their part in transcending monoculturalism. Patrick White is recognised as a satirist and ironist, who in his own words liked "to blow off" about Australia without compromising his imagination or confining himself to stage naturalism.[67] White's theatricalism is produced via a layered dramaturgy that combines the social critique of Australia in the twentieth century with outbreaks of magic and illusion in which the different planes contest the other's truth claims while destabilising and complicating realism. Across the plays, the moon, the night

---

63 Luckhurst, *Dramaturgy*, 10.
64 Fuchs, "Clown Shows", 341.
65 Raymond Williams, "A Lecture on Realism", *Afterall: A Journal of Art, Context and Enquiry* 5 (2002): 106–115
66 Fuchs, "Clown Shows".
67 Marr, *Patrick White*, 391.

sky and the spectacle of the Aurora Australis contribute to competing realities on stage. White's dramaturgy moves in the direction Eric Bentley referred to as "the open, diffuse play which starts early in the narrative and proceeds through it in many scenes".[68] Another important dramaturgical feature of White's plays and their performance is the non-textual image that combines character, action, gesture, costume and lighting in a moment of heightened significance. In *The Ham Funeral*, Mrs Lusty sits at her dressing table and takes down her hair while her husband's dead body lies on the bed beside her. In *Big Toys* Mag Bosanquet holed up in her Sydney penthouse bursts a balloon with her fingernail and in *Netherwood* Royce Best puts on Dora Pilbeam's frayed dress to play the piano for his psychiatrist. Each moment shares characteristics with the Brechtian gestus, the "quotable gesture" to use Walter Benjamin's description, that interrupts the "act of acting" with self-conscious posturing.[69] Gestus can function as a key to unlocking the social and gendered relations between character and place and the playwright's critical stance. In other words, it leads to the politics of the performative.

Theatre Studies and Methodology

The study of a single play and its theatrical production has now given way, as Marvin Carlson captures it, to a more dynamic view that considers "the fluidity of texts and interpretations from performance to performance" and "from revival to revival" over time and place.[70] R. Darren Gobert argues there is now a greater understanding that the play text is involved in "ever mutating signification over time" as history, culture and theatre practice intersect.[71] The book's focus on a single playwright may appear *démodé* in this context but it proceeds on the basis that comparative analyses of performances of the plays over time take into account the centrality of that which Erika Fischer-Lichte refers to as "the bodily co-presence of actors and spectators".[72] The reading of White's published texts in chapters one and two acts as a starting point after which variable performances accumulate in such a way that the text is no longer a fixed object. In the same vein, the social and cultural context, including racialised, class-based, gendered and sexual politics at work across the different times and places of production and reception, are considered counterpoints to the authority of the play text and the playwright's original intentions and influences.

---

68   Eric Bentley, *The Brecht Commentaries 1943–1986* (New York: Grove Press, 1981), 41.
69   Walter Benjamin, *Understanding Brecht*, tr. Anna Bostock (London: Verso, 1998), 19.
70   Marvin Carlson, "Performance Studies and the Enhancement of Theatre Studies", in *The Rise of Performance Studies: Rethinking Richard Schechner's Broad Spectrum*, eds. J.M. Harding and Cindy Rosenthal (London: Palgrave Macmillan, 2011), 16.
71   R. Darren Gobert, "The Field of Modern Drama, or Arcadia", *Modern Drama*, 58, no. 3 (2015): 299.
72   Fischer-Lichte, Erika, *The Routledge Introduction to Theatre and Performance Studies*, eds. Minou Arjomand and Romona Mosse, trans. Minou Arjomand (Oxford: Routledge, 2014), 56.

The study of the performed text is facilitated and enabled by the concept of the performative derived from Judith Butler's sense of the performative as a dramatic enactment of everyday life by a lived body. Applied to the art form of theatre and performance, Fischer-Lichte argues bodily performative acts (on stage) do not express a pre-existing identity (stipulated by the text) but "engender identity through those very acts".[73] Live performance is dramatic because it involves the body's "continual and incessant materialisation of possibilities" entwined with and embedded in historical situations.[74] Performativity is that which "manifests itself in the performative nature of acts" and which carries affective potential, that is, the capacity to create audience response.[75] The concept allows for a discussion, for instance, of Benedict Andrews' production of *The Season at Sarsaparilla* for the Sydney Theatre Company in 2006, which highlighted the effect of a bitch in season through sound, duration, and frequency that unsettles or amuses characters and audience alike.

The important point here is that the dynamic qualities of performativity replace the idea of theatre as the rendition of the literary dramatic text, which is the principal driver of the event. Recognition of the syncretic composition of theatre brings the creative energies of directors, designers, composers, and performers into view. Each of these figures plays a major role in the story of Patrick White's theatre, as the analysis of landmark productions will show. Key productions of White's plays are commonly referred to as Jim Sharman's *Signal Driver*, Neil Armfield's *A Cheery Soul*, Michael Kantor's *The Ham Funeral* and Benedict Andrews' *The Season at Sarsaparilla*. Jim Sharman had a transformative effect on White's reputation as an Australian playwright.[76] He was a driving force in Sydney's New Wave theatre scene and its commercial sector, directing Alex Buzo's *Norm and Ahmed*, a radical two-hander about racism at the Old Tote in 1968 and the New Age musical *Hair* at the Metro Theatre in 1969. Sharman became a celebrity international director while retaining his art house theatre practice, a point that was critical to his production of *A Cheery Soul* at the Sydney Opera House in 1979. Inspired by that production the baton passed to Neil Armfield who went on to direct almost all Patrick White's plays over twenty years including premiere productions of the later 1980s' plays such as *Signal Driver* in 1982.

Of particular interest is the way in which Armfield would stage and then restage White's plays often with different designers and actors, and in different venues. He liked to "dig further", seeing each play as a work in progress rather than the last word.[77] Actors working on White's characters harnessed "a certain poetic theatricalisation" consisting of "heightened effects, poetry and symbolism".[78] These

---

73   Erika Fischer-Lichte, *The Transformative Power of Performance*, trans. Saskya Jain (New York: Routledge, 2008), 27.
74   Fischer-Lichte, *The Transformative Power of Performance*, 27.
75   Fischer-Lichte, *The Transformative Power of Performance*, 29.
76   Kate Gaul, interviewed by Denise Varney, 26 September 2019.
77   Neil Armfield, interviewed by Sandra D'Urso, 9 January 2018.

poetics were frequently captured in physical imagery, which in turn allowed "a strange sculptural energy" to emerge through the interaction of the body in space or in relation to objects, sounds and light.

These important developments in theatre practice since the 1960s shape the analysis and discussion of White's theatre with his plays implicated in the changing modes of production and reception. As Armfield wrote in a tribute to White:

> His plays are unlike anything else in the Australian theatre. They have their feet in vaudeville and their heads in the stars, in the vaulted air of the cathedral. They have a crystalline hardness tempered with earth and blood. And the plays will continue to be staged, because he created parts that actors love to play. His characters are clowns requiring the finest to release them. They are comic and tragic, like life. But the language they play with obeys its own poetics.[79]

Benedict Andrews in turn worked as Assistant Director on Armfield's *Night on Bald Mountain* in 1996 and went on to direct the acclaimed production of *The Season at Sarsaparilla* for the Sydney Theatre Company ten years later.

Theatre, as a live event that involves the work of directors, actors, designers and increasingly technicians, enables the visual, spatial, performative and auditory systems to challenge the dominance of the text as the privileged stage signifier. Dramatic representation via the communicated experience of the speaking character is turned into a stage presence surrounded by the technologies of theatre. Applied to White's theatre in the 1960s, Harry Kippax was able to view a full professional production of *The Ham Funeral* by brilliant young director John Tasker, featuring rising international star Zoe Caldwell in the cast. Whereas critic Neil Hutchison, who had only read the script, could only imagine a tedious production. Here the specific aestheticism of theatre and performance produces, in the words of Fischer-Lichte, "the transformative power of performance".[80]

Dramatic representation via the communicated experience of the speaking character is turned into a stage presence surrounded by the technologies of theatre. White's last performed play, *Shepherd on the Rocks*, features a carnival of characters, a motif of the last two plays, who represent states of heterogeneity, ambiguity, puppet-like presences and correspondences. The dramatic character is no longer tied to the humanistic idea of sovereign subject, of the artist as transcendent or autonomous. Australian drama's modernism is to be found in White's movement away from realism, causality and motivation, and in its encounter with illumination, contingency, and creative forces that include landscape.

---

78 Armfield, interview.
79 Neil Armfield, "Patrick White: A Centenary Tribute", *Meanjin* 71, no. 2 (2012): 28.
80 Fischer-Lichte, *The Transformative Power of Performance*.

The Book

The concept of aesthetic modernism is central to the investigation of White's theatre that focuses on text, *mise-en-scène*, and reception in light of that which Fuchs and Fischer-Lichte, among others, refer to as the transformative experience afforded the spectator and critic.[81] At the same time, the book stages an historical account of the plays in performance that necessitates a certain amount of narrative and descriptive writing. This narrative will have significant concentrations around the number of times a play is performed as well as continuities and discontinuities around the available archive, the artists involved in the productions and the analysis that follows. The chapters on the whole identify key scenes for aesthetic and comparative analysis rather than accounts of whole performances.

Chapters one and two conduct a close reading of White's eight published play texts. My analysis of the texts is not to establish a normative reading against which their various theatrical adaptations are to be assessed. The close readings attend to the question of what the texts do, and what "makes a text theatrical".[82] These close readings will show how texts anticipate life on stage, even as they also occupy the bookshelf or the digital repository. The aim in these chapters is to develop a contemporary overview of the texts of a single author in their formative context before opening up discussion of the ways in which they have been staged over time. The close reading is not intended to establish a fixed meaning but to identify features that would later be differently highlighted in performances by different directors.

Chapters three to eight draw on archival research to analyse performances of the plays over four decades. In drawing extensively on archival sources, the book grapples with the unevenness of the collections for each production. This is partly to do with the fact that there have been many more productions of the first four plays (the later plays having had only one or two productions each), leaving an archive heavily weighted towards White's early works. This unevenness also applies to newspaper articles and reviews, which form a significant part of the archival research. The relative size of the archive has left its mark on the organisation of chapters. *The Ham Funeral* has had six productions, including three since 2000, and has a sizable print and digital archive dating back to 1961. The fact that the early productions were bathed in controversy, much of which played out in the press – both in newspapers and in longer formats in magazines and periodicals – has left a large footprint. Hence, productions of *The Ham Funeral* are awarded a chapter of their own to examine productions from 1961 to 2018. The chapter compares and contrasts the different productions of the play to conduct a detailed study of this foundational work in White's theatrical repertoire and its development as a major work over a period of social, cultural and aesthetic change.

---

81 Fischer-Lichte, *The Transformative Power of Performance*, 190–200.
82 Christopher Balme, *The Cambridge Introduction to Theatre Studies* (Cambridge: Cambridge University Press, 2008), 118–19.

Introduction

The Season at Sarsaparilla and *A Cheery Soul* have a chapter each for the same reasons. *The Season at Sarsaparilla* was first produced in 1962 and has had several revivals up to the Sydney Theatre Company's 2007 production directed by Benedict Andrews. This chapter scans White's theatre for its increasing gender fluidity that is variously elided and enhanced in subsequent productions of the plays. Andrews' 2007 production of *The Season at Sarsaparilla* cast veteran White actor, Peter Carroll, as Girlie Pogson, offering a cross-dressed version of the prissy housewife. The chapter analyses how the performance recalibrates Girlie's social anxieties as sexual ambiguity in a way that is both hilarious and sad in the twenty-first century. Chapter four considers the theatricalisation of Australian suburbia as the iconic scene of the social organisation of modernity from the 1960s to the present. The chapter considers how productions of White's plays represent new treatments of suburban spatialities. *A Cheery Soul*, also set in Sarsaparilla, and first performed by the Union Theatre Repertory Company at the Union Theatre at Melbourne University in 1963 is examined in chapter five. Revived by Jim Sharman at the Sydney Opera House in 1979, this play had its most recent revival in 2018. Although set in Sarsaparilla, the play presents a different angle on suburbia to do with morality, ethics and doing good in the modern world.

Chapter six considers *Night on Bald Mountain* and *Netherwood*, paired for their rural settings and themes of modernity's non-conformists and outsiders. *Night on Bald Mountain* is the final work in White's first quartet, first performed at Union Hall, Adelaide University on 9 March 1964. Directed by John Tasker, who had also directed *The Ham Funeral* and *The Season at Sarsaparilla* in Adelaide, the production also prompts commentary on the creative collaboration between the playwright, director, and designer. Neil Armfield restaged *Night on Bald Mountain* for Company B Belvoir and the State Theatre of South Australia, with Anna Borghesi as designer and with Benedict Andrews as Assistant Director. A new production in 2014 at the Malthouse Theatre in Melbourne directed by Matthew Lutton and designed by Dale Ferguson provides the trans-temporal comparison. *Netherwood* is a further instance of the pivotal role of the director in realising White's theatricalist vision. This large-cast play, also set in a country house and featuring the co-existence and collision of different planes of reality, was directed by Jim Sharman for the South Australian Theatre Company (renamed Lighthouse) at the Playhouse, Adelaide in 1983. The chapter highlights White's theatrical concern with damaged minds, gender play, fluid identities, corporeal otherness, places of confinement, and the power of authoritarianism. It discusses how each of these elements calls for a particular theatricalist vision that moves White's theatre increasingly towards collaborative relationships facilitated in part by the emergence of directors' and designer's theatre.

Signal Driver and *Big Toys* are discussed in chapter seven in terms of White's growing involvement in the anti-nuclear and anti-uranium movement. *Signal Driver* was first performed in 1982 by the Lighthouse Company, Adelaide in a production directed by Armfield and restaged in Brisbane and Melbourne the following year, and at the Belvoir Street Theatre, Sydney in 1985. *Big Toys* has to date had five professional productions between 1977 and 1994. It was first performed at the Old Tote Theatre Company, Sydney in 1977 with Jim Sharman as director and stage design by Brian Thomson. *Big Toys* signalled a return to the theatre for White, who had concentrated on writing novels and other pieces after the hostile response to *Night on Bald Mountain*. Sharman was intent on exploding the mainstream from within, not with radical politics but with radical theatricality, although one did not exclude the other. The cross-class erotic encounter between barrister Ritchie Bosanquet and trade unionist Terry Legge in *Big Toys* is examined as part of the increasing gender fluidity of White's theatre. The premise of the chapter is that material surfaces such as windows, mirrors, jewellery, minerals (uranium, plutonium), the shine of a Ferrari are counterposed with soft objects such as fur, flesh, sexuality, identity and an unstable idea of "humanity" in the context of economic development and investment in the post-Whitlam years.

Shepherd on the Rocks is discussed in chapter eight with reference to religion, metaphysics and enchantment, and brings together the aspect of light and illumination which is identified as a feature of White's theatre. It was written with Franz Schubert's "Shepherd on the Rock" (1828) as inspiration, just as *Night on Bald Mountain* was inspired by Mussorgsky's composition made famous by Rimsky-Korsakov. Further intertextuality occurs in the veiled conversation White sets up between artworks and musical composition within the play's extension of the genre of dramatic literature to other media. The play was first performed at the Playhouse Adelaide Festival Centre in 1987, directed by Neil Armfield with set design by Brian Thomson and lighting by John Comeadow. A second production was mounted in Canberra in 1993. Where it is not possible to compare productions of the play over time, this chapter focuses on White's last published and performed play as the most extensive realisation of the theatricalist tendencies in his body of work as a whole. In particular, it considers the interplay of image, light and sound with metaphysical themes to do with religion and spirituality as a phantasmagoria, recognising the elaboration of theatricalist tendencies throughout the whole body of work.

1
Reading the Early Plays: A Critical Reflection

The Ham Funeral, The Season at Sarsaparilla, A Cheery Soul and *Night on Bald Mountain* were first published in a volume of collected plays in 1965 following their premiere productions that took place between 1961 and 1964. Although White wrote the first draft of *The Ham Funeral* in London in 1947, it is considered here among the 1960s plays because it was revised, performed and published during that period.

Together these early plays and productions belong to the period described by theatre historian Geoffrey Milne as the first of three waves of change in contemporary Australian theatre. For Milne, the first wave, which lasted from the mid-1950s to around 1969, saw the formation of "the first genuinely enduring – if limited – network of subsidised, non-commercial professional theatre companies".[1] The modernist form and flavour of *The Ham Funeral, The Season at Sarsaparilla, A Cheery Soul* and *Night on Bald Mountain* tallied with the non-commercial profile of this niche sector. The archives show they were written with productions by the Universities of Adelaide and Melbourne with the support the Australian Elizabethan Theatre Trust, established in 1954, in mind – even if White harboured aspirations for London's West End. We can place these early play texts within the first wave of change in contemporary Australian theatre while appreciating they are more than passively positioned within the period. The formal innovations of the plays actually energised the first wave, setting it at a distance from, and in many ways in opposition to, the dominant forces of commercial and repertory theatre. Other Australian first wave playwrights including those nominated by John McCallum – Dorothy Hewett, Peter Kenna, and Hal Porter – share interests in unconventional dramatic subjects and anti-realist theatrical forms that signify further distancing from the dominant commercial and repertory theatre sector. McCallum notes in particular the artistic synergies between White and Dorothy

---

1 Geoffrey Milne, *Theatre Australia (Un)limited: Australian Theatre Since the 1950s* (Amsterdam: Rodopi, 2004), 5.

Hewett's theatre especially in relation to the use of vaudeville, expressionist techniques and Brechtian techniques.[2]

When White's four plays had their first productions in quick succession in Adelaide and Melbourne, postwar Australia was undergoing rapid modernisation at an economic and social level but was politically conservative. In 1961, Prime Minister Robert Menzies' Liberal/National Coalition was returned to office in a close federal election but the party went on to remain in power until the Whitlam Labor victory of 1972. At the same time, the long tail of colonialism excluded Indigenous Australians from the rights of citizenship, the right to vote, to equality, and to land rights while being subjected to authoritarian state-based laws that removed children from families and placed them in institutions. There was moral censorship in the arts and laws against homosexuality; unequal pay for men and women. The first wave of contemporary Australian theatre is set against a bleak period in which modernity continued to urbanise the nation but its radical offspring, modernism, struggled to loosen the bonds of patriarchy, family and the white nation.

The contradictions between modernity and modernism in parochial Australia were similarly embodied in Patrick White. This is strikingly evident in a minor incident in 1963, when he was invited to lunch with the Queen and Prince Phillip on the Royal Yacht Britannia in Sydney. There he met and admired modernist architect Jørn Utzon, architect of the highly controversial Sydney Opera House.[3] The capacity to accommodate both old imperialist ties and radical modernist architecture captures the ambiguity of White's artistic life in relation to his conservative social and political background. For instance, he voted for the return of the conservative Menzies government in 1961, at the same time as those same Liberal Party supporters and backers rejected his plays. He was a social and political conservative, and a gay man; a radical disrupter of artistic form, and a consumer of modern culture. It is interesting to see how politics came to be closer aligned with artistic practice over time rather than the other way around. As he told David Marr, his political beliefs were "forming vaguely", and by the late 1960s he would vote for Gough Whitlam's Labor Party.[4]

The Ham Funeral: Expressionist Drama

The Ham Funeral is a two-act drama set in a lodging house in East London in 1919. The play ostensibly follows the efforts of an introverted young male,

---

2 John McCallum, *Belonging: Australian Playwriting in the Twentieth Century* (Sydney: Currency Press, 2009), 114.
3 Patrick White to Desmond Digby, 8 March 1963, MS 9982/1.1/12, National Library of Australia. See also David Marr, *Patrick White: A Life,* (Milsons Point: Vintage Books, 1992), 412; and Patrick White, *Flaws in the Glass: A Self-Portrait* (1981; London: Vintage, 1998), 219.
4 Marr, *Patrick White: A Life.*

who seeks to overcome his ineffectual and fearful self in order to make his way in the world as a poet. He is distracted from this goal by the crass vulgarities, noise and disorder of everyday life. Interest is created in the ways the centrality of the male hero's artistic journey is contested by the presence of strong female characters including a mysterious girl, an older woman and two old scavengers. The young poet's dramatic life is further disrupted by a metatheatrical frame that questions the ontological status of the characters, raising the possibility that the stage figures are projections of the unconscious, fantasy or malevolent comic forces. Many critics and directors have identified the poet with the young White, who admits that he drew on his own "self-searching and experiences" as a young man in London during the interwar years.[5]

As is well known, the inspiration for the play is artist William Dobell's anecdote about the origins of his painting *The Dead Landlord* (1936). In the foreground of the darkly expressionist and comic painting, a man lies dead on an iron bed next to which his widow sits at a dressing table brushing her long hair. The image captures an episode from Dobell's London sojourn when he was drawn into unwanted involvement in the death of his East London landlord after which the landlady had sat and brushed out her hair while asking her lodger to invite their relatives to a funeral where ham and stout would be served.[6]

While revising the text, which was originally written in London in 1947, White reset the play to 1919 on the advice of his director, John Tasker. He agreed on the grounds that it increased the "air of surrealism and timelessness" that he wanted to project.[7] That a play about artistic crisis is conceived amidst "the despair and confusion" of World War Two, and then reinscribed into the aftermath of the Great War, sets the solitary male artist within wider historical forces of upheaval and change that demand new approaches to culture and social life.[8] Returning after World War Two to "the great piles of rubble" in Berlin to pick up the pieces of his theatrical work with a production of *Mother Courage and Her Children*, Brecht wrote: "All this is reflected in art, for our way of thinking is part of our way of living. Where theatre is concerned, we put forward models to fill the gap".[9] White is concerned in his postwar play *The Ham Funeral* with the ways in which theatre depicts the social alienation and ongoing consignment of surplus human labour to single rooms and empty lives. In this reading, the uneven progress of modernity is

---

5   Patrick White, "Author's Note on THE HAM FUNERAL", World Premiere Season at Union Hall (Adelaide University Theatre Guild, 15–25 November 1961), theatre program, Patrick White Collection, Series 1477, Barr Smith Library, The University of Adelaide.
6   See Denise Varney, "Australian Modernists in London: William Dobell's *The Dead Landlord* and Patrick White's *The Ham Funeral*", *Humanities* 5, no. 76 (2016).
7   See John Tasker, "Notes on 'The Ham Funeral'", *Meanjin Quarterly* 23, no. 3 (September 1964): 300. See also Elizabeth Schafer, "A Ham Funeral, Patrick White, Collaboration and Neil Armfield", *Australian Studies* 3 (2011): 7.
8   White, "Author's Note on THE HAM FUNERAL".
9   Bertolt Brecht, "From the Mother Courage Model", in *Brecht on Theatre: The Development of an Aesthetic*, ed. and trans. John Willett (1964; London: Methuen, 1984), 215.

reflected in art as the alienation felt by those hidden away in single living spaces for solitary individuals. The formal logic of the play is directed towards the Young Man's escape from a living death in an old house, but light is also shed on those who remain through the figure of Alma Lusty.

The play begins with the actor/poet, designated as the Young Man, addressing a fictional audience. He is standing in front of a stage curtain, which is drawn, and behind which we are told preparations are underway for a piece of theatre that is "a mad, muddy mess of eels".[10] In the meantime, which is also dramatic time, he confides he is uncertain about the role he is to play representing a state of creative paralysis, in which "knots" form in memories (30) to choke progress and life. He tells the audience that behind the curtain is "a great, damp, crumbling house" (15), where the walls speak, the gas fires offer advice, mirrors tell "living lies" (16), and the stairs resent "all the feet that ever trod the carpet" (30). The Young Man goes on to explain that there are some in the old house who have never been seen to open their doors but are heard to "fry little meals" in their rooms, and whose fingers by five o'clock have "turned to bones … and the sky is green" (16). At the close of the monologue he exits behind the curtain and the piece of theatre begins. Here the metatheatrical dramaturgy establishes its formal logic from the interplay of verbal, spatial and temporal elements paired with a music hall address to the audience.

When the curtain rises on Act One we meet cockney Landlord and Landlady, Will and Alma Lusty, who live in the basement of the aforementioned house and connected to the upper rooms by the resentful staircase. This space is soon established as the central location of the drama mainly due to the vibrancy of Alma Lusty. Her dialogue continues the vaudevillian elements of the dramaturgy. As she tells her silent husband, "I loved you Will. Afterwards I even got to like yer, and wanted you about" (18). Alma Lusty craves life, and loves "theayter" where she watches a "bunch of toffs in satin … gassin' about love and nothink" (17). Will Lusty remains fixed to his chair beside the kitchen table, where he sits in his underclothes with his legs apart facing the audience, smoking his pipe with dogged contentment. When he finally speaks, it is to proclaim the existential certainty of the man of the house:

> LANDLORD: I sit 'ere. I am content. Life, at last, is wherever a man 'appens to be. This 'ouse is life. I watch it fill with life, an 'darken. These are my days and nights. The solid 'ouse spreadin' above my head. Only once in a while I remember the naked bodies… knotting together … killing theirselves … and one another … Bloody deluded! (27–28)

---

10 Patrick White, *Collected Plays Volume I: The Ham Funeral, The Season at Sarsaparilla, A Cheery Soul, Night on Bald Mountain* (Sydney: Currency Press, 1985), 15. All subsequent references are to this edition and appear in parentheses in the text.

Will Lusty presents as the centred, intractable, mortal man that is soon to leave the play and the modern world. The Young Man enters and continues his direct address to the audience, declaring for example, that he loathes Will Lusty. The interruption of the dramatic world by direct address, of the dialogic with narration, is clearly Brechtian. But it also serves to enhance the theatricalism of the text in that it establishes multiple commensurate realities within the dramatic world of the play that invites or demands that the reader/spectator responds to rapid changes of mode, perspective and time differences. The interplay of these different layers contributes to the overall complexity of the text in ways that involve a pleasurable shifting perspective.

The drama is structured so that the scenes in the basement are interspersed with scenes between the Young Man and a Girl through the closed doors of their first floor rooms above. The staircase provides a passage between the two levels that also enclose different worldviews. The Girl dressed in white is an ethereal presence, which speaks to the Young Man about spectral childhood experiences:

> GIRL: [*her voice intimate, but distinct*] The mountain? The mist was cold behind your bare knees. The valleys were rolling with the white mist. The parrots flew screaming … the wedge of black cockatoos … You held the sheet of paper in your hand. You had not yet found the words … (32)

This intimacy bespeaks the figure of the double, the Jungian anima or the dualist psyche, introducing a surrealist alternative reality. While his desire is to be complete, she stands for deferral and suspension of the possibility of psychic closure. The Girl links the idea of poetic sensibility not with bucolic reverie but with the scream of parrots and the wedge of cockatoos. Later in the play, the black cockatoos are symbolically embodied in the raucous laughter and physicality of the Relatives who attend the ham funeral, and precipitate the Young Man's crisis. The affective and unsettling power of the non-human world on the human psyche recurs as a motif in several plays and includes dogs, goats, cattle, and finally lions.

The Girl insists that the unsettled world of Will and Alma Lusty offers the Young Man lessons in life that will save his poetry from merely repeating the platitudes of false realism. She urges him to return to the basement where the Landlord and Landlady enjoy an unhappy marriage filled with memories, confessions, human love and loss. There they perform the ritual airing of Alma's infidelities: the tragedy of "the little, blue-faced" (29) stillborn baby and the violence that ends the scene as Will raises his hand to his wife. The Young Man is to learn that this kind of performance is a repetition of the same story with the same outcome each night. The voice of the mysterious girl, which may be the stirrings of the Young Man's own consciousness, alerts him to the connection between poetry and the social world.

The death of the Landlord takes place towards the end of Act One. The Landlady and the poet lay out the body, after which she lets down her hair and brushes it. When the Young Man is sent to invite Will Lusty's relatives to a ham funeral he encounters what critic Dennis Carroll referred to as "the voracious vulgarity of the outside".[11] This vulgarity is embodied by the presence of two scavenger women, who divert the Young Man from his errand with macabre tales of the streets, rape, and abortion. They let him know that poor women on the streets exist beyond the purview of the law. The pivotal moment occurs when they discover with "*a scream, or series of dry, gasping retches*" (43) the remains of a foetus in a rubbish bin. With the memory of the Landlord's abject corpse still fresh, the Young Man attempts a clumsy elegy to the "[T]ender, humorous foetus!" (44). At this stage in the play he is plagued with self-doubts and deeply unsettled.

Scene Two presents the ham funeral as theatre of cruelty in terms of its ritual patterns, physical and linguistic rhythms, and its spectacle. In this theatre, Alma Lusty "*monumental in black*", presides over a large boiled ham on the kitchen table (48). Will Lusty's avian-like relatives arrive and place their black bowler hats on the bed. The stage is set for a ritual performance that begins with the relatives paying solemn tribute to Will before they turn their attention to the widow with insinuations that she "turned the knife in 'is side" (51). Having sent the widow to the edge, the mourners flick the switch from cruelty to vaudeville and burlesque, pulling Alma back into the revelry, in a comic parody of high culture in which the ham takes pride of space. A tipsy Alma proclaims with pride, "We 'ad a 'am" (58).

The staged ham funeral is a celebration of theatre. In an essay on popular theatre forms, Len Platt argues that canonical modernism erases much of what was of value in burlesque, vaudeville, melodrama and musical theatre.[12] These forms are encoded with significant expressions of resilience and solidarity in the face of bourgeois society's disapproval. In the raucous scene of the ham funeral, White reinstates popular forms playing on its iconoclastic theatricality to mark his preferences for stylistic heterogeneity.

Later, the Landlady and the Young Man are left alone in the basement where Alma is intoxicated by ham, stout and grief, and tends towards sentiment and self-pity. He is appalled and fascinated to find himself the object of her sexual advances. In this Oedipal scene, she holds his head against her breast to recollect the pleasure and power of her own desiring body:

> But I was never a slow one. Nor cold. A cold colour, but not cold. Alma Jagg breathed life into the hedges. The frost melted when I

---

11 Dennis Carroll, "Stage Convention in the Plays of Patrick White", *Modern Drama* 19, no. 1 (1976): 13.
12 Len Platt, "Popular Theater", in *The Cambridge Companion to Modernist Culture*, ed. Celia Marshik (Cambridge: Cambridge University Press, 2014).

> lay beneath 'awthorns. I touched the warm, moist earth with my
> 'and. Afterwards when flowers come, I lay back … an' crushed
> 'em. (65)

The Young Man is mesmerised by the words of the older woman, which seem to express truth without effort or artifice, unlike his own ineffectual efforts. There follows a struggle/embrace during which "*he begins to struggle against her*" (67) before attempting to strangle her as she screams, gasps and falls to the floor in a cruel outbreak of violence.

The Young Man's desire to strangle the sexualised, maternal Alma Lusty precipitates an internal crisis and he retreats to consult with the Girl in the room opposite. She advises him to act intentionally, in order to burst out, existentially, that is, "to wrest oneself from moist, gastric intimacy and fly out over there, beyond oneself, to what is not oneself".[13]

In the final scene the Young Man leaves the house to embrace the world while Alma Lusty's cries, "I don't know wot I done … to be shut up in this body … an' nobody to open an' let me out …" (67), give voice to an entrapped subjectivity that wants to be free but is denied release. She represents a pre-feminist subject that reappears in the body of the sensuous Nola Boyle in *The Season at Sarsaparilla*, as alcoholic Miriam in *Night on Bald Mountain,* and as the materialist Mag in *Big Toys*.

Although free of the house, the Young Man leaves with a divided understanding of the self; this more fluid, dualistic construction of the central male protagonist offers an advance on the solid, deadly masculinity of the Landlord. Yet White's final stage direction, which calls for the back wall of the set to dissolve as the Young Man walks towards a luminous night, underlines the imaginary construction of the theatricalist world's temporary and contingent encounter with the world.

Stylistically the play mixes metatheatrical irony with expressionist and surrealist elements, comedy, and popular entertainment forms such as cockney songs and vaudeville. Critics and scholars have commented widely on the language and modernist style. Jessie Dyce identified both *The Ham Funeral* and *A Cheery Soul* as expressionist plays that ask audiences to accept locations and actions that are not fully represented.[14] Critic J.J. Bray looked to postwar playwrights such as Dylan Thomas, Samuel Beckett and Harold Pinter to identify the technical features White used in 1947, especially the use of "cascading language", "sinister grotesqueries", "inconsequentialities", and "down-at-heel setting".[15] May-Brit Akerholt similarly notes the modern European influences, especially August

---

13 Jean Paul Sartre, "A Fundamental Idea of Husserl's Phenomenology: Intentionality", in *Critical Essays (Situations I)*, trans. Chris Turner (London: Seagull, 2010), 42.
14 Dyce, *Patrick White*.
15 J.J. Bray, "The Ham Funeral", *Meanjin Quarterly* 21, no. 1 (1962): 34.

Strindberg, for the way in which the set mirrors the psychology of the characters.[16] She is especially interested in the way the prologue "introduces a link between the stage and auditorium" in a way that we would describe today as empowering, activating or emancipating for the spectator.[17]

The Suburban Plays: *The Season at Sarsaparilla* and *A Cheery Soul*

The Season at Sarsaparilla and *A Cheery Soul* represent White's first major theatrical treatments of contemporary Australia. Both plays are set in Sarsaparilla, a fictitious outer suburb of Sydney, usually taken to refer to new developments in the 1960s at Castle Hill on the city's western edge. White and his partner Manoly Lascaris bought a property there on their return from Europe after the war before moving to Centennial Park in Sydney in 1963.

By 1961, urban growth had spread to the west of Sydney, subdividing farmland and turning rural townships into modern suburbs, which were fast becoming the place and symbol of Australian life. At the political level, conservative Prime Minister Robert Menzies delineated the suburbs' typical inhabitants as the forgotten people – "the salary-earners, shopkeepers, skilled artisans, professional men and women, farmers and so on",[18] – ordinary people, who lived in neither mansions nor workers' cottages but in neat rows of identical houses on newly subdivided land. Menzies cast ownership of the suburban home as a worthy goal for middle-class couples with modest aspirations, who wanted nothing more than "a little piece of earth with a house and a garden", where the foundational values of "sanity", "sobriety", and "frugality" could be laid down for the future.[19] Menzies' idea of the middle class was of a docile electorate, not wealthy enough to wield individual power nor poor enough to identify as victims of class. The men and women were white, heterosexual and protestant, like Menzies himself, but modest rather than ambitious. The great political and social upheavals of 1968 and the popular interest in neurosis, discontent and desire were yet to surface; globalisation had not yet opened the protectionist economy.

This conservative view gave rise, as Andrew McCann puts it, to the suburb becoming the target of satire and critique in literary and popular representations.[20] These included performer Barry Humphries' character Dame Edna Everage, an increasingly grotesque caricature of the suburban housewife, who came to embody popular anti-suburbanism. McCann finds a more complex resistance to suburbia

---

16 May-Brit Akerholt, *Patrick White* (Amsterdam: Rodopi Press, 1988), 8.
17 Akerholt, *Patrick White*, 9–10.
18 Robert Menzies, "The Forgotten People", Speech, 1942. http://www.liberals.net/theforgottenpeople.htm
19 Menzies, "The Forgotten People".
20 Andrew McCann, "Decomposing Suburbia: Patrick White's Perversity", *Australian Literary Studies* 18, no. 4 (1998): 56.

1 Reading the Early Plays

in Patrick White's fiction that "consists in staging the instability and potential perversity inherent in forms of representation that consolidate a commercialised image of the good life".[21] Staging is the key provocation in McCann's commentary here in that it points to the performativity of the ways in which concepts are brought into being via iterative processes, including theatre. The extent to which White's suburban plays, including his return to Sarsaparilla with *Signal Driver* two decades later, stage the mythico-commercial representation of the suburb and its embodiments in dramatic characters is a key consideration for reading the plays today and their productions over time.

At one level *The Season at Sarsaparilla* and *A Cheery Soul* appear as satires of suburban life, heightened mimetic charades of normative values. Roy Child, a teacher and aspiring poet, appears as a spokesman for anti-suburban sentiments, commenting to the audience on the stultifying ordinariness of Sarsaparilla and his desire to escape into a more stimulating world to "London … Paris … the Galapagos Islands … It doesn't much matter where" (177). But this is revealed as shallow anti-suburbanism born of blindness to the particularities and unconventional behaviours that fill the days and nights on its streets. It is apparent from the opening moments of the play that the inhabitants of Mildred Street conform only outwardly to Menzies' ordinary people. The play begins with "*an outburst of* BARKING *as from a pack of dogs somewhere in the distance*" that draws young Joyleen known as Pippy out of her house while her mother, Girlie Pogson, calls her back (79). The intrusive sound of barking dogs cuts through the ordinary with an insistent reminder of the presence of the non-human other in their midst. Another ontological reality to co-exist with human and non-human life is activated through a razzle-dazzle lighting effect, giving pause for reflection on daily life. News of other places filters in. Clive Pogson, a middle-aged husband, father and company manager, reads aloud from the morning newspaper that "something is happening in Laos …" (83), a phrase that floats in the air like matter out of place, opening up a connection with abject spaces of suffering and danger. The satire can be directed against those who would condemn moral lapses and flights of fancy, and those who would homogenise the suburb.

The Season at Sarsaparilla takes on a modern two-act format and offers a series of ironic, absurdist and symbolic caricatures of life in the newly emerging spatial formation of Australian suburbia. The play features three modest families – the Knotts, the Pogsons and the Boyles – who live side by side in three similarly sized and shaped iconic representations of the homes of the era. The play intertwines short scenic moments across the lives of the three families and their encounters with others including a post-office clerk, an ambitious young beauty named Julia Sheen, and the local city councillor, Mr Erbage. There is some suggestion of minor corruption and scandal at the Town Hall and a fatal accident, which might be a

---

21 McCann, "Decomposing Suburbia", 59.

suicide, involving the pregnant Ms Sheen. Corruption, unwanted pregnancies and violence are incorporated into Mildred Street, whose inhabitants go about their daily life often under the watchful gaze of family members and neighbours. Beyond that the fourth wall is breached by direct address to the audience, as indicated, by Roy Child, who doubles as a narrator. There is little by way of conventional narrative and plot. The condensed mode of simultaneous action draws on cinematic editing techniques and is a precursor to the television sitcom that would appear in 1966 to become the dominant representation of suburban life in twentieth-century Australia.

Family, work and home are central interests as befits the idea of suburbia with culture in the form of music, literature, art, and even religious observation largely absent. Teenage Judy gives up playing the violin after melodramatically discovering "the music has died in me" (136). For the three housewives meals consist of "Steak, chops, chops, steak" with echoes of "food means steak and cake" in White's 1958 essay "The Prodigal Son":

> In all directions stretched the Great Australian Emptiness, in which the mind is the least of possessions, in which the rich man is the important man, in which the schoolmaster and the journalist rule what intellectual life there is, in which beautiful youths and girls stare at life through blind blue eyes, in which human teeth fall like autumn leaves, the buttocks of cars grow hourly glassier, food means cake and steak, muscles prevail, and the march of material ugliness does not raise a quiver from the average nerves.[22]

In the play, food production regulates time but its uniformity is threatened by the barking dogs. Actions such as birth, a fatal accident, an infidelity, and a flirtation break the routine of meals and work across the three homes but are assimilated within the comic genre of the satirical play.

It is apt then that the play is called a charade, suggesting a series of tableaux in a game of heightened pretence or comic entertainment, while retaining the individualised quirks of the character/performers. Charade carries a further suggestion of the populism of amateur theatre and anti-elitism, theatricalism over the realist representation of Australian suburbia, while allowing that the suburb gives rise to more complex human emotions than discerned behind the "blind blue eyes" of "the Great Australian Emptiness".[23] Stylistically, there is a mixture of melodrama, realism, the absurd and the poetic with interludes of illumination by means of razzle-dazzle lighting effects.

The barking dogs are a rich source of extra-linguistic meaning offering directors and designers infinite possibilities for opening the dramatic world to errant forces both within and beyond. Sporadic barking unsettles, interrupts

---

22 Patrick White, *Patrick White Speaks* (1958; Sydney: Primavera Press, 1989) 15.
23 Patrick White, *Patrick White Speaks*.

conversations, keeps people awake at night and threatens the separation of the human and non-human worlds. The perverse barking conjures the carnal instincts and energies that belong to sentient beings. Girlie Pogson fears the unsettled atmosphere in the streets, which she attributes to the dogs, and to the school holidays, when the linoleum is marked by children running in and out of doors. The barking dogs provide others such as Nola and Ernie Boyle with an opportunity to reflect on human sexuality and the codes that govern desire and reproduction. They fascinate and then frighten Pippy and her friend Deedree. White gave prominence to the intentionality of the barking dogs' provocations when he wrote:

> [It] is about the effect a bitch in season has on a certain suburban street. It has allowed me to blow off a lot of what I have been feeling about Australia.[24]

He is referring specifically to the Adelaide Festival's rejection of *The Ham Funeral* for the 1962 drama program but more generally to a culture of censorship and authoritarianism, accompanied by hypocrisy and self-interest. The broader satirical target is not the people on Mildred Street, but the oppressive civic and political governance that curtails freedom of expression in art and life. The dogs signify the agents of repression and denial in contemporary Australia.

Along with the barking dogs, the curiosity of the two little girls plays a significant role in defamiliarising a way of life evolving in modern Australia. When released from induction into family routines, Pippy and her friend Deedree scout quietly underneath the houses to observe with increasing uncertainty the ways of the adult world. Pippy is especially drawn to Nola Boyle's kindness and warmth, qualities lacking in her own authoritarian mother, but which expose her to adult emotion and sexuality with all its confusions. The razzle-dazzle lighting effect initiates further variations of Brecht's *Verfremdungseffekt* – it interrupts linear progress to mark interior spaces in which the lure of modernisation and its productivity is suspended. Nola Boyle, for instance, likes to go outside at the end of the day and take in the evening:

> NOLA: This is the best time of day. Before the men come ... Even in the summer, at the end of the day, when you feel you could have been spat out, when the hair is stuck to your forehead, it is best, best. A time to loiter. The flowers are lolling. The roses are biggest. (*Stoops to smell.*) The big, lovely roses, falling with one touch ... (*Laughs.*) I could eat the roses! (125)

The razzle-dazzle prompts historicising and nostalgia in Girlie Pogson:

---

24 Marr, *Patrick White: A Life*, 391.

> GIRLIE: When I was a girl, at Rosedale, oh, the evenings were lovely then! Playing rummy on the mosquito-proof veranda. With the young fellers who would come in. Off the neighbouring properties. Oh, the light beneath the willows! Oh, the lamplight at Rosedale, when I was a girl!" (175)

Girlie's speech gives voice to perceptions of the bush as a lost paradise amidst the materialism spreading to the outer suburbs of Sydney, transforming rural properties into modern streetscapes. Despite the nostalgia, she holds to the pact in which she exchanged "the big verandas" and "willows" of her girlhood "property" for "a man and a washing-machine" (87). Adulthood means interior spaces are surfaces on which branded consumer objects are displayed and Rosedale recedes from view.

The Australian vernacular is familiar but also shown to be efficiently minimalist. A typical example occurs in Act Two. Nola Boyle is serving breakfast to Masson, a visiting Digger mate of her husband Ernie. She has just slept with Masson while her husband has been out on night shift collecting the neighbourhood's sanitary cans. She despises Masson, and herself, and puts his plate down on the table with disdain. Then she asks if he would "Like a termarter with it?" (146). The grammar and the accent capture the gesture of hospitality, familiarity and dismissal all at once drawing attention to the elasticity and humour of vernacular language.

In another mood, the vernacular becomes epic when Ernie Boyle narrates the procession of the bitch in season and the barking dogs in a direct address to the audience:

> There she was. A little bit of a blessed thing. 'Er tongue almost hangin' on the ground. Lickin' the dust she was. And gunna get a whole lot drier. 'Er eyes 'uv turned glassy. (96)

Ernie's "*messenger's speech from a Greek tragedy*" (96), elevates the man who deals with abject human refuse to the classical heritage of modern drama but also to its origins in ancient ritual, which deal with more bodily matters. White endows the sanitary man's speech with linguistic powers that reside in the capacity to find the heroic in the abject reality of the other. This enables him to transcend the everyday in ways denied the mildly ambitious self-regulated middle-class men, Clive Pogson and Harry Knott, who are his neighbours and social superiors. Having forgiven his unfaithful wife his language is performative:

> ERNIE: I feel good. I feel warm. *He kisses hungrily–bite–kisses–down her neck.* I ate! (172)

These linguistic variations add richness to the repertoire of the dramatic vernacular in ways that exceed the utilitarian functions of realist dialogue. The contrasting postwar lives of Ernie and Digger Masson are key markers of the transition from the society of farmers and soldiers to city workers and consumers. Our classical messenger, Ernie Boyle, a returned serviceman, works nightshifts as a sanitary man to enable him to fill a home with a wife and goods. The dialogic exchange with Masson brings to the surface previously unseen angles of self-reflexivity in Ernie, who shows he is well aware of emerging codes of postwar masculinity vested in the possession and consumption of consumer goods. Yet he is not aware of the adverse effect on his wife, who freed from the necessity of work, fills the long hours of the day sleeping, dreaming, shopping and loitering. Her shopping is not so much related to the purchase of household necessities as an escape from the quiet of home.

Roy Child, the young teacher/narrator figure dreams of becoming a writer of the type found in mid-century American drama in Tennessee Williams' *The Glass Menagerie* and in the bookish Toby Raven in Nick Enright and Tim Winton's *Cloudstreet* (2009) set in 1940s and '50s Perth. Roy Child's ambivalent relationship to place, to family and to the ties that bind a community hint at a social reality that is stretching further afield. Roy describes the feeling of physical, intellectual and psychic entrapment:

> Here I am, then ... smelling of salt, sun, and seaweed capsules popped in the heat of the day. Wearing its glaze of summer, my body is more or less renewed ... while my mind lurks in stuffy corners, filled with Genoa velvet and silky oak veneer. Where the body ignores, the mind reminds ... that the radio hasn't let off playing in empty rooms ... that the TV will continue to dissolve human personality, like gelatine in tepid water. (99)

Roy Child, as indicated, is a similar kind of narrator figure to the Young Man in *The Ham Funeral* and makes his final appearance as Denis Craig in *Night on Bald Mountain* before disappearing from White's plays. Unlike the Young Man who becomes embroiled in Alma Lusty's tragedy, Roy Child and Denis Craig represent "the untragic hero", Walter Benjamin's term for the undramatic character, a dispassionate observer or thinker, who is detached from the dramatic elements of the play. They are non-participant figures that Bertolt Brecht adapted, for example, to show the contradictions that make up the social world. In *The Season at Sarsaparilla*, having observed that nothing will change on the Mildred Streets of Australia, Roy feels his skin itching for "London ... Paris ... the Galapagos Islands" (177), but knows he can't shed his skin and his path will wind back to Mildred Street eventually and he will have to find a way to live.

White's charade of suburbia announces the arrival of a new type of theatre that would no longer, as Polish playwright and essayist Stanislaw Witkiewicz once put it, be "bottled up" with realism and psychological "truth".[25] *The Season at Sarsaparilla* is aligned with the quickening pace of suburban modernity, where the self is no longer considered determinable by an act of the will or creativity.

White's satirical treatment of the families is not without sympathy for the longing to escape the confines of suburban life but is critical of mediocre aspirations and unexamined lives. Mildred Street represents modern life as anti-idealist and anti-expressionist, materialist and only mildly anguished. Its streetscape belongs to instrumental rationality drilled down to the micro level of everyday living, while managing occasional outbreaks of resistances in the present and imagining more to come as the children grow.

A Cheery Soul

A Cheery Soul is adapted from a short story of the same name first published in *The Burnt Ones* in 1964. White wrote in a letter: "I am now roughing out a play version of the same story, and find things fall into place as though the original idea had already been in mind as a play".[26] The play features an aging woman, sixty year-old Miss Docker, over several months from summer to the following spring, as she is moved from private to public residences in Sarsaparilla. Orphaned as a young child and suffering homelessness as an adult, Miss Docker hides a deep loneliness beneath an overlay of self-regard, feigned cheerfulness and menacing goodliness encapsulated in the rhetorical refrain: "Everyone'll tell you I'm the cheerfulest person. Normally." (193) The action follows a series of social encounters that shift between the present and the space of memory.

One of the first questions about the play concerns the meaning and interpretation of the title and in particular its use of the word "soul". In Act One the charitably minded of the town refer to her as "a cheery soul ... always so helpful" (185), and the "soul of goodness" (187), but over time her unwanted help and tactlessness drive her victims to declare she has the "soul of a bulldozer" (199), or one that is blighted by "disease" (223). In a Brechtian style gestic contradiction, Reverend Wakeman, the Vicar of the local church, accuses Miss Docker of having a soul that is afflicted by the "sin of goodness" and displays a "*militant* virtue" (258). Miss Docker is however a complex figure that allows White to critique the values that govern suburban life especially its domestic rituals and to explore the effects of social isolation on a marginalised and disadvantaged woman in modern Australia.

Act One begins with the premise that charity needs to be bestowed on poor Miss Docker, whose last employer, old Miss Baskerville, has died. The parishioners of Sarsaparilla are aware that the old lady's house, in which Miss Docker was the live-in help, is soon to be sold leaving the poor soul with nowhere to live.

---

25 Stanislaw Ignacy Witkiewicz, "From On a New Type of Play (1920)", in *Twentieth-Century Theatre: A Sourcebook,* ed. Richard Drain (London and New York: Routledge, 1995), 35.
26 David Marr, *Patrick White Letters* (Chicago: University of Chicago Press, 1996), 207.

1 Reading the Early Plays

Mrs Custance, a housewife with time on her hands, offers Miss Docker modest accommodation in the "little glassed-in veranda room" (186) of her suburban home. When Miss Docker enters for her first appearance in the play, she alarms her host with non-stop chatter and interminable instructions. What is more, dressed in her Sunday best, her face caked in thick layers of beige powder and her mouth defined by plenty of purple lipstick, her appearance startles modest Mrs Custance. The stage directions describe her odd pieces of furniture and garish ornaments that speak perhaps of the charity of a string of employers she has served throughout her life. Only a rocking chair that Miss Docker describes as being "just about part of my own body" (190) seems to offer comfort and rest. However, like the body of its owner, the rocker soon becomes an ominous presence pitching of its own accord with gothic malevolence. While comically gauche, Miss Docker's furniture is an important signifier of homelessness and what will be the failure to fit into a house that is already occupied and furnished by its married owners. On stage the objects will become symbolic of Miss Docker – oversized, mismatched, odd items, tending towards mayhem and inviting rejection.

Miss Docker expresses the required gratitude to Mrs Custance for her charity but unsettles the nervous hostess with a bitter observation: "Don't some people have the luck!" (189). Miss Docker rightly assesses that luck is a commodity that is unequally distributed. Ever observant of the plenty of others, evidence of her covetous eye is presented at dinner when she notices the "nice piece of rump. Tender, I bet. Good and thick" (193) that is served to Mr Custance by his self-denying wife. Meanwhile, White describes Mr Custance, who takes an instant dislike to Miss Docker, somewhat blandly as a banker but with a "*Nietzschean moustache*" (183), as if he is some steak-eating *Übermensch*. Miss Docker endears herself to the reader by taking his measure:

> MISS DOCKER: (*to* MR CUSTANCE) You know what's the matter with you, don't you?
> *He doesn't answer. Messes about with his pudding.*
> (*Hunching her shoulders, lowering her eyelids*). Your posture is all wrong. And posture is nine-tenths. According to Indian philosophy. Mind you, there's a lot of that isn't altogether healthy, but you can pick up a wrinkle here and there. Now posture … Remind me to show you, some other time. (*Pauses*) I've got to be without me corsets.
> MISS DOCKER *nearly bursts*. MR CUSTANCE *gets up, goes out* BACK *looking rather tense.*
> Moody type. (197–98)

Miss Docker's intrusiveness, her drooling over the steak and finally her savage pruning of Mr Custance's tomato plants, lead poor Mrs Custance to ask her to leave, fearing her husband's symbolic castration and the end of her happy and lustful marriage.

Act Two opens with Miss Docker in residence at the Sundown Home for Old People, a genteel place for middle-class ladies. Miss Docker's garrulous nature and vulgar ways disrupt the quiet orderly lives of the docile residents. The pivotal scenes in Act Two concern Miss Docker's reminiscences of the time she helped to care for a gentleman named Tom Lillie as he lay dying. These recollections prompt his widow, Mrs Constance Lillie, now also a resident at the home, to recognise Miss Docker as the intrusive woman whose unwanted care of her husband robbed the couple of their final goodbyes. This recognition prompts the appearance of two young actors, who enact the love story of the glamorous Mr and Mrs Lillie, who toured the world on their honeymoon and lived a life of privilege. This scene is followed by a re-enactment of Tom's decline, the intrusive ministrations of Miss Docker and his helpless endurance of her care. A third scene tells the story of the funeral that followed as narrated by Miss Docker with the help of the residents who take on the role of the mourners and double as a Chorus. Uppermost in Miss Docker's mind is how she was shunned by the mourners at the funeral and abandoned on the side of the dusty road between the cemetery and the town. It was "the worst of all" the things that have happened to her (222). The Chorus has taken Mrs Lillie's side in a conspiracy among the widow and mourners but asks:

> Was it necessary? Was it kind? She did so want to watch Tom Lillie's polished casket stagger down the ramp towards the curtain. She would have wrung the widow's hands. She would have cried professionally. So, was it necessary? Was it kind? Who can say? (230)

As Miss Docker sees it, having charitably attended the bedside of a dying man, she was never thanked and was given "the slip" at his funeral (222).

The scenic interludes in Act Two are constitutive of a theatricalist mix of the everyday with "commensurate" worlds of competing memories, and the metaphysical, to create complex effects.[27] These effects highlight the conflict between Miss Docker's self-regard and the different viewpoints that form around the realities experienced by the others. The distance between the competing worlds, here Miss Docker's and the Ladies', is represented by the dusty road on which the cheery soul finds itself alone "with the dust, and the blow flies, and the dead heads of the banksias ..." (230). Act Two ends back at the Chinese room in the present with Miss Docker shrieking with laughter as she shows some old photographs to the ladies while Mrs Lillie looks on.

In Act Three Miss Docker again offers unwanted voluntary services this time to the Vicar, Mr Wakeman. She arrives at the vicarage to mow the lawns as he struggles to write his sermons. The stage directions indicate:

---

27 Fuchs, "Clown Shows: Anti-Theatricalist Theatricalism in Four Twentieth-Century Plays", *Modern Drama* 44, no. 3 (Fall 2001), 340.

1 Reading the Early Plays

> *... the clatter and slash of a push-mower is heard outside.*
> SCENE FADES *for a moment.*
> LIGHTS UP *on some scene later in the afternoon.* MR WAKEMAN *sitting hunched at his desk, hands over his eyes. Continuous sound of lawn mower outside.* (247)

Finally inspired, Wakeman's Sunday sermon asks how often the sin of luxuriating in one's own goodness turns " grotesque and ugly in other people's eyes" (258). White's stage directions are attentive to the spatiality of the nave of the church, its symbols of power and authority, and the ordinary people who are present in the act of worship.

Once again, a commensurate world opens up in the everyday. Lighting design and textual references indicate an extra-theatrical world where a different kind of militancy is active. Not long into Wakeman's service, the congregation turns to contemplate the end of the world. As they imagine the end, the stage notes specify the appearance of *"clear white Sunday light"* deepening into the *"golden glow of inwardness"* as in a *"brooding light"* (254) after which the worshippers fall to their knees *"in a gust of terror"* and *"look back terrified over their right shoulder"* (256). The stage space accommodates the shift between present and future with lighting effects but also the shift in mood amongst the worshippers from a mundane service to existential threat. Inspired by the vision, the congregation, including Miss Docker, cower before the spectre of: "the great mushroom … growing … and growing …" (256). The two commensurate ontological worlds then dissolve and the clear light of the Sunday morning returns. But the memory lingers in the everyday – later one of the worshippers repeats the fear of the bomb: "We'll never have peace while they go on piling up those bombs" (259). These unexpected references to the postwar nuclear era seem remote, like Clive Pogson's reference to Laos in *The Season of Sarsaparilla*. They are interesting for the ways in which they interrupt the minutiae of daily life, find their way into prayers about death and everlasting life, and underscore the wider context of Miss Docker's world.

The brooding light and Laos signify the presence of what Timothy Morton refers to as hyperobjects, objects that have a spatiality and scale that is beyond the reach of humans but which have the capacity to act as the primary cause of "the end of the world" as humans know it.[28] In White's second phase of playwriting the hyperobject reappears in *Signal Driver* in the form of the Aurora Australis that portends the expansion of nuclear power enabled by Australian uranium mining as White begins to identify existential threats on a universal scale. In a letter to designer Desmond Digby, Patrick White writes that he saw the lighting in the church scene as "a womb like saffron light" suggestive of a dream, a vision or a deep

---

28 Timothy Morton, *Hyperobjects: Philosophy and Ecology after the End of the World* (Minneapolis: University of Minnesota, 2013), 2.

religious experience when "all the thoughts and fears of the characters come to the surface". As he writes, "Then they all cringe and look back over their shoulders in the same direction, at the source of some mass fear – the Bomb implied".[29]

The scene in the church reaches an abrupt and unexpected end when Miss Docker's constant interruptions and corrections during the service cause Vicar Wakeman to dramatically expire, falling lifeless over the edge of the pulpit like *"one of the conventional figures of the Punch and Judy show"* (260). Goodness has shown its militant side and the agency attached to it; Miss Docker exults in her power – "My thoughts could light a fire!" (260) she thinks as a gauze scrim descends behind her for the final scene.

The scene at All Saints is worth considering in detail for it shows White's theatrical sense of the interplay between scenic space, lighting and thematic intentions. The narrative enlarges upon Miss Docker's destructive goodness, conveyed as inane non-stop dialogue, leading to the unfortunate death of the vicar. But thematically, the broader point is about inner experience, including the fears that rise to the surface in moments of reflection. The novelist, whose modernist prose masters the art of free indirect discourse, adapts by imagining, as a playwright, how scenic writing captures interiority. Many critics such as Harry Kippax highlight the gap between White's prose and playwriting, criticising the latter for its failure to achieve the same mastery. This scene and the extra-theatrical discourse around it, demonstrates White's exploration of theatre's modes of communicating the unspoken.

In the final scene, Miss Docker returns to the dusty road on her way back to the Sundown Home for Sunday lunch after the death of the Vicar. As she is battered by the weather, an invisible blue cattle dog appears and urinates on her leg. The cattle dog had previously witnessed her humiliation at Tom Lillie's funeral and now reinforces it. A Swaggie looks on while two boys enter and laugh. Miss Docker struggles to overcome the doubts triggered by the dog before vowing to go home and pray. With nowhere else to go and despite the humiliations and rejections, she stays in Sarsaparilla, destined to continue as before.

The key to approaching the representation of Miss Docker is the non-naturalist absurdist form of the play. The dramaturgy breaks up the naturalist form in Act One, becomes more overtly theatricalist in Act Two, and in Act Three stages multiple scenic encounters for virtuoso comic and grotesque performative utterances and action. The play is structured around key symbolic images such as the manic rocking chair in Act One and a series of tableaux involving temporal shifts in Act Two. These scenes incorporate Brechtian distanciation but also Artaudian features of ritual humiliation and cruelty. In Act Three when Miss Docker is buffeted by wind on the dusty road, one of her stockings hangs down around her ankles and the dog appears. The scene turns into a spectacle of

---

29 Patrick White to Desmond Digby, 2 June 1963. Papers of Desmond Digby, MS 10056/1/1, National Library of Australia.

abjection, a sudden loss of self for Miss Docker and an experience of adverse judgement by the dog, or God.

Critics have commented on both the shortcomings and possibilities of the adaptation of *A Cheery Soul* with Akerholt finding weakness in the play's translation of the interiority and emotions of the story's characters.[30] Judith Barbour, on the other hand, considers the play offers infinite opportunities for the character's autonomous self-expression. As she writes, the difference between narrative and drama resides in the greater autonomy the play offers the character, where she no longer "yields to the narrator-author the ulterior vision of how she operates".[31] This relative autonomy translates magnificently into theatre through performers such as Robyn Nevin and Sarah Peirse, whose embodiments of Miss Docker generate powerful visual and visceral presences that exceed the authority of the text.

Barbour also offers an historicist reading of Miss Docker's character as a remnant of English patterns of social and family life. In this view, she is a modern Australian version of the nineteenth century "spinster parishioner", who survives in a succession of live-in placements as the help in Christian homes, while privately existing outside the "exclusive domicile of marriage". Now frail and elderly she finds herself in a precarious social position, homeless and lonely. In terms of the longer tradition of English literature, Barbour sees her as a picaresque character, a "patchy conformist" and "chameleon-like" figure who, by necessity, "wedges herself into others' lives".[32] In particular, she inserts herself between middle-class and childless couples – the Custances, the Lillies and the Wakemans – where she is both the rival female and female child, and as such, an object of resentment and the instigator of guilty consciences.

Miss Docker's soul inhabits a figure who is an outsider without family, inheritance or home. The cheery soul denotes a harmless minor character, who lacks tragedy's gravitas and death. Yet contradictions between cheerfulness and resentment, kindness and cruelty, and selflessness and selfishness mark her social intercourse. The effects of want and envy complicate the struggle to remain cheery and are driven by gender and class. These elements support a monstrous femininity but also a damaged soul. At the end of the play, she feels she is "the last soul alive" (261) and leaves the reader caught between sympathy and horror. The evocation of Miss Docker's soul softens the character and binds the character and the play to a theme of abandonment.

---

30 May-Brit Akerholt, "Story into Play: The Two Versions of Patrick White's *A Cheery Soul*" *Southerly* 40, no. 4 (1980): 461.
31 Judith Barbour, "Cheery Souls and Lost Souls: The Outsiders in Patrick White's Plays", *Southerly* 42, no. 2 (1982): 140.
32 Barbour, "Cheery Souls and Lost Souls", 139.

Night on Bald Mountain

Night on Bald Mountain is the third of White's 1960s Australian plays and the fourth in the sequence of first productions that took place in succession between 1961 and 1964. The representation of bitter social relationships based in class, previously explored in the singular character of the disadvantaged Miss Docker in *A Cheery Soul*, now encompasses a professor, an archetypal failing patriarch, who withholds love, imprisons his wife and preys on the innocence of youth. The play is set on Bald Mountain, a fictional location in the highlands west of Sydney, with the action taking place in a twenty-four-hour time frame. The overall structure operates at the symbolic and the domestic level offering contrasting perspectives on the natural and human worlds. The intricacy of character, plot and action invites the audience into a dramatic world of intrigue, where timing and deception, arrivals and departures, deferrals and revelations sustain a high degree of tension.

The main characters are educated Australians, whom White thought should "intrigue those snobs" who complained about his typical "low-life characters".[33] In turning his attention to educated characters with the capacity and motivation to conceal rather than reveal, White presents audiences with a critique of the repressed and abandoned dreams, and perverse desires of the Australian middle class. In the playwright's words, the drama is a bitter conflict "between a university professor [Hugo Sword], who is also incidentally a writer of pornographic verse, and his dipsomaniac wife [Miriam], a woman of frustrated talent, her beauty and charm gone sour. Between them they destroy the person they respect the most".[34] The destroyed character is the innocent Stella Summerhayes, a nurse brought to the house to care for the professor's wife, but who becomes the symbolic sacrifice in an attempt to restore the ageing patriarch's power. The classical forebears are Agamemnon and his daughter, Iphigenia, sacrificed to appease the gods and secure the winds to drive the Greeks to Troy.[35]

While the Swords live in a large house on top of the mountain, a rival household lower down, absurdly figured as a shack with a goat yard, is ruled by a "low-life character" in the form of an old female goat keeper, Miss Quodling. She is a foil and moral counterweight to the middle-class world of the play. Her story frames and mitigates the human drama of the bitter professor and his wife as they reprise the failure of their intellectual and artistic ambitions with a mixture of coldness and disgust. The Swords' drama is enacted as psychological realism, but its denouement is inflected by the poetry of the mountain setting and its "*suggestion of vastness*", on a scale beyond that of the human being's daily life and dreams.[36] The two sets of characters and locations allow White to delve into the

---

[33] Patrick White to Beryl Sheasby, 10 February 1964. Patrick White Collection, Series 1477, Barr Smith Library, University of Adelaide.
[34] White to Sheasby, 10 February 1964.
[35] Euripides, *Electra, Phoenician Women, Bacchae, Iphigenia at Aulis*. Trans. Cecelia Eaton Luschnig and Paul Woodruff (Indianapolis: Hackett Pub., Co., 2011).

dark interiority of psychological realism and the symbolic resonance of landscape. Bald Mountain represents the natural environment as a powerful presence, silent and barren beneath the blue sky by day, and distant from the "the rhinestones [lights] of Sydney" that it overlooks by night (348). The house has all the comforts of wealth and privilege but is a deeply unhappy and conflict-ridden place.

The outer frame is articulated in Miss Quodling's monologues and dialogues with her goats. A hermit, she has developed a deep relationship with the natural world of animals and landscape. Life is regulated by sunrise and sunset, seasons and geography, out of which she has fashioned an ethic of human and non-human co-existence. The key to the performance of the scenes at the goat yard is how they interrupt the conventionally anthropocentric stage in which the human story takes precedence to introduce an ecological consciousness.

The outer and the inner narrative frames connect three times: at the beginning when Stella and Denis Craig, a young lecturer from Sword's university department, meet Miss Quodling at her shack; during an interlude later on when Miss Quodling visits the house and indulges in a subversive drinking session with Miriam; and at the end when the characters assemble at the goat yard to learn the tragic fate of Stella Summerhayes.

The first scene is located at Miss Quodling's shack. Like Miss Docker, Miss Quodling is in the English spinster tradition, but is proudly independent and self-sufficient. Rather than attaching herself to a life of good deeds and service, she is highly protective of her solitude. There are hints of a troubled childhood and adolescence – memories of an aunt, a broken china ornament, Holland blinds pulled down, a feather duster, and young fellers – but Bald Mountain is a burrow offering the multiple comforts of home, a livelihood, companionship, emotional warmth, spiritual succour and scenic pleasure; in short, it meets all her needs and wants. The stage directions describe her as a large woman, wearing layers of stiff dirty clothing, gumboots and a man's hat. Like Miss Docker, she has "*a large, leathery-brown face*" (269) connected to the many years spent outdoors, exposed to the elements, and perhaps to a concealed racial or ethnic identity.

The opening speech is a dawn monologue, which reads as a hymn to the morning and encompasses the mountain, the dew, the rocks, and the miracle of life. The hymn is accompanied by music, and is presented by Miss Quodling:

> Bald Mountain! I wasn't born here. Oh no! But know it, how I know it! I've learnt to understand the silences of rocks. Only the barren can understand the barren. I came, because I couldn't help it. I tasted the little runty apples … and sour apricots … that

---

36 Patrick White, *Collected Plays Volume I: The Ham Funeral, The Season at Sarsaparilla, A Cheery Soul, Night on Bald Mountain* (Sydney: Currency Press, 1985), 269. All subsequent references are to this edition and appear in parentheses in the text.

> somebody planted before they died. On Bald Mountain, nobody else has survived. Nobody else. I've lived here so long, I've forgotten now. (*Pause*) I don't go down ... (*Pointing behind her*) ... not down there ... though I watch the lights ... at night ... that glitter too much to be trusted. In the end, you can't trust anythun but goats and silence. Oh, yes, I know now! I've seen the mountain from a distance, too ... moisture glist'nun on its bald patch ... on bare rock. Sun on rock ... that's the kiss that never betrays ... because it doesn't promise nothun ... (272)

The hymn is rich in detail about the capacity of the human subject to enter into a relationship with the landscape and to develop an emotional, physical and spiritual connection to it. Here the ellipses allow time for silence in anticipation of an audience that might empathise with Miss Quodling's emotional connection to and respect for nature. The emotional connection to the land resonates with contemporary understandings among settlers of European descent of Indigenous relationships with country. Although Miss Quodling, whose name indicates British ancestry, keeps an introduced species, she admires the mountain for rejecting more extensive cultivation. Critic Robert Brissenden, who had problems with the inconsistencies he saw in the formal aspects of the play, nevertheless offered insight into the prescience of White's imagining of the natural world:

> Dramatic tension and interest are generated in his work not only out of relationships of the characters with each other (as is the case in most plays) but also out of their involvement with these larger biological and physical forces: the ideal state is clearly one in which man can exist in fruitful communion with the environment.[37]

But White is less idealist than Brissenden suggests, showing the reader instead that the environment remains quite indifferent to human-centred emotion.

Into this opening scene steps Stella Summerhayes, a Melbourne nurse, who is a few days into her position at the Swords as the live-in carer of Mrs Sword. In that lonely house surrounded by "sour" soil (274), Stella will be the catalyst for unleashing psychological realism's repressed desires and will be its victim. For now, the older woman quickly intuits that the nurse is "as good as a sound apple" but at risk of being cut into, especially by the professor (276). Stella's background is established and sets up a parallel situation in which having been raised by her widowed father to whom she is attached but from whom she wants to break free, she finds employment in the house of another paternal figure. The scene between the Goat Woman and Stella is interrupted by the arrival of Denis Craig, who has

---

37 R.F. Brissenden, "The Plays of Patrick White", *Meanjin Quarterly* 2, no. 3 (September 1964): 246.

1 Reading the Early Plays

been sent from the house to find the nurse who has not appeared for breakfast. Miss Quodling, Stella and Denis establish a sympathetic relationship that will be critical to the moral divisions between goodness and corruption among the characters. The non-appearance of members of the household at meals greatly upsets the housekeeper, Mrs Sibley, whose strict domesticity is continually undermined by the irregularity of the day that unfolds. With her growing anxiety about the disorder and lack of routine in the household, the housekeeper functions as a choric reflection on the capricious behaviour of the middle class. Her anxiety is also a device to stoke the rising tension in Acts Two and Three by means of connection to the outside world and her desperate attempts to send a telegram to her family to come and get her.

The scenes in the house realise the Swords' tormented marriage, their adult daughter who escaped to London, the professor's turn from poetry to religion and to pornographic verse, and Miriam from art and beauty to alcoholism, quaintly referred to as dipsomania. Professor Sword is a domineering man of the patriarchal kind, memorably described elsewhere by Virginia Woolf in her account of the male professor figure:

> Nobody in their senses could fail to detect the dominance of the professor. His was the power and the money and the influence ... With the exception of the fog he seemed to control everything. Yet he was angry.[38]

Privilege, power and anger is a lethal combination for the women who cross Sword's path. In vernacular terms, Miss Quodling thinks Sword is "stuck-up", "full of self-*importance*" (275), and dangerous. His wife resorts to deception to avoid his censorious gaze. In Act Two, he dramatically discovers Miriam's secret stash of whisky and shouts as he smashes the bottles in a spectacle of righteous outrage. In Act Three he prays on his knees before succumbing to the urge to visit Stella in her room late at night where the scene of sexual abuse takes place between the powerful male professor and the young female nurse. Sword is thoroughly self-serving as he ignores the nurse's distressed attempts to push him away and breaks her by assuming the role of father/lover, insinuating a primal scene of abuse that is deeply disturbing to the young woman. His actions precipitate her death by suicide, fulfilling Miss Quodling's fear that Sword would destroy her.

The final scenes bring Sword and Quodling together in moral battle over his treatment of Stella and Miriam, both of whom seek refuge at the goat yard at different times during the long night and early morning. Miriam has slipped out of the big house and spent the night at Quodling's fireside. After Sword leaves her in her room, she has taken her cloak from the wardrobe, put it over her nightgown, and walked downstairs and through the living room before leaving the house by the glass doors. These movements are conveyed as stage directions. She is next

---

38 Virginia Woolf, *A Room of One's Own* (1945; London: Penguin, 2000).

seen briefly approaching Miss Quodling's yard in the early morning repeating the words "My own father" (350), before disappearing again. Neither Miss Quodling nor Miriam have noticed Stella come and go.

The discovery of her body is dramatically deferred. Sword arrives looking for Miriam, not knowing Stella has left the house, and ask for Miss Quodling's pity, causing her to burst out laughing. Then a hiker enters to report a woman has "gone …" (353) over the edge of the mountain and later describes how she stood "against the light … a rare glare around her … She seemed to topple out of the sun" (353). The sequence of events works to deny Sword the knowledge that he wants, and in doing so brings about a change of demeanour in the tyrant.

In the final scene the cast assembles at Miss Quodling's shack to respond to the discovery of the body. Sword confesses indulgently to killing Stella Summerhayes, while Miriam recognises they are both destroyers of the innocent and good. They return to the house to try again as Miss Quodling begins her final monologue.

Alone on stage, she mourns Stella's death before returning to the present where it is once again morning on Bald Mountain. The outer frame narrative is reactivated as Miss Quodling speaks lyrically about rocks, the scrub, and the prickly flowers as she opens the gate to let the goats out to run, skip and jump. Her momentary joy is interrupted when her favourite goat Dolores, the bringer of sadness, loses her footing and goes over the edge of the mountain. Finding words again and steadying herself, Miss Quodling's final monologue expresses a fatalistic view of the co-presence of the generative and destructive principles of life on earth.

> (Shouting) But when there is nothing left … not even Bald Mountain … after they've ground it into dust … and all livin' things with it … like they tell yer … if you can believe … (*Beside herself*) But you can't! Can yer? You can't! There is no such thing as *nothun*! (*Softer*) The silence will breed again … in peace … a world of goats … perhaps even men! (356)

The evocation of "nothing left" and "dust" have been interpreted as references to nuclear power and the bombings of Hiroshima and Nagasaki just twenty years earlier in 1945. The reference gains further traction through White's later involvement in the campaign against uranium mining, and flows through the early and later plays including *A Cheery Soul* as well as *Big Toys* and *Signal Driver*. The notion of nothing left is also expressed by Denis Craig, another version of the young writer from the earlier plays. However, the vision is less positive. Where there is a sense of hope at least for the young poet heading into the luminous night at the end of *The Ham Funeral,* and an expectant sense of departure and return for Roy Child in *The Season at Sarsaparilla, Night on Bald Mountain* theatricalises a state of despair in which the young man is left after the death of his love interest asking "how shall we believe … in life?" (353) as Miss Quodling wavers between hope and "nothing left" (356).

Critics such as Harry Kippax argue that the play lacks the necessary unity of elements, a point also made by Akerholt[39] but the formal dissonance between the house and the mountain may also work in performance as a more integrated aesthetic achievement. Axel Kruse finds several examples that support an argument about the internal coherence of the play by means of repetition, doubling and allusion. He goes further to argue that this internal unity shares common thematic and poetic features with the novels.

Dyce is more receptive to the symbolism of the landscape, which she links to precedents such as the heaths in *King Lear* and *Macbeth*, and the slopes of the Norwegian fjord in Ibsen's *Brand,* where interiority is projected, "without impeding dramatic progress".[40] Dyce highlights White's use of Mussorgsky's composition "Night on Bald Mountain" as source material for the overall narrative and symbolic frame of the play. Also known as "Night on the Bare Mountain", Mussorgsky's composition is based on the theme of the witches' Sabbath that begins at dawn, when the witches and evils of the night are banished, and ends the following dawn, after a night of mayhem. In White's time frame, the second dawn brings the tragic discovery of the death of Stella Summerhayes.[41]

The combined effect of the dramatic events indicate that which Artaud describes in his essay on theatre and alchemy as matters on their way to destruction and fiery purification. With this aspect of the scenario, White returns theatre to its archetypal, primitive form where the essential drama is the "underlying menace of chaos as decisive as it is dangerous".[42]

Elin Diamond has eloquently pointed out in her landmark study of realism that rationalist, secular drama never quite manages to suppress the hysteria that it inherits from the melodrama it replaces.[43] In *Night on Bald Mountain* secular knowledge is incomplete and readily disrupted by the animist beliefs of Miss Quodling, the Dionysian alcoholism of Miriam, and Stella's hysterical flight into the night. When realism uncovers the repressed sexual history of Sword and entangles it with the young live-in nurse, the young woman's tentative romance with the young lecturer is ruined. Given the forces that upset the narrative of the upper-class weekender and the restorative retreat from the city, it is possible to see how realism is disrupted with elements of violence and myth, and embodied memories that send mortal flesh over the edge. The Artaudian-style mix of ancient and modern, and the innate cruelty that drives the narrative to its tragic resolution, embroiders White's

---

39 Akerholt, *Patrick White*, 102.
40 White, "Author's Note on THE HAM FUNERAL". See also Simon During, *Patrick White*, (Melbourne: Oxford University Press, 1996), 85–91, on the novelist's shift from diegesis to mimesis.
41 J.R. Dyce, *Patrick White as Playwright* (St Lucia: University of Queensland Press, 1974), 108.
42 Antonin Artaud, *The Theatre and Its Double,* trans. Mary Caroline Richards (New York: Grove Press, 1958), 51.
43 Elin Diamond, *Unmaking Mimesis: Essays on Feminism and Theater* (New York: Routledge, 1997).

modernism with threads that take the play beyond its contemporary moment. Here the title is a further index of its range. White was insistent that the title remain unchanged despite the misgivings of Harry Medlin, his staunchest supporter in the staging of the work.

***

At their worst critics equated White's early plays with the writings of a wrong-thinking misanthrope. Children's author and drama editor of the Australian Broadcasting Commission, Leslie Rees, complained that White's plays lacked the "'common touch' – a true respect for ordinary humanity ... which is ultimately necessary to warm the cockles of playgoers on any level, especially in Australia".[44] On the opposing side younger critics such as Katharine Brisbane argued that White and the younger generation of playwrights that emerged in the late 1960s and constituted the New Wave, were "not wrong – just different" and criticised stifling rejections of the "broad, loud, extremely agile and all-enveloping theatricality" of the 1970s.[45] Dennis Carroll writing in *Modern Drama* in 1976 argued sensibly you could think two things at once. You could praise White's break from "the plodding naturalism then pervasive on the local theatre scene" while also recognising the productive challenge they posed to directors, actors, audiences and critics as an asset.[46] Roger Covell concludes that however much White's early plays disconcert or discomfort, "he must be granted recognition as the only figure of our theatre to be unmistakably of major creative force and as a playwright with the vision and gifts to write a masterpiece".[47] He connected White's modernist form, themes and characters with Auden and Isherwood's plays of the 1930s (*The Ham Funeral*), and Arthur Miller's *After the Fall* and T.S. Eliot's *The Cocktail Party* (*Night on Bald Mountain*).

Under this influence, Peter Fitzpatrick gives muted recognition to White's contribution to Australian theatre describing it as "quite distinctive, in its eclecticism and its idiosyncrasy" while noting the European influences.[48] Yet of White's overall dramaturgy in the four early plays, Fitzpatrick remains concerned that arbitrary fabrication, stylistic impurity and incongruity take precedence over coherence. Carroll makes the critical point that the question of White's arbitrary or gimmicky artifice should be tested against the ways in which the staging elements reinforce the play's action, structure and thematic meaning, in other words, how cast and crew discover the relationship between the parts and the whole within

---

44 Leslie Rees, *The Making of Australian Drama: A Historical and Critical Survey from the 1830s to the 1970s* (London: Angus and Robertson, 1973), 351.
45 Katharine Brisbane, *Not Wrong – Just Different: Observations on the Rise of Contemporary Australian Theatre* (Sydney: Currency Press, 2005), 166.
46 Carroll, "Stage Convention", 11.
47 Roger Covell, "Patrick White's Plays", *Quadrant* 8, no.1 (April–May 1964): 12.
48 Peter Fitzpatrick, *After 'The Doll': Australian Drama Since 1955* (Melbourne: Edward Arnold, 1979), 48.

the syncretic systems of the theatre.[49] The Brechtian notion of the separation of elements of text, music, image and fable is also relevant to the understanding of the conscious "structural disruption" of form to account for new conditions of social life.[50] In a recent overview, John McCallum nominates White as "the first successful modernist dramatist" in the Australian sense of being a "non-naturalistic" playwright who stages an "exultant rebellion against realism".[51] David O'Donnell similarly argues Patrick White's experimentations, although once considered "modernist rubbish", paved the way for acceptance of New Wave theatre and drama later in the 1960s.[52]

In a 1965 review of the publication of White's four early plays, Harry Kippax named *Night on Bald Mountain* as the "most ambitious and subtle" of the four but also the most "fatally" flawed: "[H]ere is the basis of the case for the prosecution".[53] Kippax wants a representation of the essential conflict between "idealism" and "vitalism" that he found satisfying in the first three plays. These oppositions are presumably adapted from the classical Apollonian and Dionysian opposition between reason and passion that drive and explain the conflicts that drive Western civilisation to the brink of destruction. Kippax praises the idealism of the Young Man in *The Ham Funeral* in conflict with the vitalism of Alma Lusty. These same forces drive Roy the idealist teacher in *The Season at Sarsaparilla* and the vitalism of Nola Boyle, although the two do not come into direct conflict. Miss Docker embodies a perverse idealism driven by misplaced vitalism. These oppositions, according to Kippax animate the dramatic conflict in these plays. But in *Night on Bald Mountain*, Kippax appears to be saying that the conflict between idealism and vitalism should play out not as a mundane conflict between the husband and wife but between the hermit Miss Quodling and the idealist Professor Sword. That it finally plays out in an "arbitrary" way between Sword and Nurse Summerhayes, Kippax argues, reduces the dramatic impact. Is this because Kippax views the young woman as childish and lacking in gravitas or is it because she does not represent an opposing force? He writes:

> we are given patterns of dialogue, analysing different kinds of failure, which at the best expose character but fail to jolt it into action. At the climax the catastrophe, being virtually unprepared, seems arbitrary.[54]

---

49 Carroll, "Stage Convention", 11.
50 David Barnett, *Brecht in Practice: Theatre, Theory and Performance* (London: Bloomsbury, 2015), 51.
51 McCallum, *Belonging*, 132.
52 David O'Donnell, "Staging Modernity in the 'New Oceania' Modernism in Australian, New Zealand and Pacific Islands Theatre", in *The Modernist World*, eds. Allana Lindgren and Stephen Ross (London: Routledge, 2015), 283–5.
53 Harry Kippax, "The Novelist as Dramatist", 19.
54 Kippax, "The Novelist as Dramatist", *Sydney Morning Herald*, 23 October 1965.

This critique makes little sense. It is not an arbitrary event that an ageing male professor forces himself on his young female employee. On the contrary, this scenario is perfectly credible, as is its outcome. This is the dramaturgy that turns Kippax against White's theatre that escalates in his reviews of the later plays.

With this play, the dramatic world remains paramount but the wider framework is the mountain as a feature of the relatively untouched Australian landscape. The gothic dimensions of the house and the brooding presence of barren rock offer rich atmospheric and visual possibilities for producers and directors to exploit. This text reveals the theatricality of White's vision beyond language.

The support of a small group of friends, critics, academics, and artists was pivotal to White's entry into the theatrical arena. Reviewers and writers filled the reviews pages of newspapers, while commentary in monthly literary and theatre journals developed a context and explanatory discourse around the apparent novelty and audacity of White's theatre. The conservative backlash led by the Governors of the Adelaide Festival, and critics such as Kippax, however, represented the dominant forces in Australian theatre. The Australian Elizabethan Theatre Trust, J.C. Williamson's Theatres, the Australian Broadcasting Commission, the Adelaide Festival and even the combined power of amateur theatre lobbies remained wary if not hostile to White's theatre. Retreating from the conflict and drama of theatre, White returned to the solitude of the novel, where he would remain for twelve years.

In conclusion, this chapter has not sought to tie White's 1960s plays to a mode of modernist theatre for the sake of the history of Australian theatrical modernism. Rather it attempts to understand White's aesthetic modernisms as a way of finding the patterns and links within and across the plays and to identify a body of work that seeks to interpret, shape, heighten and intensify aspects of modern life rather than merely mirror it. The aim is to connect the plays to the wider movement of modern drama in order to recognise the Australian experience of modernity and the critical modernisms it generated. White's achievement with these remarkable early 1960s plays was to stitch the Australian scene into global modernism. It is ironic as this book will make clear that these early works have acquired a longevity through recurrent productions that have so far been denied the later plays of the 1970s and 80s.

2
Reading the Later Plays: Anticipating Revival

Patrick White returned to the theatre in the late 1970s and up to 1987 to write four more plays and the draft of a fifth. These later plays span the second and third waves of Australian theatre.[1] The second wave, better known as the New Wave had won the case for Australian drama on the mainstream stage and produced a number of critically respected playwrights including Dorothy Hewitt, David Williamson and Alex Buzo, among many more. Moreover, the New Wave began to diversify "the Australian play" from its masculinist-nationalist origins to include political, feminist, avant-garde, diverse and experimental theatres that challenged with some success the continuing dominance of realism and naturalism. Recent scholarship now recognises that White's theatre in the early 1960s "paved the way for a broad acceptance of theatrical modernism in the 1970s and 1980s, emerging from the new wave".[2]

White's later plays were written for a changing Australia. In his autobiography *Flaws in the Glass*, White reflects that the passing of the sixties into the seventies saw a quickening of pace during which money (new money) becomes more visible, and less discrete than his own inheritance about which he enjoyed the luxury of ambivalence. The "social climate", as he describes it, had changed with the privileges of class replaced by the power of money, and with it bribery and corruption.[3] By the mid-1970s, White had become more politically active in the anti-uranium movement and its co-ordinates Indigenous Land Rights, the Green Bans and the conservation movement.

National politics had also become more volatile. The impact of the postwar "Great Acceleration", which had brought more wealth, and rapid increases in population, migration, consumption, pollution, and urban growth produced a

---

1   Geoffrey Milne, *Australian Theatre (Un)limited: Australian Theatre Since the 1950s* (Amsterdam: Rodopi, 2004).
2   David O'Donnell, "Staging Modernity in the 'New Oceania' Modernism in Australian, New Zealand and Pacific Islands Theatre", in *The Modernist World*, eds. Allana Lindgren and Stephen Ross (London: Routledge, 2015), 284.
3   Patrick White, *Flaws in the Glass: A Self-Portrait* (1981; London: Vintage, 1998), 152.

more agonistic political culture.[4] Often applied in relation to its adverse effects on the environment and climate, the Great Acceleration is the context within which these later theatrical works express opposition to endless growth. Political volatility was in evidence when the long period of Liberal National Coalition governance came to an end in 1973 with the election of the Whitlam Labor government, and then again with its dramatic dismissal in 1975.

During this period, White became more actively engaged in public discourse than before and spoke out on politics, the environment and the arts. He joined a list of prominent writers, actors, academics, and sporting champions to speak at the Opera House at a rally in favour of Whitlam's re-election in the 1974 federal election campaign, but threatened to withdraw his support a year later over Labor's approval of mining permits on Fraser Island.[5] When in 1975, the Governor General of Australia, John Kerr, dismissed the Whitlam government, White spoke at an artists' rally for the Labor Party declaring that "the arts had flourished as never before under Labor – if the Liberals come to power I am afraid that we would slip back to those Philistine days that we had in their previous days of rule".[6] The socially progressive Whitlam period was accompanied by new anxieties to do with inflation, the global oil crisis and unemployment that contributed to its downfall.

Despite the return to conservative governance, a decade of cultural production in the arts, social activism and legal reforms including the abolition of censorship meant that theatre did not retreat to the conservative values of the past. *Big Toys*, *Signal Driver*, *Netherwood* and *Shepherd on the Rocks* landed in a less censorial and hostile critical landscape than the first four. Long-standing social taboos had been overturned.

In 1973 White won the Nobel Prize for Literature but declined an invitation to take an honorary seat in the House of Representatives.[7] He accepted the plaque for Australian of the Year in 1974, but named three other men, who in his view, had an equal right to the award: historian Manning Clark, builder's labourer and environmentalist Jack Mundey, and satirist Barry Humphries.[8] As White developed a public profile for speaking on matters of national and local concern, he resisted the push by governments to bask in his literary glory. He returned his Companion of the Order of Australia award in protest at Malcolm Fraser's move to restore the Knighthoods that Whitlam had abolished.[9] As well as taking a radical stance in the public sphere, White's later plays became more daring, more poetic and

---

4   Will Steffen, Wendy Broadgate and Lisa Deutsch, "The Trajectory of the Anthropocene: The Great Acceleration", *The Anthropocene Review* 2, no. 1 (2015): 84.
5   Brian Jones, "Whitlam and the Stars Draw 11,000 to Opera House Rally", *Sydney Morning Herald*, 14 May 1974, 1; *Australian*, "Patrick White Protests to PM", 28 May 1975, 9.
6   Ian Frykberg, "Patrick White Sees 'Sinister' Overtones", *Sydney Morning Herald*, 29 November 1975.
7   *Sydney Morning Herald*, "White Declines Honour", 30 November 1963.
8   *Australian*, "Patrick White Names the Men Who Matter", 26 January 1974.
9   *Sydney Morning Herald*, "No Knights for Patrick White", 23 June 1976, 24.

more politically motivated than his previous plays. They anticipated and stimulated directorial inventiveness and entrepreneurial risk-taking, while reaching out to audiences prepared to tolerate theatricalist over narrative-based drama. Critics continued to find the plays "structurally awkward" as Leonard Radic wrote, "combining as they do a variety of styles and impulses".[10]

Big Toys and the Return to Theatre

Big Toys first performed in 1977, marks Patrick White's return to writing for theatre, thirteen years after *Night on Bald Mountain* received mixed reviews. Critic and publisher Katharine Brisbane attributes White's return to writing for theatre to the success of Jim Sharman's revival of *The Season at Sarsaparilla* at the Drama Theatre at the Sydney Opera House in 1976.[11] David Marr similarly describes Sharman's production as critical to this "second time around" for White.[12] For his part, Sharman believes that the positive reception for *The Season at Sarsaparilla* by the mainstream public and press encouraged White to write for theatre again.[13]

Big Toys is a play about a city and its wealth, its harbour and its modernity. It is a tightly written three-act character and place driven drama set during the winter and spring of 1976 in a penthouse apartment with panoramic views over the Sydney skyline, including the Opera House and the Harbour Bridge. The penthouse belongs to wealthy QC Ritchie Bosanquet and his beautiful and stylish wife Mag. White's proposition in the play is that the Bosanquets covet and ply influence through conspicuous displays of luxury with the finest toys money can buy: clothes, jewellery, penthouses, cars, trips and so on. The moral point of the drama is that luxury is a commodity that preys on the finer emotions leaving those who covet it unhappy in a loveless marriage or an impending existential crisis, symbolised by the westerly winds that blow across the harbour at the end of the play. A third character, Terry Legge, a socialist and a trade union official, is a critical counterpoint to the couple, drawn into their lives, as history would have it, through his past connections to a fourth character, Sir Douglas Stannard, who is an offstage presence in the play. Legge becomes the focal point for the couple's attentions, and an opportunity to compete for his favours, both sexually and juridically, because he is also a key witness for the Crown prosecution case against Stannard that Ritchie is defending. The interlinked past between Legge and Stannard evokes the figure of the class traitor – Stannard is a former labourer and Legge's one-time friend and mentor, now a successful and benighted property developer, who is about to stand trial on bribery charges. The complication interweaves White's anti-uranium stance

---

10 Leonard Radic, "A Satirical Side of White", *Age*, 1 October 1983.
11 Katharine Brisbane, *Not Wrong – Just Different: Observations on the Rise of Contemporary Australian Theatre* (Sydney: Currency Press, 2005).
12 David Marr, interviewed by Sandra D'Urso, 25 October 2017.
13 Jim Sharman, interviewed by Hazel de Berg, 19 February 1976, NLA.obj.192631976. Tape 3.

with an account of corruption at the upper levels of corporate culture. Stannard is seeking to become the Chairman of Intermond Mining, which has plans to develop uranium mining export interests that a conviction for bribery would stymie. As his defence barrister, Ritchie Bosanquet will dig up anything that comprises the witness. The plot and the intrigue that follows is activated by Stannard's offstage presence and, as a parallel, the offstage presence of a red Ferrari "that Doug and I [Ritchie] wanted to make a gesture of".[14]

This dramaturgical move breaks with the convention of the onstage protagonist and the discovery of a body, the guilty party or a lost object, with the effect that the drama is concerned with how events play out behind the scenes. There is no courtroom drama in Act Three in which the characters' moral struggles are enacted within the dramatic world. Instead, the action takes place in a confined interior space. The mood is leavened by witty and playful talk rather than tense or dramatic scenes.

The exchange of dialogue in a glorious setting is the central action and feature of the play. Mag as indicated is a glamorous and yet slightly inscrutable character. The stage notes initially describe her as she is "*discovered lying on the bed, either in bra and very brief panties, or a dressing-gown over these, according to how much the actress can effectively reveal*" (5). Clearly aiming for a sexualised image, and inviting the audience to gaze and eavesdrop, the extra-dialogic text is also signalling its awareness of decisions made by the theatrical team in the context of production. Nevertheless the stage notes are highly prescriptive. She is described as "*stylish*" and "*feverish in her manner*" as she chats on the telephone while playing with a large balloon. Soon, she pricks it with a fingernail so that it sags like "like some ugly old wrinkled scrotum" as she tells Eileen on the other end of the line. She has joined the Labor Party, partly as a provocation to her "true-blue" Liberal husband (5–6). Mag is seen to enjoy the luxury afforded by her marriage to the powerful QC but likes to go to Labor Party meetings. We later learn that her own upbringing was in a rural working-class family in Tibooburra, a town in far northwest New South Wales over a thousand kilometres from Sydney, where her mother died young and from where she escaped as a teenager from her sexually abusive father. The joke in Act One about the balloon as a scrotum resonates later with the trauma of her father's attempt at rape. This background provides the important context for her marriage to the QC in which she has compromised her emotional, and sexual life, for an opulent life in Sydney.

Mag soon meets Terry Legge at a Labor Party Town Hall meeting and brings him home to seduce, and introduce him to Ritchie, who finds something from his past to compromise the Crown witness. Legge is offered big toys, of which Mag is one, and interest is directed at the power, appeal and the will to withstand the second, highly reified material object, here signified by a red Ferrari. In this

---

14 Patrick White, *Collected Plays, Volume II: Big Toys, Signal Driver, Netherwood, Shepherd on the Rocks* (Sydney: Currency Press, 1994), 50. All further references to these plays are given in parentheses in the text.

most Marxist-oriented of White's eight plays, the agency of capital, the division of labour, commodity fetishism, and the politics and economics of uranium mining are central to the unfolding story.

The prominence given to commodified objects in *Big Toys* is signalled through the play's title and reiterated through stage objects such as the enormous balloon, an emerald necklace, the keys to the Ferrari, and the glittering Sydney lights. They mark the scenes in which they appear as pivotal points in the narrative and show the pressure points and contradictions of the 1970s. When Bosanquet attempts to reward Legge with the keys to a Ferrari, the moment is gestic, indicative of the social relations of class but also sexuality in that the QC had previously clasped his wife's emerald necklace around Terry's neck as an erotic object, a plaything or toy for diversionary amusement.

The interaction between character and symbolic object reveals social and emotional states, including unspoken desires and secrets. The passing of objects from one character to another (who gives a gift to whom and how it is received, or rejected) all play a part in a series of interlocking moves from seduction to bribery. In Act Two Ritchie is witheringly indifferent to having "walked in" on Mag and Terry in bed in the mid-afternoon. Ritchie and Terry then engage, on the one hand, as competitors on the opposite side of politics and class, and on the other as males, whose diverse personalities and socio-economic circumstances provide an attraction of opposites. Each is curious about the other but it is Terry who drops his barrier and becomes more porous. A whisky-fuelled encounter condenses the elements at play into a single image: Terry, wearing Ritchie's dressing-gown, sits looking at the mirror on Mag's dressing table while Ritchie slips her emerald necklace around his neck. The inter-connectedness among the three points of the triangle is sealed by the mediation of the erotic object. Terry can merely offer his bodily self up in the transaction. This mutually reinforcing system assists with the gestic content of individual scenes and the overall political commentary embedded in the dramaturgy. Bertolt Brecht wrote that gestus embodied actions that express the complex social, historical, affective and ideological relations among characters. As he wrote, "expressions of a gest are usually highly complicated and contradictory, so they cannot be rendered by any single word",[15] so the body, situation, action, and, as now acknowledged, gender play their part. *Big Toys* is not a piece of Brechtian theatre but White and Sharman were familiar with the plays and the techniques of epic theatre that are part of the repertoire of modern theatre, especially in socio-political dramas. White's gestic theatricalisation of everyday objects fills in the gaps in what is left unsaid on the realist stage; the range of interpretations it activates gives the audience plenty to think about.

White's key interest in *Big Toys* is arguably to expose the corruption in the investment, mining and minerals sector, especially those with interests in uranium

---

15 Bertolt Brecht, *Brecht on Theatre: The Development of an Aesthetic*, ed. and trans. John Willett (1964; London: Methuen, 1984), 198.

mining, then the subject of mass public protests. But there is also an interest in the relationship between sexuality and money. While the drama mimics the intrigue that underpins the corporate world, it does so by means of a game of ritual courtship initiated by Ritchie towards Terry. His ritual ordination by means of the robe and the jewel inducts Terry into the transactional relations among the rich, played out against a background of the city's glittering lights. The corruption case is duly resolved in Stannard's favour and Ritchie wins another high-profile defence of the morally indefensible, leaving the former free to become the new chairman of Intermond Mining, a company with major interests in uranium mining.

Big Toys (and later *Netherwood*) plays provocatively with gender fluidity and homosexual desire to destabilise the performed identities of civic philistines. In distinguishing between artists and civic philistines in this later period, White's criticism is primarily directed at members of the Establishment – corporate capitalists, corrupt politicians, developers and so on – not the lower middle and working class whose compromised lives are satirised but not condemned in *The Ham Funeral*, *The Season at Sarsaparilla*, *Cheery Soul* and *Night on Bald Mountain*. The plays' narratives are sympathetic to Alma Lusty and Nola Boyle for their sensuality under the conditions of social and cultural constraint, and to the Young Man, Roy Child, and Denis Craig for their artistic aspirations. They are in turn critical of bullies like Will Lusty, opportunists like Digger Masson, and sexual abusers such as Professor Sword.

Mag's story is of an empty marriage compensated by luxury. Observing her husband's body in its expensive suit, Mag declares, "you've never ever been a human being – although you're dressed as one" (7) in a line that could be delivered deadpan to the audience while concealing emotional distress. Later, Ritchie appears in "*an unexpectedly way-out jump-suit*" (33) that Mag has bought for him as a joke. The emphasis on costume in the dialogue and stage directions, enhances the sense in which Ritchie is cast as a type whose surface acts as a second skin, thickening the exterior against ruptures from within, whether from the conscience or the soul. The drama proposes that the other side of the Ritchie of the legal-corporate world is the clown and toy-master, a frightening figure laden with sinister intent. Mag begins to express frustration at being "smothered by all this expensive drag" (19) indicating the emerald necklace.

Brisbane writes in the preface to the play "that *Big Toys* takes up where *Night on Bald Mountain* left off in 1964", with Mag and Miriam Sword, both Hedda Gabler figures trapped in hollow marriages. Mag fills her days with shopping, lunches and gossip, and is the resentful acceptor of life's big toys but social class plays its part in her malaise. In line with White's female characters, she is a sober version of the unhappy Miriam Sword, a pre-feminist subject lacking agency, a job and her own money. White ends the play with Mag looking out over the harbour as the westerly winds blow, with the palms of her hands pressed against the glass, whispering "Christ … oh, Christ …" and soundlessly crying (58).

Signal Driver: The Ordinary, the Astral and Uranium

Signal Driver, was written in 1981 after Jim Sharman, who had been appointed artistic director of the 1982 Adelaide Festival of Arts, invited White to write a play for the festival. The invitation consolidated the regime change at the festival, which had, twenty years earlier subjected White's plays to hostile treatment. The play premiered at Sharman's Lighthouse Theatre, Adelaide, in 1982, directed by Neil Armfield.

Just as *The Season at Sarsaparilla* calls itself a charade of suburbia, *Signal Driver* is denoted as "A Morality Play for the Times". Here the "pre-given reference"[16] is to the medieval morality play, an allegorical form, which precedes Elizabethan drama and captures the figure of the Everyman, a typically ordinary character, who seeks salvation. The medieval Everyman sets out on a journey that has its ups and downs, friends and foes, but he achieves salvation and eternal life in heaven in the end. *Signal Driver* represents the modern Everyman and Everywoman as an ordinary modern couple: "middling sort of people", sober, steady and seemingly lacking the artifice of the theatrical.[17] They are Theo Vokes, a carpenter, and his wife Ivy, a mother and later an antique dealer. Medievalist Leanne Groeneveld notes that the morality play was revived and adapted by expressionist dramatists, especially Hugo von Hofmannsthal's *Jedermann* (1911) and Georg Kaiser's *From Morning to Midnight* (1915), to express "the plight of an early twentieth-century Everyman".[18] These expressionist dramas utilise the pre-given references in the medieval morality play to investigate what Groeneveld refers to as "the plight of a modernist subject searching for and failing to find fulfilment", and thereby "providing a modern perspective on familiar human anxieties and challenges".[19] In the late twentieth century in which the play is written, the search for and failure to find fulfilment plays out as tragi-comedy, or absurdist comedy. With its comic and parodic representations of human subjects, *Signal Driver* can be read as a late modernist adaptation of the subgenre of the morality play for Australia in the 1980s. As morality play, the drama suggests that the fate of the Vokes offers a theatrical demonstration of a wrong state of affairs intended to prompt questions about alternative ethical, moral and political stances.

The play begins in the evening with two timeless, supernatural Beings, described as a pair of "*super deros*" (57), lying on either side of a transport shelter calling out to each other as they wait for Theo and Ivy Vokes to appear. Theo approaches first through the audience to wait at the shelter. He carries a large wooden chest by its handle. The Beings advise that he routinely arrives of an evening at the shelter and then watches as the tram disappears from view. White's

---

16 John Frow, *Genre* (London: Routledge, 2005), 19.
17 Alex Eric Hernandez, *The Making of British Bourgeois Tragedy: Modernity and the Art of Ordinary Suffering* (Oxford: Oxford University Press, 2019), 3.
18 Leanne Groeneveld, "Modernist Medievalism and the Expressionist Morality Play: Georg Kaiser's *From Morning to Midnight*", *Film and Media Studies* 16 (2019): 83.
19 Groeneveld, "Modernist Medievalism", 98.

stage directions indicate that "*THEO half-raises his arm, then lets it fall impotently*" (68), in other words, he may fail to signal the driver. This melancholic figure then prepares to wait for the next tram while cautioning himself against the sentimentality that would drive him back to Ivy and the domestic routine at home. The idea is that he is to leave his wife for a room by the ocean where he will live a solitary but meaningful life as an artisan. When Ivy comes to fetch him, as she always does, he succumbs to her embrace and they set off back through the audience in the direction of home. Ivy wants to have children; all she has ever wanted. After they have left, the Beings chime in noting the unequal distribution of labour and power accorded to each of the Vokes:

> FIRST BEING: By and large, the Vokes couple are happy in their ad hoc relationship.
>
> SECOND BEING: … resigned to the quid pro quo of marriage.
>
> FIRST BEING: They don't realise that the situation in which they're involved …
>
> SECOND BEING: … currently…
>
> FIRST BEING: … is not exclusively theirs.
>
> SECOND BEING: Hopefully they will not become too drastically disillusioned when the scenario begins to …
>
> FIRST BEING: … clot. (69)

It is not so much that the scenario of marriage and children is opposed to the elevated world of the artist and his work, but is enmeshed in a matrimonial economy that functions as a micro version of economic relations. Theo's theatrical escapes are unsuccessful because as the Second Being explains: "Presently at least, in a sociological context, they are wholly dependent on each other" (69). Lacking awareness of philosophy, ideology, and history, the Beings declare with bitter irony that the naïve Vokes / Everyman and Everywoman, represent the "Lucky Australians" (70). The Beings continue to develop their sociological commentary with irony.

Act Two sees the Vokes in their fifties in the 1950s. It is again evening at the transport shelter but "*Random buildings have appeared on what was the stark hill behind the shelter*" (72), signalling urbanisation is turning the environment into spaces of production and consumption. The trams of the 1920s have been replaced by buses but the shelter itself – the symbolic heart of the play – remains the same. The Vokes' social status has changed: Ivy has traded up to an antique furniture business and Theo no longer carts his box of tools around. Ivy has changed her name to Jasmine to fit her new persona and has taken up with the "sophisticated" and business-savvy Sol, who is referenced but never appears in the play. Theo is now "a fine figure of a man" (72). Following the structure in Act One, Theo arrives at the shelter as the Beings sing:

> Not running, but on the run,
> not waving, but drowning ...

Ivy arrives to take him home again but appears as if in drag, a socially aspirational version of her younger self. White imagines her cruelly as "*an artificially preserved, menopausal fifty*". She has acquired a cultivated accent. Although she is on her way to her dinner date with her lover, and wears a supper hat in coral, she worries about Theo in what the Beings muse is "the daisy-chain ... of marriage and adultery ..." (74). He is bitter and filled with remorse. Another development is that the Vokes have had children who are a great disappointment to them, and grandchildren. Theo persists in a melancholy way with his identity as an artist:

> THEO: What you ought to realise is that the secrets of the artist – or craftsman – connect with that secret life of the woman, creating the child she carries in her womb; this pocket of dark-green moss with a pearl of flesh lying in its moisture, growing, expanding, till no conspiracy between you can hold back its embryo conscience from facing life. (78)

When the bus arrives, Ivy dares Theo to signal it to stop. Again, in a repetition of the half-raised hand gesture in Act One, he lets the bus charge past. In a scene that introduces a space of memory, White softens the harshness of the cynical, bitter marriage by introducing a lyrical element as they return to the point of origin in which they reminisce about a soldier returning from the Western Front, who meets a girl, sheltering from the rain under a paperbark. This foundational moment of love triggers a flickering consciousness in Ivy:

> IVY: I don't know. Everytime the bell rings and I open the door – I expect to find someone who's been shadowing me, who's never taken shape, man or woman, all my life ... (83)

But poetics fail her.

In Act Three tower blocks with illuminated windows provide the backdrop for the bus shelter. The Morality Play for the Times has arrived at 1982. Theo and Ivy are now elderly. The traffic is more obvious and imposing than before; the straggling trees from Act One have now disappeared. This time the roles are reversed. Ivy arrives at the shelter first but is terrified of the traffic and can't remember why she is there. While the Beings reflect on the ongoing treatment of Indigenous peoples and the colonial past, Theo arrives with her coat. Ivy has plans to buy a ticket to Bourke, the apocryphal back of beyond. Theo is resigned but Ivy, having lost her inhibitions through dementia, swears and rocks in despair as she recalls how she gave up life for marriage. Uttering thoughts she has never had until now, she declares "I want to rub my hands in the dust, rub it on my cheeks, find out what I've been living for – in this country" (88). The flicker of consciousness of alienation soon subsides into the gentle comedy of elderly comradeship. They reflect on adultery and disappointments as the bus approaches for the third time. The Beings are quite drunk but get up to watch as they intone:

FIRST BEING: The dero's express …

SECOND BEING: … The Bourke connection…

FIRST BEING: … for runaway couples…

SECOND BEING: … and neglected poets…

FIRST BEING: …and masturbators…

FIRST AND SECOND BEING: [*with the scepticism of the all-knowing*]
… and those who've failed to signal the driver – but this time will … will …? (90)

Now it is Ivy whose gesture lacks the will to signal the driver. As the play moves towards the end, the stage directions describe "*a pale, cold ineffable light*" that grows to bathe the stage. It is the Aurora Australis, the false dawn, that lights up the sky of a night. The sight of it makes Theo wonder why he never put his head in the oven. What the audience sees is an elderly couple illuminated by an atmospheric light as they exit supporting each other as they cross the road. White makes the case for love and asks the audience to empathise with the couple. This empathy is quickly interrupted by the Beings, who refer to Ivy and Theo as two blind mice returning home. The Beings are about to set off to check the four cardinal points of the land, and move downstage for a final song and dance act. The switch to vaudeville parodies the Vokes' lack of awareness of uranium and the nuclear power it produces that might blow us all up. The final moment sees nature in the form of the spectacular Aurora Australis take possession of the whole theatre.

Each of the three evenings is presented as a variation on a paradigmatic event. An anxious Ivy comes after Theo, they argue, make up and then go home. The key moment in each variation sees the approach of the transport, the decision to signal the driver or not, and then the failure to do so. The transport passes and the couple go home. This symmetry is made interesting by the variations on the theme that develop over the three time frames.

White's interest in outsider figures continues with the Beings, who drink copious amounts of alcohol and are prone to obscenities. They are contemptuous of both the simple Vokes' mundanity, and "Whitey", mining magnates digging up uranium in the Northern Territory to feed a nuclear hungry West (58). The dero figure appears across multiple plays from the two old scavengers in *The Ham Funeral*, the Goat Keeper in *Night on Bald Mountain* and the carnivalesque parade of prostitutes and addicts in *Shepherd on the Rocks*. In White's autobiography, *Flaws in the Glass*, deros are transmitters of sacred art works, their fallen state a bitter reflection of the status of the artist in modern Australia. In their rifling through trash and recovering of discarded objects, White discovers the principle of vitality crucial to a work of art; these inventive practices of survival bestow upon the dero a liminal presence in a society largely driven by materialism and commerce. The Beings in *Signal Driver* perform a function that affirms the presence of the metaphysical or virtual within and among the real, showing that being is not a reduction to a single real world based on resemblances. In terms of the morality play, they represent the absence of God in the modern world, while their dereliction speaks to the degraded status of the metaphysical in the rational world.

Theo Vokes, whose name suggests a theological disposition, and also *evokes* the German word for folk (*Volk*), does not seek salvation by religious means. Rather in the age of individualism, he seeks personal fulfilment through asceticism. The premise is that by becoming a solitary artisan, sleeping alone on "a monk's palliasse" (65), he can inhabit an idealised space. The moral of the story then follows. Failure to escape is related to the temptations of sexual and material comfort in the modern world. Towards the end of the drama, Ivy too identifies as a subject who may have sought more but has failed to achieve fulfilment in life, giving expression to Everywoman's perspective on regret. The questions the morality play asks for the times is how do Everyman and Everywoman find fulfilment in the modern world? What has secular modernity got to offer a human subject? Is personal fulfilment a modern version of redemption and salvation? Finally, through the agency of two metaphysical Beings who comment on human actions, the more political question about whether the world can survive the nuclear age is presented. If the morality takes a final position it pitches the consolations of old age when the basic expression of love boils down to Theo bringing Ivy's coat to the shelter.

In the first act the shelter is located in a sparse semi-rural setting populated by "two or three native trees" giving the impression of a place largely untouched by urban development. Sounds such as a horse-drawn dray and the occasional car break the silence while the tram is heard approaching in a shower of sparks on newly electrified tracks. As time progresses buildings appear behind the shelter and the tram is replaced by buses. By Act Three the sound of cars whizzing by "viciously" is heard, the native trees have all but disappeared and tower blocks with illuminated windows frame the shelter, which now has a sign "Signal Driver" on its front (85). The Vokes' failure to progress, to experience more than mere "flickers of perception through their half-consciousness" (Notes 55), as White writes in the description of the setting, is presented at times empathetically in ways that make the play more than a critique of Australian suburbia. The repeated failure to "signal driver", sent up in bawdy song and poetic quip by the Beings, is also couched in a sentimental love of home and companionship that feeds into the play's ideological purpose of exposing the existential threat to human life of uranium mining and nuclear arms.

That time passes differently for the two couples, one terrestrial and one metaphysical is crucial to White's framing of the fragile human condition in relation to the existential threat of nuclear war. Here the Vokes' lack of intellectual striving is a warning about Australian apathy and a call to awaken to nuclear threat. In the case of the Vokes, a sense of obligation to the other, as well as a sacrifice of self has allowed them to form a fraught yet solid bond. They have traded much happiness and creativity in life for something they consider more superior – their marital legacy. But that sacrifice and sense of obligation to the other will amount to nothing if Australians condone by silence the escalation of uranium mining and export. This is, as the subtitle hails it, the moral of the Morality Play for the Times.

In terms of the theatrical context, there are indicative sensibilities shared by other late modernist artists and playwrights. At the 1982 Adelaide Festival of Arts, where *Signal Driver* premiered, American realist painter, Edward Hopper, and actor, playwright and screenwriter Sam Shepard were also featured. The Whitney Museum of Art Touring Exhibition of Hopper's major works showed the artist's rendering of a growing malaise in urban America in a series of paintings featuring empty cityscapes and isolated human figures. Two of Shepard's Family Trilogy, *The Curse of the Starving Class* and *Buried Child*, appeared in a double bill both referencing the "the physical, emotional and spiritual starvation" of the family on modern America.[20] White had been working with these themes in the Australian context during his early phase and they combine with the mythic and metaphysical in the later plays. In terms of form, the overt theatricalist style of *Signal Driver* and the two final plays – the agnosticism of the carnivalesque, the fantastic, and the rupture of narrative – would seem to be well suited for revivals.

Netherwood: "Loonyland" in the Southern Highlands

Netherwood is a comic grotesque drama about fragile identities and institutional violence. It features an assemblage of socially marginalised figures and those who would contain or help them such as social reformers, healthcare workers, police

---

[20] Thomas P. Adler, "Repetition and regression in *Curse of the Starving Class* and *Buried Child*" in M. Roudané (Ed.) *The Cambridge Companion to Sam Shepard*, (Cambridge: Cambridge University Press, 2002), 112.

and, improbably, self-styled nationalists whose task it is to defend country life. The drama is nominally set within the context of the de-institutionalisation of psychiatric care in the 1970s, which saw the shift from confinement to community-based care. But White broadens the theme to consider the fluid boundaries between rational and irrational behaviour amidst a period of social and cultural change. The play imagines a scenario in which social change drifts into rural communities via urban dwellers seeking a better lifestyle and moving onto abandoned farms. In this respect the play articulates conflict between old landed money and modern urban wealth, and between the values of rural workers and bourgeois professionals.

In a slow-burning drama that escalates in its final moments, the play begins in early spring, lingers over summer and gathers pace as state-sanctioned violence is realised amidst aggressive assertions of national sovereignty. *Netherwood* stages the different ontological claims of realism, masquerade, and absurdity to arrive at a hyperrealist finale. This theatricalist format activates themes of identity and difference as well as the field of psychoanalysis and the politics of nationalism.

To explore these themes the drama is contained in a secluded space set at a distance from town and city. White deploys another large house – this time a dilapidated country dwelling in rich grazing country in the Southern Highlands of New South Wales, not unlike the locality in which the playwright's family held extensive properties. The house has a history of personal loss that has led to its current state of neglect in the period following the departure of the previous owners, the Du Faurs, who were born and bred in the district and well known in the community. It was widely understood that after their only child had tragically drowned in the property's dam, the grief-stricken parents lost interest in the farm, sold up and left the district. The pre-history of the house aligns the play, and its present inhabitants, with Chekhov's comic-melancholic turn of the century drama *The Cherry Orchard* in which the past loss of child haunts an assemblage of characters left behind by the passage of time. Like the crumbling London house in *The Ham Funeral*, White's modern Australian characters arrive in a country house marked by the past and imbued with an atmosphere of neglect.

The new owners are former Sydneysiders, Royce and Alice Best, who aim to make a new life in the country based on service to the damaged souls of modern civilisation. Royce is a former banker and footballer, who has abandoned a rising career, for a change of lifestyle. They turn the house into a live-in community facility for three guests, all former inmates of the nearby asylum drolly known as Bonkers Hall. The unwanted arrival of the Bests' Austrian psychoanalyst, Rolf Eberhard, reveals the fragile state of their own psyches and suggests they may also be part of the social experiment they manage.

The play initially follows the daily rituals of the household. Alice, whom White describes as a middle-class woman in her early forties, refers to her care work at Netherwood as a "sacramental service" that reaches a high point in acts of washing "excremental sheets" (133). These acts of contrition turn out to be a down payment on the liberties she later takes with Mog, Alice's favourite guest, who has been released into her care from the institution she has lived in since she was very young. On her entrance, Margaret Figg (Mog) is described as a *"girl in her mid-twenties, dark, heavily built, slow moving, what some might call a slob."* (103). She cradles a dead chicken, announcing she has "rung its neck" because it was crooked and others were picking on it (104). This act is followed by play in which Mog feeds an imaginary baby, possibly an incarnation of the newborn she may have smothered in Bonkers Hall, fathered by a priest she refers to as Mr Fatty Belly. Mog is unsurprisingly resistant to Alice's attempts to provide love, tuition in bourgeois politeness and "edumacation", having been let down by so many people including her own mother, who sent her to the institution. These brief scenic moments are indicative of how gender and intellectual disability intersect in the figure of Mog, whose learning has amounted to compulsory adaptation to a performed life that is not of her own choosing. This point has implications for the agency exercised by Mog in her games with Alice later in the play.

Another guest is Harry Britt, an ex-boxer, now an alcoholic, and an arch misogynist with a *"bruiser's face, broken nose, a cauliflower ear, scars from healed cuts, an alcoholic's skin"* and a stubbornness that provides *"the something which helps the desperate survive"* (112). He is also incontinent and confined to a wheelchair. The challenge he presents is taken up by Royce. Mrs Dora Pilbeam, an ageing diva, pianist, and pill addict, completes the household. She is under the illusion that her presence at Netherwood is arranged so she can "introduce music therapy to the mentally deranged" (105). Each of the guests resents the other, although alliances are temporarily mobilised, while overall the scenes among them reveal a bitter comic past of institutionalisation and abuse.

The narrative moves along with the entrance of unexpected visitors such as Dr Eberhard, who has tracked down Alice. Entering the house through the open terrace door and startling Alice, far away from his Sydney rooms, the ensuing conversation confirms that Alice and Rolf were his patients:

ALICE: [*coldly*] I was never your patient.

EBERHARD: You came to me, however, and returned every other day.

ALICE: I was what you created. The case you wanted.

EBERHARD: One always hoped for an interesting case, and you were that.

ALICE: [*turning on him passionately*] I'd like to know what you want from me here at Netherwood? All you stand for is behind me. I've started living positively. What you amounted to, Rolf, was the dregs of life.

2 Reading the Later Plays

> EBERHARD: You needed to paddle, shall we say, in the dregs. When you weren't in my rooms, pouring out your confidences, my telephone never stopped ringing. If it wasn't you, it was your alter ego.
>
> ALICE: My alter ego?
>
> EBERHARD: [*interrogatively*] Your husband?
>
> ALICE: Preposterous!
>
> EBERHARD: Didn't he tell you he consulted me. (109–110)

The dialogue recalls Sigmund Freud's famous case involving a young woman known as "Dora", whom he treated in 1900 and deemed a therapeutic failure. The case was controversial for Freud's suggestion that the foundations of the hysteria she denied were to be found in the complex psycho-sexual dynamics that underscored her familial relationships. Alice denies she was Eberhard's "patient" and denies his current insinuations about her attachments to the guests. When he strokes Alice's neck with the back of his hand in a gesture that she rebuffs, White underlines the predatory behaviour of the psychiatrist.

After a brief pause, during which the lights fade and come up again some months later, it is summer. The next scene begins with the arrival of the second set of visitors, Fred and Flo Stubbs, a local farming couple, who identify as upstanding country figures. The scene has a suspicious Stubbs slyly wondering what people get up to in the big house as he enters through the terrace doors to momentarily lie on the daybed that will soon be the site of the sexual games that take place in the house. This ironic implication of desire and complicity adds to the drive that sees him return to "Loonyland" (132) in the final scene to enact his unseemly interest in their social and sexual lives. The brief entrance and exit of the Stubbs is crucial to the narrative that begins to move towards a violent end.

In between the departure of the Stubbs and the final scene, White creates a liminal space for masquerade, gender ambiguity, homoeroticism, and mimicry. Identities are adopted and discarded with the assistance of lighting changes and objects such as costume, hats and scarves, the daybed and chairs. These objects and effects delineate the theatricalist text in terms of its anticipation of staged performance.[21] As Stubbs departs, Alice re-enters in "*a long, white, floating transparent robe over bra and scanties, also white. The robe is open*" (133) for a performance in which she co-stars with Mog. In this new playful role she is

---

21 Christopher Balme, *The Cambridge Introduction to Theatre Studies* (Cambridge: Cambridge University Press, 2008), 119.

uninhibited as she admires her reflection in the upstage mirror. The presence of a sombrero and scarf on a chair (also noted by Stubbs) is the sign that a game of masquerade will soon begin. Into this summer afternoon walks Royce in red bathers, thongs and a towel ready for a swim in the dam. He experiences a rare feeling of attraction to his wife, as if to flirt for a moment with the idea of a sexually active marriage, but Alice is keen to deflect his attentions. When Mog appears, the younger woman has changed into a "*glistening apparition*" in a white silk tunic and slacks and embraces Alice who responds ecstatically to her (134). Sexual play leads on to dance, raunchy songs, and mimicry – Alice plays a prostitute with Mog as her client, Mog plays Alice's mother, and Alice rebels. Harry joins in to relive his boxing heyday as Alice and Mog take on the roles of Nettie and Myra, two women who vie for his attentions. The scenes of masquerade and lesbian desire come to an end when they hear Royce returning from his swim in the fateful dam. Alice rushes off to change while Mog's actions dissolve in the following way: "MOG, *the apparition, literally vanishes (if possible) or disappears through the door leading to the inner house*" (140–1). This liminal scene is designed to ask questions about reality and realism, and appearance and deception within the realms of desire and sexual play.

Left alone in the room Royce, as Alice has throughout the play, checks his reflection in the mirror as the lights darken to enclose him in a "*womb of light which suggests another reality*" (143). Netherwood is now a space where he rehearses a new identity that seems to involve a return to an adolescent state, where he refers to Harry as Dad, and gazes narcissistically into the mirror admiring his bare chest, and imagining the feminine within. The former golden boy of banking and football concedes a penchant for tapestry and cross-dressing. The ever-watchful Eberhard reappears to find Royce passive on the daybed and willing to talk in alternately defensive and surprisingly revealing ways about identity but he resents Eberhard's recourse to the cliché of the homoerotic basis of male sport:

> ROYCE: [*groaning, putting on the ocker act*] You get on my tits, mate. Just because I enjoy – or used to enjoy – a game with the boys, you find all sorts of *significance* in it. That might go down in Vienna, Budapest, but this is Australia. (145)

A little later Royce utters the rhetorical xenophobic question: "If you don't like it here, why don't you go back where you came from?" (145). The men are combative and manipulative. When Royce reveals he and Alice wear each other's clothes, he finds one of Dora's tatty dresses on the floor, gets into it and goes to the piano to play brief pieces of Bach, Beethoven, Liszt and Debussy under the fascinated gaze of Eberhard. The gestus constituted by Royce wearing Dora's tatty dress to play Bach draws attention to the prohibition on the arts and music for upper-class boys. The voice that asks if playing the piano is "Too *sissy*?" (147) is that of the man who played rugby. Royce now plays defiantly for Eberhard, who becomes the father figure in the reperformance of boyhood trauma. Jim Sharman's premiere production of the play featured cross-gender casting of Dora so that the scene parodically realises the feminisation that playing the piano is said to initiate.

The scene places the inner reality and self-deception of Royce and Alice under scrutiny and gradually produces further revelations. Mog reappears beside the baby highchair to recall the image of her dead baby's abject face and wonders if the child of an intellectually disabled girl and a priest would have been a monster or a man. Royce and Harry enter a surrealist space in which they sit on baby high-chairs from which Royce unfurls a tapestry depicting "*a heraldic monster, part bird, part animal, of Australian origin*" (151). This long sequence of masquerade and homoerotic desire finally runs its course as the outer frame reasserts itself at Netherwood.

During the intervening middle section of masquerade, Stubbs calls the police to check on the goings on at Netherwood and the slide into massacre is activated. The critic Harry Kippax could not accept the play's ending because in his view it lacked a rationalising motive that reduced the ending to " mayhem perfunctorily prepared".[22] But to read the arrival of the Stubbs as initiators of the gradual build up to mayhem is to arrive at the play's symbolic and ideological rationale. The rural couple, stereotypes of battling farmers, provide an intrusive and judgemental outer framework for the inner dramatic world of the house, and they embody and enforce a colonial view of the land as a human resource to be farmed and made productive by good Christian people. He voices a resentment of city folk "movin' in all over the country. Buyin' up the land. Takin' the bread out of the mouths of decent farmers" (132). Faith in cattle grazing takes on the air of moral principle and White critically presents this view as bigotry clothed in entitlement. It is also offered to the reader and audiences as the rationale for the violent intervention that takes place at the end of the play. The idea of good grazing land providing a culturally therapeutic environment for damaged people is beyond tolerance in Stubbs' world. The critique of ordinary neighbours found to be judgemental and violent is carried to comic extremes but it also contributes to claims of an elitist White who is as intolerant of the other as the subjects of his satire.

The dramaturgical demarcation of inner and outer worlds has by now become a characteristic feature of White's plays. The frames perform a number of functions but primarily indicate different modes of address, behaviour and belief, and are often identified as physical settings.[23] The street in *The Ham Funeral*, the barking dogs that roam the streets in *The Season at Sarsaparilla* and the invisible dog in *A Cheery Soul*, the dual narrative frames of the mountain and house in *Night on Bald Mountain* are examples of such frames. In the later plays, the westerly winds blow across Sydney Harbour, the Beings in *Signal Driver* fly around the universe, and now the outside world represented by Eberhard, the Stubbs, and later Miss Jelbart and the police, encroach on the house. In one sense these outer frames

---

22   Harry Kippax, "White Play Still Disappoints Under Sharman Direction" *Sydney Morning Herald*, 23 January 1984, 10.
23   See John Frow, *Genre* (London: Routledge, 2005), 9–10.

simply refer to the social and environmental setting of the texts but in another important way they function dialectically as estrangement devices, unsettling the natural world with evidence of its man-made and arbitrary structure. White pairs the mobilisation of a rights discourse with a white farmer, anti-intellectual, yet armed with the protections and privilege of the authorities. They will never admit that property ownership was determined by a violent legacy of white European property law over Indigenous sovereignty. The casting of the Bests' house as a threat to national sovereignty is emblematised in the Arcadian surrounds of Netherwood, and later its interruption by a skirmish of inexplicable violence.

As the inhabitants of the house return to the stage dressed as themselves, Stubbs also returns, heralded comically by the sound of a lowing beast. Speaking of Du Faur, compared to whom Royce and Alice's household of "well-heeled drop-out nuts" falls short, Stubbs explains:

> STUBBS: 'E was one of us – a real Australian.
>
> ALICE: What's real?
>
> [MOG *plumps down at the far side of the table, yawns, buries her head in her arms.*]
>
> STUBBS: [*astounded*] Real? Well, *real*! See that 'and? Those scars I got diggin' fence-post 'oles in a drought – through bloody stones – strainer slipped on wire – nearly took me thumb off. I could show yer me foot a steer trampled – or me groin that the *barbed* wire savaged when a brumby got me cornered. That's real enough. That's Astraylia – held together by wire, bags, and politicians' promises. (154–55)

As a parting shot Stubbs remarks: "Now we got maggots bred on city garbage – swarming over good Australian country" (155). To the rest of the household, Stubbs represents unwanted attention and the encroachment of the outside world. By the final scenes of the play, as a party including the police, Stubbs, Eberhard and Miss Jelbart from Bonkers Hall approach the house, Mog, Harry and Dora fear capture by the authorities and their forcible return to the institution where they had previously endured electric shock treatment. With their capture imminent, they prepare to face off against an armed hostile police force, medical health experts and Stubbs in an inept but fatal shootout. At the end of the play, the scene is one of cruelty and mayhem with dead bodies and wrecked furniture littering the room. Alice and Royce survive to face an uncertain future.

Netherwood poetically invokes a sovereign power that requires the ejection of abject figures who are manifestly queer and deranged from national space and the maintenance of their removal through violent policing. In this imagined scenario, the division between real Australians and outsiders leads to state-sanctioned death. The play can be read as a poetic realisation of the kind of thinking that has marked Australia's political and legal history, especially its anxieties about contamination by outsiders.

Shepherd on the Rocks: A Phantasmagoria

Shepherd on the Rocks was first performed in 1987 and as White's final published play, it is his most ambitious stylistically and thematically. Its dramatic arc encompasses an epic tale on biblical, social, artistic and philosophical themes combined with high degrees of theatricality, humour and pathos. It has additional moral elements akin to a modern fable and a parable that ends in the repudiation of institutional religion. The fantastic is delivered through carnivalesque characters, visionary escapades, magic and a stunning Grand Guignol. The text revisits themes explored in White's earlier plays such as the inner world of artists, eccentrics and dreamers, the ordinary lives of those without wealth or power, and the role of fate and religion in a modern secular world. The key figure in the play is Reverend Daniel Shepherd (Danny), Rector of Budgiwank, a small rural town in New South Wales. His journey takes him from life as a vaudeville entertainer, to an extended period as a clergyman with unconventional ideas, to being an outcast wandering along coastal shores, before he returns to entertainment in a travelling circus where he delivers a manifesto and meets a biblical fate.

The play has two likely sources. Franz Schubert's melancholic *Lieder* for clarinet, piano and soprano entitled "Shepherd on the Rock" (1828) gives the play its title just as *Night on Bald Mountain* drew for its title on Mussorgsky's composition. The other source is Alan Jenkins' *The Thirties* (1976),[24] a book which contains the story of the real-life Reverend Harold Davidson of Stiffkey in Norfolk, England. In Jenkins' intriguing account, the vicar, also a father of five, would catch the train to London on Monday mornings, conduct special missionary work with Soho prostitutes during the week and catch the last train back on Saturdays. While the missionary work was intended to save the souls of those who had fallen by the wayside, one lost soul made a complaint against the vicar to the Bishop of Norwich, who had Davidson tried and convicted for immoral conduct. Afterwards, defrocked, bankrupt and jobless, Davidson went on to become a sideshow Lion Tamer, and was almost killed by one of his charges.[25] This improbable story was cited in the program notes for the premiere of *Shepherd on the Rocks*, alongside Neil Armfield's director's note explaining that:

---

24 Alan Jenkins *The Thirties* (London: Heinemann Books, 1976).
25 *Shepherd on the Rocks* (The State Theatre Company of South Australia, Adelaide, 1987), theatre program, Patrick White Collection, National Library of Australia.

Patrick, stimulated by this story and perhaps drawn to it by the fact he had been at Cambridge with one of Davidson's sons, and seeing good roles for John [Gaden], Kerry [Walker] and Val [Levkowicz] from the *Signal Driver* cast, began work on a play.[26]

The result was an Australian version of the story written for many of White's preferred actors, and a platform for experimenting with a large-scale work of theatre. David Marr adds that White was also motivated by the opportunity to provoke his critics, especially Harry Kippax, having told Kerry Walker, "I am writing this for all of us and everything we stand for".[27] Here the implied stance is one that asserts artistic freedom, both to experiment with form and give expression to a socially critical voice, against the critics who decried his plays for their lack of aesthetic unity and narrative plausibility.

A further contemporary source may have been the story of the Bhagwan Shree Rajneesh, an Indian guru whose teachings promoted polyamorous sexual freedom and abandonment of earthly attachments as a meditative first step on the path to enlightenment. His teachings drew large numbers of American, Australian and European followers in the 1970s and '80s who flocked to his ashram in India and later set up a commune in Oregon, America. His followers were referred to as the Orange People, on account of the saffron robes they wore.[28]

Originally entitled The Budgiwank Experiment, the play is comprised of fourteen scenes, each set in a different location. A News Team provides media commentary and acts as a chorus assisting with the narrative trajectory of the play and the passing of time. The world of the play follows Shepherd's progress as a clergyman who reaches out beyond his dwindling rural congregation to gather a band of prostitutes, circus performers and drug addicts from King's Cross, Sydney, to join an experimental congregation at his parsonage. In this respect, the character has much in common with fiction's picaresque anti-heroes. Shepherd undertakes his mission in the midst of a personal crisis of faith and a fervent desire to connect with a more humanist, outgoing, even theatrical God. The church for its part is concerned about reputation and begins an investigation into his behaviour. In the words of Erroll Dick, the private eye hired by Archbishop Wilfred Bigge to spy on the wayward Rector:

> He's planning to take a mob of … prostitutes and junkies – blacks – a metho artist or two, down to his parish – and turn the rectory into a kind of boarding house. The idea is that by rubbing

---

26 *Shepherd on the Rocks*.
27 David Marr, *Patrick White: A Life* (Milsons Point: Vintage Books, 1992), 626.
28 Susan Palmer, "Charisma and Abdication: A Study of the Leadership of Bhagwan Shree Rajneesh", *Sociological Analysis* 49, no. 2 (1988): 121.

> shoulders with what the Church sees as decent people the outcasts will be converted to, well, Christian virtue. (188–89)

White's extensive extra-dialogic commentary describes the Archbishop projecting an air of "*indignation*" belonging to those who feel themselves to be "*a defender of morality*" (188). Bigge has links to business and a morbid fear of viral infection, which functions as an expression of a discrete spiritual authority and sovereignty, not to be breached by infectious, foreign, or other incursions of any kind, such as Shepherd's scandalous ministry. The Archbishop's secret liquor cabinet, "for medicinal purposes", is a minor example of greater hypocrisies (190).

The action begins with Shepherd leaving Budgiwank to catch his weekly train to King's Cross, a place known for its night-life and seediness. During the journey, he changes costume as indicated in the stage directions: *He is now in shorts, T-shirt with motto 'I luv Everybody', and joggers*" (178). He is unaware that he is under the surveillance of the Archbishop's private detective. On arrival, it is night time and buskers can be heard singing dated pop songs while the voices of Americans clamour from out of the darkness as they negotiate the cost of street opals. A "VOICE OF SEX TOUT" advertises the services of women sex workers: "It's live, gents. Performance just starting. Watch 'er take it ... plenty close up seats!" (179). In the doorway stands a woman by the name of Mrs Lily Thripp, "*a dark, moustachy madam, probably of Mediterranean origin*" (180), who guards the entrance to the establishment. Thripp sells tickets while Queenie, a sex worker, emerges from a room upstairs: she is described as "*an elegant figure*" wearing a "*neo-mini*" and clutching a "*large gold handbag*" (180). A second sex worker by the name of Bee strolls along the street while being followed by Krish, "*an Indian youth, probably a student*" (180). Here White signals the multicultural population of Kings Cross as distinct from the white congregation back at Budgiwank, while also representing the race politics taking shape in a bustling Sydney environment. Thripp asks, "Who's this boy, Bee? You know I don't allow black followers" (180) while warning Queenie not to shoot up heroin on her stairs – "Do it in private if you must" (181).

Shepherd enters, and we catch glimpses of Dick shadowing him as he makes his way toward Queenie and Bee. Released from his conventional ministrations, Shepherd is engaged in a recruitment plan based in what John McCallum refers to as "his peculiar combination of carnality and faith" in the rooms of the two sex workers, Queenie and Bee.[29] It is clear that Shepherd has the women in his thrall. They respond to the carnality rather more than his faith in God. Stage directions indicate that Queenie is seen "*lying naked on an unmade bed, moaning as she tosses from side to side; SHEPHERD in profile seated on the floor at the side of the bed, lolling, as he soothes her body*" (183). The nature of Shepherd's spiritual work is

---

29   John McCallum, *Belonging: Australian Playwriting in the Twentieth Century* (Sydney: Currency Press, 2009), 110.

now made explicit as his charisma works its magic over the residents of the Kings Cross business. Additional characters include Puss, a lion-taming circus strong man *"wearing loose baggy trousers, gathered at the ankles, above heavy boots"* (183), who introduces himself to Thripp as Bee's boyfriend. Sounds of a roaring lion, traffic and pedestrian voices contribute to a fantasia effect just as the conversion of the sex workers becomes an act of proselytising Christianity in which seduction, submission, bodily ecstasy and performance all coincide.

Shepherd remains at a distance, apparently unaffected by the ecstatic sexual experiences he instigates while crossing several ethical boundaries: he betrays his faithful wife, Elizabeth; he uses his clerical position to take advantage of vulnerable women; and he lacks the capacity for self-awareness and empathy with the other. The adulation of the women, as May-Britt Akerholt notes: "feeds his ego and his faith in his mission to unite the worlds of flesh and spirit."[30] He fails to understand or conveniently underscores the sexual relations he has initiated and will soon suffer the consequences of the jealousy he unwittingly provokes. Shepherd is cast as a cerebral figure, unworldly, naïve and deluded; and an unwitting vehicle for White's investigation of the modern idealist and dreamer.

Later in the play the Kings Cross congregation, including Queenie, Bee, Krish Karma, and Puss, arrives in Budgiwank to take up residence in the church. Soon the press, followed by hordes of tourists, arrive in Budgiwank to report on and peer at the unconventional band of followers. But the arrangements soon fall apart as the Archbishop's investigator bribes the now disaffected and jealous female congregants, corrupt local officials and the police into painting a negative picture of their saviour. The aim is to gather enough evidence against Shepherd for the Archbishop to withdraw his pastoral licence, and limit the reputational damage to the church.

On losing his licence, and after an impassioned speech followed by a public dressing down in a courtroom, Shepherd is declared bankrupt and is forced to leave Budgiwank with his loyal wife Elizabeth. After a brief stint performing at the Glitz Palace in Sydney, they head for the coast, where after several days wandering along the eastern beaches, they join a travelling circus, where they find Queenie, Bee and the Lion Tamer from Kings Cross. Shepherd resumes his career as an entertainer, signifying that his performative transformation from stage to pulpit to stage is complete.

The final act sees Shepherd play two more roles. First, he performs in a Dick Whittington costume to amuse audiences with tales of streets paved with gold. Then, the adaptable and still idealistic Shepherd appears in a monk's cassock to deliver a final sermon on the theme of magic and the quest for grace as a crescendo of multi-faith religious music fills the circus arena. He asks:

---

30   May-Brit Akerholt, *Patrick White* (Amsterdam: Rodopi Press, 1988), 195.

2 Reading the Later Plays

> SHEPHERD: Are you for magic? I am. Inadmissible when we are taught to believe in science or nothing. Nothing is better. Science may explode in our faces. So, I am for magic. For dream. For love. That pervasive dream which becomes more reality if we have faith in it. If we can resist abusing them, all our dreams can amount to a *world* faith. If we can pursue our dream of faith to the end, to the death if necessary. Whatever death is remains to be seen. Another facet of life? Not – I refuse to believe – what certain scientists, academics, and a variety of non-human beings try to persuade me – I should say US – because you are part of ME – and we are all part of one another. At the gates of death – which is not hell, as Church voices have so often promised, I hope to shed my doubts, fears, obstinacy, lust … I pray for grace – for the deceived shrimps – the monsters of power – and the least deserving creature – myself. (229)

Then he unbolts the gate to the lion's cage and disappears into an apocalyptic blaze accompanied by "*a roaring of vengeful beasts*" (230). Queenie and Bee grieve with Elizabeth, Shepherd's faithful wife, amidst the turmoil of police and ambulances. The circus proprietor captures the culture of greed by demanding to know if he can claim insurance. But Shepherd's Grand Guignol takes him to a plateau that is more than the self-aggrandisement of a fantasist in ways that authenticate his vision of a progressive or enabling credo.

The final speech is critically and, arguably, historically significant in terms of White's theatre. Within the theatricality of the drama the speech or sermon precedes the staging of the final Grand Guignol, wherein Shepherd is mauled to death in front of the terrified circus crowd. Within the endgame of Shepherd's life, it is a suicide note in the order of a manifesto. But then as the last great dramatic speech penned by Patrick White the dramatist, it takes on further significance as a statement that repudiates scientific modernity, that which "may explode in our faces". Picking up the theme of uranium mining in *Signal Driver* and White's own anti-nuclear activism, Shepherd's naming and rejection of the paradigm of "science or nothing" warns that the world should recognise other knowledges, typically those disparaged as magic or dreams. Reading the speech in the twenty-first century in the midst of not a nuclear but a global climate crisis, Shepherd's speech resonates with the belated but slowly emerging acknowledgement in Australia of the "old ways", of pre-colonial forms of knowledge accumulated over 60,000 years of Indigenous occupation of the land. The rejection of the singular dominance of Western systems of knowledge and religion is suggestive of that which in contemporary discourse is referred to as decolonisation, in which traditional knowledge co-exists in a more holistic multilateral approach to mitigating climate change, water and land usage and land and fire management. On this view,

Shepherd's speech anticipates future reorientations in Western and Indigenous knowledges that become readable in the third decade of the twenty-first century, if not before.

White's contemporary critics are not averse to this view. Akerholt, for example, is sympathetic to a message that she couches in more neo-Romantic terms. Nevertheless, she interprets the speech as White's critique of a society in which "visionaries and dreamers" are "mauled", and where Shepherd's idealism makes him vulnerable.[31] McCallum finds in *Shepherd on the Rocks* the culmination of White's attempts "to fracture the artificiality of … [the] old genres and forms" of Australian theatre, opening it up to "fresh ideas, innovative styles and a new concern with the transcendent."[32]

Yet this new vision has limits that come into focus in the twenty-first century. Despite its environmental foresight, White's final work does not advance a progressive view of female subjects. From the imprisonment of Alma Lusty in her basement apartment to the loyalty of the saintly tolerant and loving Elizabeth Shepherd, there is a retraction of the restless rebellion hinted at in Nola Boyle. *Shepherd on the Rocks* ends with a tableau that resonates in an unsettling way with the old ways of Western patriarchy. In the aftermath of Shepherd's spectacular end, the audience views a biblical gathering of the Three Grieving Woman – Elizabeth, Queenie and Bee – who embrace and support each other (capitals my own).

> ELIZABETH: … we knew, we knew how it would end …
> QUEENIE: … from the beginning.
> ELIZABETH: The women.
> BEE: … Always the women. (230)

They are offered a classical solution in the form of Cassandra-like intuition and the solace of a Christian assemblage at the foot of the cross of the great martyr. On the one hand there is the call for greater recognition of non- scientific and academic epistemologies and values. On the other, the image of the Three Grieving Women portends more grief. The path for each woman has been delimited by the persistence of a patriarchal vision that has been subject to critique but not advancement or resolution.

***

This chapter has sought to position White's later plays within the expanding cultural framework of modern drama in the late twentieth century in which a more pluralist society engages with new ideas circulating within and around global modernity. As indicated at the end of the last chapter on the early plays, it is ironic that the later plays

---

31 Akerholt, *Patrick White*, 196.
32 McCallum, *Belonging*, 112.

of the 1970s and '80s, closer in form and content to our present, and anticipating its concerns with fluid identity, secularism and religion, as well as the polarisation of urban and rural interests among other themes, have not been revived.

This second period of playwriting finds an increasingly socially engaged and politicised theatre in the making. Culminating in *Shepherd on the Rocks*, the play can be seen as ahead of its time in terms of the large-scale anarchic postdramatic theatre that would emerge in the UK and Europe in the 1990s and 2000s. Christoph Schlingensief's anarchic multimodal performative events at the Berlin Volksbühne Theatre, Berlin, and in outdoor venues made political points in irrational ways.[33] British theatre company Forced Entertainment's *Bloody Mess* created in 2004 was, as its title suggests, a piece about not making a coherent theatrical work.[34] *Shepherd on the Rocks* has common ground with postmodern and postdramatic theatre, but the key to understanding White's continuing modernism is that the plays retain the conventional dramatic form of character, dialogue, plot, coherent themes and scenic action even as it experiments with these elements. White is of the generation that lived through two world wars and the acceleration of industrial modernity in the West in the postwar era. His influences remain those of modernist theatre: Expressionism, Surrealism, Brecht, the Theatre of the Absurd, Beckett. But it is the case that White becomes increasingly and politically anti-modern. Danny Shepherd's final sermon quoted above, which can be understood as a manifesto in the manner of the historical avant-garde, stages a performative adoption of an anti-modernist position against rationality, science, and the rule of logos, in favour of magic, dreams, love and faith.

---

33   Anna Teresa Scheer, *Christos Schlingensief: Staging Chaos, Performing Politics and Theatrical Phantasmagoria* (London: Bloomsbury, 2019).
34   Beth Hoffmann, "Bloody Mess Review", *Theatre Journal* 58, no. 4 (December 2006): 701–3.

3
Expressionist Theatricality: *The Ham Funeral* 1961–2017

The Ham Funeral has had multiple stagings since its premiere in 1961, generating a critical mass of archival material and commentary, as well as rich opportunities for comparisons across time.[1] The world premiere was at the Union Hall Theatre, University of Adelaide, on 15 November 1961, followed by a transfer to the Palace Theatre, Sydney in 1962. Controversy surrounding the Adelaide Festival of Arts' rejection of the play for its 1962 program gave the production an historic significance that lasts to this day.[2] Important later productions include Neil Armfield's for the Sydney Theatre Company in 1989, Michael Kantor's at Belvoir Theatre Sydney in 2000 and the CUB Malthouse Melbourne in 2005, Adam Cook's at the Adelaide Festival of Arts in 2012 and Kate Gaul's for The Stables, Griffin Theatre Sydney in 2017. In between, there are smaller productions and a play reading directed by Lucien Savron in 1995. The volume of material on this most performed of White's plays supports this chapter's sole focus on performances calibrated with broad social, cultural and aesthetic changes in Australia and abroad over sixty years.

Premiere Production, Adelaide, 1961: "It's Not a Naturalistic Play"[3]

From the premiere in 1961 directed by John Tasker to Kate Gaul's 2017 production, stage interpretations have worked to realise the play's subjective, eccentric and comic view of the world in striking and transformative ways. The premiere was

---

1   These restagings feature leading Australian directors (John Tasker, Jim Sharman, Neil Armfield, Michael Kantor, Kate Gaul), designers (J. S. Ostoja-Kotkowski, Wendy Dickson, Brian Thomson, Anna Tregloan) and actors (Zoe Caldwell, Peter Carroll, Geoffrey Rush, Robyn Nevin, Pamela Rabe, and Julie Forsyth).
2   For a detailed account see Denise Varney and Sandra D'Urso, *Australian Theatre, Modernism and Patrick White: Governing Culture*. (London: Anthem Books, 2018), 31–58.
3   Patrick White, cited in "Drama has Force", *Sunday Mail*, 18 November 1961.

at the Union Hall, a modern proscenium theatre that opened in 1958 for student and some semi-professional productions, including those funded by the Adelaide Festival of Arts. The semi-professional premiere of *The Ham Funeral* as well as the other early plays suggest that there was to be no privileged access to the Australian stage for Patrick White, who by 1961 had published six novels and was an internationally recognised writer. The prejudices of the Adelaide Festival aside, White needed to prove himself as a playwright as well as a novelist by doing the rounds of small theatres. In critical terms, we can see a White-led acceleration in the speed at which Australian theatre begins to form itself into, as Julian Meyrick puts it, a "project" and a "narrative", with entry tests and a degree of border control.[4] The critical test of White's theatre on the amateur stage is important for the way it begins to establish the values by which modern Australian theatre will judge itself then and now.

The staging for *The Ham Funeral* was designed by abstract expressionist painter, Stanislaus Ostoja-Kotkowski, whose set was as critical as Tasker's directorial vision to the stage realisation of a play that was experimental in visual design as well as structure and language. Ostoja-Kotkowski had studied at the Dusseldorf Academy of Fine Art in Germany before migrating to Australia in 1949 at the age of twenty-seven, where he worked in theatre design for drama, opera and ballet. Notably he designed the set for the first South Australian production of *Waiting for Godot* in 1958. Ostoja-Kotkowski's compact set design for *The Ham Funeral* drew on expressionist and film noire influences while Geoffrey Ward's lighting design created dark shadows for the play's gloomy atmosphere and gallows humour.

The staging interpreted White's highly specific stage directions that foreshadow the interplay of a fictional space that is simultaneously revealed as unreal. For Act One, for instance, the stage directions follow the Young Man's prologue about being in a play. The stage directions indicate the set, lighting and props but also an invisible dressing table:

> *The curtain rises on Scene One. The basement of the lodging house – that is, the lower half of the picture; for the present the stairwell, back, and the hall and two ground floor bedrooms, above, remain in darkness. Back centre is a door standing open on the darkened stairwell. Right and left are the area windows, through which the light palely filters. Against the wall, right, is an enormous iron bedstead with brass knobs. A kitchen table centre. At least six kitchen chairs, some at the table, some dispersed. Against the wall, left, a gas stove of an antique variety, and a dresser. The action of the play will also reveal there is an invisible dressing table against the 'fourth wall', so that anybody making use of the mirror must expose themselves fully to the audience. An invisible sink against the same 'wall', to the left, on the kitchen half of the basement. The whole is lit by an isolated, unshaded electric bulb.*[5]

---

4   Julian Meyrick, *Australian Theatre after the New Wave: Policy, Subsidy and the Alternative Artist* (Leiden: Brill Rodopi, 2018), 2.

Hedley Cullen's photographs of the 1961 production show the built set with the basement living quarters of Mr and Mrs Lusty set on the stage floor. The Young Man and the Girl's rooms, without walls and separated by a door frame, are on an upper level. The upper bedrooms' rear walls are removable to create a third space for the street scene in which the Young Man meets the Two Ladies under the soft light of an elegant Edwardian lamp. Mismatched furniture in the basement dwelling, including the wooden kitchen table with odd chairs and a bed, present audiences with cramped down-at-heel living conditions. Cullen's photographs reveal the expressionist influences on Ostoja-Kotkowski's atmospheric two-tone design. The staging supports the contrast between the raised consciousness of the Young Man and the Girl, and the mundane existence of the Landlord and Landlady, "those human symbols, Mr and Mrs Lusty, the figures in the basement with whom he [the Young Man] wrestles in his attempt to come to terms with life".[6] Naturalistic conventions lead quickly into abstractions with invisible objects and the dressing table with its mirror, into which Alma Lusty will gaze, breaking the 'fourth wall' of the stage. Five decades later in the Stables production at Griffin Theatre, Sydney, in 2017, the built set is replaced by darkened space with only the kitchen table and a few chairs surviving.

The cast included relatively unknown actors with Joan Bruce as the first Alma Lusty and Cullen, the production's photographer, as Will Lusty.[7] Seventeen-year-old John Adams played the Young Man with Anne Dibden as the Girl.

For this premiere production, Tasker was also an unknown talent, who saw *The Ham Funeral* as a unique opportunity to make his mark. Laura Ginters reminds us that unlike their European counterparts, theatre directors in Australia were not yet professionally trained.[8] Tasker, for example, had studied acting at the Central School of Drama in England and had visited key modernist centres of theatre, arts and culture in Paris, Berlin and Vienna. This international experience was enough to provide "his passport" into Sydney theatre where he was hired to direct semi-professional productions of *Love's Labour Lost* and *Peer Gynt* at the newly opened National Institute of Dramatic Art (NIDA).[9] *The Ham Funeral* was

---

5 Patrick White, *Collected Plays Volume I: The Ham Funeral, The Season at Sarsaparilla, A Cheery Soul, Night on Bald Mountain* (Sydney: Currency Press, 1985), 16–17. All subsequent references are to this edition and appear in parentheses in the text.
6 Patrick White, "Author's Note on THE HAM FUNERAL", World Premiere Season at Union Hall (Adelaide University Theatre Guild, 15–25 November 1961), theatre program, Patrick White Collection, Series 1477. Barr Smith Library, University of Adelaide.
7 Joan Bruce (1928–2014) had a long career in Australian theatre and television. Her performance as Mrs Lusty launched her career and was followed by her role as Miriam Sword in *Night on Bald Mountain* in Adelaide in 1964. See her obituary, Sue Baden-Powell, "Actress Was Rarely Out of Work in Stage and Screen", Obituary, Joan Bruce (1928–2014), *Sydney Morning Herald*, 20 June 2014.
8 Laura Ginters, "Before The Ham Funeral: 'The Young Man Appears' – John Tasker Returns Home", *Australasian Drama Studies* 71 (October 2017): 21.
9 Ginters, "Before The Ham Funeral", 21.

therefore only his third directorial experience. This was quickly followed by requests from Patrick White to direct the premiere productions of *The Season at Sarsaparilla* in 1962 and *Night on Bald Mountain* in 1964.

Tasker's preparation for the production can be pieced together through reviews and longer pieces of analysis augmented by Cullen's photographs, which provide extensive records of the stage production. White and Tasker collaborated and argued over rehearsals and rewrites. For an inexperienced director whose early experiences were with Shakespeare and Ibsen, *The Ham Funeral* seemed to be a disorderly mixture of styles. High modernist expressionism and symbolism around the Young Man and the Girl switch to popular theatre forms such as melodrama, vaudeville and clowning in the basement. Shifts from standard educated English to colourful cockney between lodgers and landlords make the play as the Young Man warns, "a mad muddy mess of eels" (15) whose logic is not to be found in the truth or accuracy of its representations but in what might be brought into view. In an essay he wrote a year later, Tasker reflected:

> Usually the 'total view' [of the whole] is obtained before rehearsals of a play begin, but with *The Ham Funeral* it had to be continuous. We were finally able to achieve this 'total view' by rehearsing each scene against the text, against every emotion and attitude we had been carefully developing. As well as providing a necessary distancing and 'Verfremdung' effect, such rehearsals often unlocked the pathos in a scene of comedy and the element of farce in a scene of tragedy. These sudden changes are intrinsic in White's plays and are exhilarating; but we found they demanded a wide freedom of experiment and close discipline, physically and emotionally.[10]

As his references to 'Verfremdung' suggest, Tasker found a stylistic resonance between *The Ham Funeral* and Bertolt Brecht's Epic Theatre. But if one of the key elements of Epic Theatre is the view that human behaviour has more to do with circumstances and situations than inherent human nature or psychology, then you can see how Tasker struggled with the Girl as an anima figure. But Brecht also offered Tasker a model of episodic structure as opposed to realist plot, in which, as David Barnett puts it, "interconnected acts are replaced by free standing scenes".[11] In so far as the dramaturgy of *The Ham Funeral* incorporates episodic, selective and stylised scenic fragments, Tasker was right to build the total view of the play scene by scene. The distancing effect of White's stylised characterisations and contradictory (dialectical) presentations of pathos and comedy, are especially suited to Alma Lusty.

---

10   John Tasker, "Notes on 'The Ham Funeral'", *Meanjin Quarterly* 23, no. 3 (September 1964): 300.
11   David Barnett, *Brecht in Practice: Theatre, Theory and Performance* (London: Bloomsbury, 2015), 28.

3 Expressionist Theatricality

As Tasker's experimentations with Brechtian techniques indicate, the work undertaken to bring *The Ham Funeral* to its premiere performance was slow, careful and detailed. He recommended the time frame be shifted back to 1919, and Patrick White agreed, as indicated in his Author's Note in the program. (Since then some directors and designers have shifted it back to the 1940s and forward again to the present.) In Tasker's view sections of dialogue sounded too "literary" for the stage and White was asked to rewrite lines. Some characterisations, especially that of the Girl as the anima figure, as indicated above, and the extent to which she is real or a figment of the Young Man's unconscious, were difficult to resolve on stage.[12] How future directors stage the Girl and her room is a point of comparative interest. On the other hand, directors have embraced the comic opportunities offered by the Relatives. Tasker commissioned Adelaide composer, Jeremy Wesley-Smith, to write music to underscore the lyricism of the Relatives' dialogue, in acknowledgement of their vaudevillian style.

> RELATIVES: [*singing, to any drunken tune, all together*]
> 'Oo can tell
> Of the light'ouse bell
> 'S ringin for the wreck
> We only know
> That the undertow
> 'S strong as hell
> Round the rocks …
> *Cheers and jeers from* RELATIVES *as they go out to the stairs.*
> (60–61)

Composers would continue to be attached to productions as the musical interludes have expanded over time, especially in Michael Kantor's 2005 production at the Malthouse Melbourne.

Tasker was attuned to the physicality and sensuousness of the play noting several references to sight, sound and smells, each of which could be more or less emphasised by directors and designers, especially around the representation of the iconic "large boiled ham" (48). For Tasker, these extra-textual, non-literary elements made the play "theatrically electric" in a way that imagines an audience using more than the sense of sight to engage with the stage action.[13] One of the more physical if not sensuous scenes involved the seduction in Act Two of the Young Man by the widow, Alma Lusty, within Ostoja-Kotkowski's compact set. Despite the modernist features of the set – the house without walls and windows, the flexibility of its backdrop – the limitations of the built immovable set become apparent. Adolphe Appia as early as 1902 had written about the limitations of

---

12 Tasker, "Notes on 'The Ham Funeral'", 299.
13 Tasker, "Notes on 'The Ham Funeral'", 301.

scenic illusion based on "the principle of immobility" that left the actor "a most inconvenient necessity for our scene painters".[14] The immobility of Ostoja-Kotkowski's set meant there was not enough open space for the actors to perform the scene as a sequence of movements. Instead of the bed, as indicated in the text, which is off in a corner of the stage, Tasker moves the scene to the kitchen table, which is better positioned at centre stage:

> Thus Mrs. Lusty and the boy played their scene perilously on top of the kitchen table. And inside the play it did have a certain logic. Will Lusty had pounded that very table ("this table is love") in Act I: the savagery and pathos of the moment thus became more strongly underlined.[15]

Tasker was concerned with the practicality of staging the scene, which becomes more exaggerated and comic over time as set design becomes more movable and "the excruciating emptiness" or void of an open space is better tolerated. This openness achieves its full realisation in Kate Gaul's production of the play in 2017.

The scene itself contains all sorts of pitfalls in terms of gender stereotypes, the comic reversal of the woman chasing the young man, and the sudden turn to violence. Indeed, Geoffrey Dutton described the Landlady's failure to hold onto the object of her desire as her being left on the floor "tragically unraped by the Young Man".[16] Whatever made Dutton construct such an oxymoronic phrase, we shall never know. But the salient point is the extent to which White and Tasker, as well as subsequent directors and actors are sympathetic to the lives of female characters, who are tied to specific class and gender roles. For example, visual records of the 1961 production include images from Scene One in which Will and Alma Lusty play out their combative and violent marriage. In one image Cullen's Will Lusty sits at a table in dark grey underwear holding his pipe close to his chest while looking at his wife as she leans forward to speak.[17] The image appears naturalistic – a married couple sit at a table placed centre stage – but the visibility of the upstairs rooms and the street situates them in a wider context that exposes their reduced and stagnant lives. Another photograph shows Will stepping forward towards Alma with his hand raised to strike her. The photograph captures the moment before the slap in which Will holds the gesture in an attitude of threat while Alma protects her stomach as she leans away from him. The audience imagines this is part of a daily routine and wonders about their stillborn baby. The gestural system highlights unspoken violence in which the silent Will Lusty sits passively in his underwear but suddenly flies into a rage. The assault here

---

14 Adolphe Appia, "From A New Art-Material (c.1902)", in *Twentieth Century Theatre: A Sourcebook*, ed. Richard Drain (London: Routledge, 2005), 14–15.
15 Tasker, "Notes on 'The Ham Funeral'", 300.
16 Geoffrey Dutton, "Ham Funeral in Adelaide", *The Bulletin,* 25 November 1961, 31.
17 Hedley Cullen, Folio Series 662, Box 5, Patrick White Collection, Series1477, Barr Smith Library, University of Adelaide.

functions as a critical sign of the inviolable rights of the patriarchal figure to impose arbitrary rule over the domestic sphere. The underwear also represents him as the off-duty General, an angry impotent figure, who likes to have a woman cower before him, and constituting a gestic figure of male rage. Tasker's realisation of the character provides the enduring image of Will Lusty that is reproduced with only minor variations thirty, forty and sixty years later. To continue with the Brechtian comparison, the text demonstrates, without naturalising it, the limitations on Alma Lusty's options compared to Will Lusty and to the Young Man who can walk free into the luminous night.

With reference to the composition of William Dobell's painting, photographs also capture the scene of the dead landlord on the iron bed as the Landlady brushes her hair. In an image from the 1962 Sydney production, the widow is dressed in black as she leans over her husband's body in an attitude of grief.[18] The gesture shows a passionate woman suffering the loss of a bad husband she once loved.

The world premiere was a gala event attended by Patrick White, Theatre Guild Chair, Harry Medlin, civic dignitaries and guests. Such was the occasion that guests were welcomed by the University's Chancellor, Sir George Ligertwood. The controversy over the rejection of the play for the 1962 Adelaide Festival had generated extensive national interest in the premiere. Many were keen to see, as Max Harris put it, "if Patrick White's genius in the novel was matched by a similar talent for drama".[19] The press came over from the eastern states and several favourable reviews were published. In the Adelaide press, Harold Tidemann proclaimed the production "a brilliant success judging by the reaction of the capacity audience".[20] After all the excitement, Harry Medlin captured the mood drolly in a letter to White that "it was a great success and everyone pleased with everyone else", in full expectation that the pleasure would be short lived and future battles would be fought.[21]

If the Young Man holds the play together as the mediator between the eccentric figures in the basement and the audience, and if his artistic sensibility renders him superior to their 'base' characters, the stage versions have invariably been enlivened by the performative presence of the various actors who have played the role of the Landlady. As early as the first performance critic J.J. Bray comments:

> Joan Bruce's superb handling of Alma Lusty was beyond all praise. John Adams played the poet: clearly he had a sensitive understanding of the part but at times he failed to attain the necessary stature and resonance. Hedley Cullen's landlord in long underpants had power as well as solidity.[22]

---

18 Photos, Adelaide Theatre Guild, Patrick White Collection, Series 1477, Barr Smith Library, University of Adelaide.
19 Max Harris, "The Ham Funeral", *Theatregoer* 2, nos. 2/3, (December–January 1961/62): 14.
20 Harold Tidemann, "A Dobell Canvas Comes to Life", *Advertiser*, 16 November 1961.
21 Harry Medlin to Patrick White, 30 September 1962, Theatre Guild Collection, Patrick White Collection, Series 1477, Barr Smith Library, University of Adelaide.

Harry Kippax, at the *Sydney Morning Herald*, wrote "Joan Bruce would not be bettered in the east. Her Landlady had the weight this monumental character demands and a surging vitality".[23] Harold Tidemann offered future productions a vivid image of the Relatives as "four black crows moving in unison ... almost balletic in their team work",[24] while Dutton applauds the "frock-coated knockabouts ... [with their] perfect timing reflecting the general discipline of John Tasker's production".[25] The premiere production was restaged at the Palace Royal Theatre in Sydney in 1962 with Wendy Dickson as the set designer and Zoe Caldwell joining the cast as the Girl. Joan Bruce won Best Actress for her Adelaide and Sydney performances and went on to play Miriam Sword in the Adelaide and Sydney productions of *Night on Bald Mountain* in 1964.

Neil Armfield in November 1989

The next significant revival was directed by Neil Armfield in November 1989 for the Sydney Theatre Company. A recording of the production for the ABC is now available on YouTube, providing a lasting record of the performance.[26] The development of first video and then digital recording runs parallel to the stagings and restagings of White's plays, adding to the archive that underpins performance analysis while subject to the limitations of a mediated version of the live event.

The passing of time also positions the two productions within different political as well as technological contexts. In 1961, Robert Menzies' postwar Australia is a socially and culturally conservative country, but in 1989 Australia's longest serving Labor Prime Minister, Bob Hawke, is approaching his fourth federal election victory. The centre-left Labor government inaugurates a period of economic deregulation in which it adopts a neoliberal agenda while reaching an accord with the trade unions over wages and conditions. Nevertheless, opposition to the Labor government sees new players enter the political field including the environmental movement to which Patrick White adds his support.

Internationally, European politics is undergoing radical change. In 1961 when *The Ham Funeral* was first performed, barbed wire fencing was being rolled out onto the streets of Berlin to divide the Soviet-aligned Eastern side of the city from the European-aligned West. The Cold War was in full force shaping Soviet and Western politics, society and culture for the next three decades. In 1989, the Berlin Wall's solid concrete edifice was breached in a popular uprising. Rehearsals for

---

22 J. J. Bray, "The Ham Funeral", *Meanjin Quarterly* 21, no. 1 (1962), 34.
23 Harry Kippax, "White Play Still Disappoints Under Sharman Direction", *Sydney Morning Herald*, 23 January 1984, 10.
24 Tidemann, "A Dobell Canvas Comes to Life".
25 Dutton, "Ham Funeral in Adelaide", 31.
26 Patrick White, *The Ham Funeral*, Dir. Neil Armfield, STC, 1989. Screened on 'Sunday Stereo Special' ABC TV 1990. https://www.youtube.com/watch?v=5DHZ1R1qd1U.

Armfield's *The Ham Funeral* were taking place as the West watched anti-Soviet demonstrations in Berlin and Leipzig. Reviews of Armfield's opening night show were printed in newspapers filled with several correspondents' reports and photographs of young men and women sitting and dancing on the wall. The unfolding politics precipitated the collapse of the Soviet Union and the end of the Cold War, the dominant view of which was the triumph of freedom and the liberal-capitalist-democratic order over communist oppression. But 1989 was also disrupted by scenes in China of hundreds of students campaigning for democracy in Tiananmen Square and the massacre that followed. Prime Minister Bob Hawke shed public tears for the dead and offered asylum to Chinese nationals on student visas in Australia. These epoch-changing events in real time reminded theatre-goers they belonged to a global order and that seemingly inviolate structures and institutions were subject to change. The narrative of this geopolitical context was that the overthrow of oppressive regimes is successful in some areas and a tragic failure in others. Whereas the premiere season of *The Ham Funeral* took place in conservative Adelaide, immersed in parochial controversies to do with moral standards, censorship and the purity of form, its revival found itself resurfacing in the global era, where epochal change was taking place.

Neil Armfield's production remained faithful to the 1919 setting of *The Ham Funeral* in terms of Edwardian costume design but its staging at the Wharf Theatre was contemporary. Brian Thomson's design began with the naturalistic premise that the audience observes the behaviour of characters on stage from the darkened auditorium. But that also made him think of animals in a zoo. He took Armfield to visit the old cement animal enclosures at Sydney's Taronga Zoo he remembered from childhood. These long narrow enclosures had two levels, one on ground level closer to the bars of the cage and the other an upper mezzanine level set further back with openings into interior spaces for sleeping and shelter. He made the imaginative leap from the old cement animal enclosures at the zoo to images of crumbling Soviet-era concrete buildings and mausoleums.[27] The design for *The Ham Funeral* grew from these images. The basement living quarters were located on the stage floor area and a mezzanine level above provided spaces for the Young Man and Girl's bedrooms. In a theatrical gesture, the stage was divided by a steep central staircase, which provided both an elevated space for the Young Man's Prelude speech, the street scene with the Scavenger Ladies and the entrance and exits for the Relatives. Patrick White reportedly considered the zoo motif in which characters are trapped like animals to be "brilliant".[28] The rooms of the house are not enclosed by walls but are open to audience view.

The staircase is illuminated against the darkened spaces on the upper and lower levels, emphasising the Young Man's vertical movement down into Will and Alma Lusty's basement dwelling and up into his room. The Girl occupies the upper level

---

27 Brian Thomson, interviewed by Sandra D'Urso, 18 May, 2018.
28 Thomson, interview.

and looks down on the action below. The basement features a central kitchen table and chairs, a bed to the side and with Alma's dressing table and mirror offstage in the auditorium, as White imagined. Music was composed for the production by Carl Vine. There were no curtains to open and close the play.

Kerry Walker performed the role of the Landlady with Max Cullen as the Landlord, Tyler Coppin as the Young Man and Pamela Rabe as the Girl. The Two Ladies were played by Robyn Nevin and Maggie Kirkpatrick, in full voice and dressed to excess in layers of Edwardian dress, feathers and pearls. The Relatives included comic actors Bob Hornery and Paul Blackwell, who had also performed in Armfield's revival of *The Season at Sarsaparilla* in Adelaide in 1984. As with the Two Ladies, the Relatives are theatricalist figures in black mourning suits with gelled hair standing on end, white faces, exaggerated eyebrows, dark lips, comically agile movements, cockney voices and raucous laughter.[29] The costume designs by Julie Lynch and Jennie Tate are exuberantly theatricalist for the Two Ladies and the Relatives. The youthful skin of the Young Man and the Girl contrasts with the aged, bruised and scarred features of the older generation. The relative innocence of youth and the corruptions of age adds a generational dimension to the differences in social class. Elizabeth Schafer notes that the actors' accents are confusingly variable ranging from educated for the Young Man and the Girl, working class Australian for Will and Alma Lusty, and cockney for the Relatives. Schafer interprets the accents as an attempt by Armfield to Australianise the text for audiences.[30]

Armfield's production adheres closely to Patrick White's stage directions, especially in the crucial final scene between the Young Man and Alma Lusty, which he moves back to the bed. The scene develops slowly in keeping with the low key, dialled down performance of Kerry Walker's Alma Lusty. She interprets Alma Lusty as a subdued and depressed woman with low energy and limited expressivity, who is bewildered by her husband's untimely death. In this respect she departs from White's description of Alma Lusty as "a large woman in the dangerous forties, ripe and bursting". Critic Rosemary Neill describes her delivery as "dramatically and comically lethargic" which she attributes to "deficiencies in the play itself".[31] This is not necessarily the case. Walker's Alma Lusty has a heaviness and slowness of movement, and lack of physicality that runs counter to the text. Her Alma gives additional emphasis to the limitations of a life that has sapped her energy and vitality. The challenge for the actor who plays with low energy is how to create presence and affect in such a way that the character is still alive for the audience. Walker emphasises the social dimension of Alma's character – her lack of education, the impact of childlessness, and the lovelessness of her marriage – and in doing so makes her a more naturalistic than expressionist or symbolic figure.

---

29 *The Ham Funeral*, ABC, 1990.
30 Elizabeth Schafer, "A Ham Funeral: Patrick White, Collaboration and Neil Armfield" in *Australian Studies* 3 (2011), 8.
31 Rosemary Neill, "Drama Falters in House of Words", *Australian*, 16 November 1989, 12.

The seduction of the Young Man is more comic than maternal or sexual overall. When she chases him around the table, she pulls up the skirts of her voluminous Edwardian funeral dress to reveal a large pair of white bloomers. Although she gasps and groans, she appears surprised by the forwardness of her sexual behaviour.

In this production there is a marked contrast between the exuberance of the Ladies and the Relatives and the toned down performance of the Landlord and Landlady. Anne Pender describes Nevin's Mrs Goosgog as a wonderful burlesque display of "gritty comic sensibility and 'vigour'".[32] Armfield had advised Walker to "beware Alma's clichés", suggesting she speak the lines "totally truthfully springing new-minted" with "a mixture of ordinary and poetry".[33] But the question of authenticity and truth hangs awkwardly over Will and Alma Lusty as expressionist figurations, and threatens to stifle their theatricalist elements. The Young Man, on the other hand, maintains a confected manner throughout while Pamela Rabe's Girl offers an interesting interpretation of the Jungian anima by giving her a strong physical and vocal presence.

This production presents the audience with a privileged Young Man, who maintains his performative persona and remains theatrical to the end. His interior artistic crisis is underplayed. He embodies the figure, outwardly male but possibly more fluidly gendered, who is both self-conscious and lacking the capacity for reflection. The Young Man has arguably become a neoliberal subject – an ambitious, mobile, free, and self-regarding agent – whose lack of crisis undermines the play's interest in this character's interiority. The audience is asked to adjust to the hero they cannot admire and with whom they do not empathise as he exuberantly exits through the stalls. Critic Paul McGillick praises the artistic team especially Armfield and Walker but admits he "found the play more than a little tedious".[34] The open stage design is contemporary but it also enhances the late nineteenth-century convention in which the audience is the privileged observer of human behaviour. They occupy a distanced vantage point in the darkened, quiet auditorium. The point here is that the 1989 production is interesting for the way in which it remains faithful to the dialogue and dramatic structure of the play while radically redesigning it in a brutalist modern style. The temporal dissonance raises questions about the audience's experience of the performance and its themes.

---

32 Anne Pender, "Robyn Nevin, Patrick White and the Art of the Modern in Australian Theatre", *Australasian Drama Studies: Special Issue, Patrick White and Australian Theatrical Modernism*, 71, no. 2 (2017): 84.
33 Annotations in Kerry Walker's *Ham Funeral* script. Kerry Walker Papers, 1979–2004, Mitchell Library, MLMSS 7566 1 (2).
34 Paul McGillick, "The Image as Performance", *Financial Review, Weekend Review,* 25 November 1989, 11.

The Ham Funeral Enters the Twenty-First Century

Since 2000, there have been four major productions of *The Ham Funeral* with two by Michael Kantor in Sydney (2000) and Melbourne (2005), one in Adelaide directed by Adam Cook (2012), and another in Sydney (2017) directed by Kate Gaul, the first woman to direct a Patrick White play in a mainstage production.

From 2000, productions of *The Ham Funeral* embrace the heightened theatricality of the text and loosen remaining ties to stage naturalism. Expressionist elements such as the inner struggle of the Young Man are now embedded in a more extroverted, absurdist, comic stage world. Above all, the metatheatricality of the play, its bringing together of different worlds from the poet's to the scavengers', are given full force. *The Ham Funeral* is performed as a reflection of twenty-first century anxieties about how to live in the world as an artist and a human being. In other words, contemporary productions mark a shift in consciousness from the world inhabited by Patrick White, and engage with the play as a platform upon which current issues and concerns might resonate.

Michael Kantor's production for the Belvoir Theatre in 2000 and the Malthouse Theatre in Melbourne in 2005 renewed and re-energised the expressionist theatrical imagination of the play. The 2005 production carried additional weight as it featured in the launch of Kantor's first season at the renamed and revamped Malthouse Theatre in a double bill with Tom Wright's *Journal of the Plague Year*, both staged with the same ensemble of performers and designers, and the same set. Kantor hoped to redress the negativity attached to White's reputation in the field of Australian theatre. Jonathan Marshall cites an interview in which Kantor explains that White:

> Hovers over Australian theatre as this sort of naughty godfather in the cupboard who whispers 'It doesn't have to be this way! It doesn't have to be naturalistic! It doesn't have to be logical!' White was a great writer who had great thoughts about the theatre and he merged the two into these messy theatrical events, offering up volatile Australian worlds. But they're not well made plays. They're actually kind of awkward things. But they have the tactility of great works, and when you're dealing with something conceptually great in that sense there is an inherent strength that means you can take risks as you tear into it. One thing we should be doing is looking back at our theatre history and saying, 'What are the things that need to be thought about again?'[35]

Kantor eloquently captures the "quintessence" of White's theatre in terms of its formal experimentation, its theatricalist orientation and its abiding value to Australian theatre today. He also offers an important insight into that which had

---

35 Jonathan Marshall, "Michael Kantor's New Malthouse Brew", *Realtime* 65. http://www.realtimearts.net/article/65/7751.

Figure 3.1 Dan Spielman, Lucy Taylor and Julie Forsyth as the Young Man, Anima/Girl and Alma Lusty in Patrick White's *The Ham Funeral*, directed by Michael Kantor, Malthouse Theatre, Melbourne, 2005. Photo: Lisa Tomasetti.

appealed to Tasker, Sharman and Armfield, that is, the risks you can take as an artist with the plays. Melbourne critic, Cameron Woodhead would later use White to denounce Kantor: "When Patrick White said that the enfeebling vice of Australian theatre was amateurism, he couldn't have picked a better example than Kantor".[36] This was on account of his apparent adherence to postdramatic theatre that according to Woodhead devalues text, narrative and character. But Kantor well understood how characters are imaginary beings, outward facing symbols of inner states of mind.

Julie Forsyth's Alma Lusty in both productions was as exciting and revealing as Robyn Nevin's Miss Docker. Backing her was John Cousins as the Landlord (at Belvoir) and Ross Williams (Malthouse), Ben Rogan as the Young Man (Belvoir) and Dan Spielman (Malthouse), Lucy Taylor as the Girl and design by Genevieve Blanchett (Belvoir). At the Malthouse in 2005, Anna Tregloan is set designer with lighting by Paul Jackson, and sound design and composition by Max Lyandvert (Figure 3.1). Dialogue, action and character are unaltered leaving the interplay of the actors' performances in relation to set, light and sound as critical to the

---

36 Cameron Woodhead, "It's Been a Golden Year on the Stage: The Year in Theatre", *The Age*, 27 December 2010, 12. See also Alison Croggon, "In which TN Discourses at Length", *Theatre Notes* (blog), 29 December 2010.

production's interpretation of the text. Both productions place the basement and the upper lodging rooms on the same level. Trapdoors provide entrances and exits at the Belvoir Theatre. Scenes are unmoored from fixed spaces such as rooms with each scene overtaking what has gone before creating greater continuity for a play that critics in the 1960s found discordant. Critic Bryce Hallett finds the Belvoir Street stage unfurls "a variety of wonders, be it the dead landlord's cajoling clan who, slippery as 'eels', ascend from the murky depths or the trashy vaudeville ladies who ply their trade among the audience".[37] Julie Forsyth's Alma Lusty is "lavishly crude, desperately sensual" and commands much of the attention, and sympathy, in the production.[38] Ben Rogan's introspective Young Man struggles in this exuberant display suggesting that the secondary characters have finally fulfilled their destiny and taken over the play.

At the Malthouse, the audience enters the theatre to see a red curtain drawn across a raised platform that occupies the full width of the stage. A thin narrow strip downstage remains available for the Young Man's Prologue, and for exits and entrances. A short staircase is located left and right down into the auditorium. After the Prologue, the Young Man opens the curtain to reveal an empty space with Will and Alma Lusty seated at a kitchen table at one end and an empty mattress at the other. This performance space represents the basement and the ground floor of the lodging house. The stairs are represented by blocks of rectangular light projected onto the floor space between the table and the mattress. The space is framed by an upstage perspex wall behind which is another curtain that is variously bathed in blue and yellow light, and opens onto a second interior performance space. The perspex wall contains a door and doubles as the Relatives' house. Microphones amplify voices inside adding to the anti-naturalist distorted dream-like atmosphere of the performance. The overall effect of the stage design is a series of depths within depths and alternating reveals and concealments.

The Girl and the Relatives appear in the upstage interior space behind the perspex wall, evoking the expressionist idea of the dream picture as representing aspects of the interior workings of the Young Man's psyche. As Claire Warden points out in her study of German playwright Ernst Toller, "dream pictures" are "visionary aspects of reality" that impinge on the everyday world of the central character.[39] This space is the area where the subconscious resides, marking the Relatives, as well as the Girl as figments of the imagination. Will and Alma Lusty are both imaginary beings as White intended, and real in so far as they interact with the Young Man, who maintains his semblance of the real through direct address to

---

37 Bryce Hallett, "Out of the Darkness, A Pioneering Play", *Sydney Morning Herald*, 4 August 2000, 18.
38 Hallett, "Out of the Darkness," 18.
39 Cited in Claire Altree Warden, "The Shadows and the Rush of Light: Ewan MacColl and Expressionist Drama", *New Theatre Quarterly* 23, no. 4 (November 2007): 319.

the audience. The two Scavenger Ladies perform in front of the red curtain and the Relatives enter and exit through the same space.

Time and place are non-specific. The actors use Australian accents, and the costumes vary from a dark suit with sneakers for the Young Man, underpants and singlet for Will Lusty and a knee-length woollen skirt and v-neck t-shirt for Alma Lusty – all suggestive of the contemporary period. The Girl wears a pale party dress and the Scavenger Ladies are dressed in costume as music-hall figures in satin and feathers. The Relatives arrive at the funeral in long eastern European black coats which they remove to reveal themselves as doubles of Alma, the Girl, Will Lusty and the Young Man creating the impression that Act Two is a dream sequence which draws attention to the operations of the subconscious within the play. Julie Forsyth builds the character/caricature of Alma Lusty before the audience's eyes, revealing, showing, embodying a larger than life stage presence. The voice is loud, and part childish and part femme fatale. But its rhythmic cadence aims to seduce the listener. Her body is in constant motion in the space – talking, gesticulating, touching, laughing, shouting and teasing as a woman with all the time in the world to fill in. In profile her hips tilt forwards and her arms are bent with lazy hands hanging down in front of her stomach. In Act Two she wears a little black dress and high heels for the funeral, and becomes increasingly dishevelled.

The seduction scene utilises the comedy of the chase in which Alma pursues the Young Man in her high heels accompanied by fast playing piano music. They laugh as they cross and re-cross the space until he collapses onto his mattress. Alma delivers her "Alma Lusty breathes life" speech as she sinks to her knees towards the Young Man, and he pushes her away before succumbing and then pushing her away in a strangle-hold. She weeps as he makes his escape through the door to the Girl. Alison Croggon describes the sexual encounter between the Young Man and Alma Lusty as played with "a raw passion that makes it devastatingly tragic", while Owen Richardson finds Forsyth's Alma Lusty a "demonic devouring force" that makes her more of a femme fatale than the text suggests.[40] John Bailey notes "Forsyth's Mrs Lusty is a delirious rendition of the monstrous feminine".[41]

The denouement the Young Man is visible behind the perspex wall as a rain-effect signals his retreat from Alma's world. She remains on the floor where she has fallen. As the Young Man speaks Phyllis Pfither enters and sits in her room. Kantor heightens the mystery around the ontology of the Girl by drawing on Alma Lusty's reference to a young woman named Phyllis Pfither, who leaves for work every morning and returns in the evening. In contrast to the Young Man's imaginary conversations with the exotic Girl, Phyllis is an ordinary girl in work clothes. Her appearance seems to trigger a return to the everyday for the Young Man, who has

---

40 Alison Croggon, "The Ham Funeral/Journal of a Plague Year", *Theatre Notes*, 19 April 2005, http://theatrenotes.blogspot.com/2005/04/ham-funeraljournal-of-plague-year.html; Owen Richardson, "The Ham Funeral", *The Age*, 24 April 2005, 32.
41 John Bailey, "Malthouse: Vision and Delirium", *RealTime Arts* 67 (June–July 2005): 29.

become less priggish and more anxious in the midst of absurdist, even nihilist forces that threaten to overwhelm while, on the other hand, the pathos of Alma Lusty's life, stuck in some hellish replay of the past, becomes more apparent.

The Malthouse production of *The Ham Funeral* took place at a pivotal moment when debates about what constituted Australian theatre centred on the question of origin, setting, character and story. As Yoni Prior points out, *The Ham Funeral*, set in London in 1919, and influenced by European Expressionism, attracted questions about its provenance as an Australian play. Yet the response of the production was to show that "whatever its subject, theme, language, form or perspective, if the work is made by Australian artists, it is an expression of 'the Australian voice'".[42] In the context of this debate, Julie Forsyth's Alma Lusty appears as the quintessential Australian voice, just as much as she does in the Malthouse Theatre's later production of *Night on Bald Mountain* in 2014.

2012 Adelaide Festival of Arts

The State Theatre of South Australia production in 2012 is a notable revival of *The Ham Funeral* in its own right as well as an act of redress for the Adelaide Festival of Arts' rejection of the play in 1962. The revival carries the additional signification of coinciding with the centenary of the playwright's birth. The spirit of this revival is the desire to pay homage to the play but also to bring it to life with a contemporary twist. Director Adam Cook and designer Ailsa Paterson acknowledge the original twentieth-century expressionist style by setting it in the pre-World War Two era but update it with a gothic punk aesthetic. Expressionist angst gives way to subversive humour and theatrical display amidst ghostly shades of black, white and grey. The gothic punk aesthetic incorporates circus imagery at the same time as the energy and presence of the cast and crew resonate with contemporary tastes for immersion in the theatrical experience. This effect is enhanced by the location – the Odeon Theatre in Adelaide is a small-scale theatre with a wide stage enabling a closeness between stage and audience. The cast is led by Amanda Muggleton and Jonathan Mill as Mrs Lusty and Mr Lusty, with Luke Clayson as the Young Man and Lizzy Falkland as the Girl (see Figure 3.2).

The production begins with the prologue in front of a shimmering white curtain with the Young Man dressed plainly in brown trousers and shirt, and standing next to a light bulb on a microphone stand. The interplay of the naturalist and the absurd releases the Young Man from earnest introspection. The curtain rises and hangs over the stage like a Magritte cloud. Mr and Mrs Lusty sit at a wooden kitchen table centre stage. The white curtain comes down at the end of Act One for the street scene featuring the two Scavenger Ladies (Jacquy Phillips and

---

42 Yoni Prior, "Reclaiming the Middle Ground: The Case of the Malthouse Theatre", *Double Dialogues* 'In/Stead', 2 (Winter 2008).

Figure 3.2 Amanda Muggleton as Alma Lusty in Patrick White's *The Ham Funeral*, directed by Adam Cook. Adelaide Festival of Arts, State Theatre Company of South Australia, 2012. Photo: Shane Reid.

Geoff Revell) after which it becomes a façade for the house of the Relatives, whose clown-like faces appear through openings in the cloth.

Ailsa Paterson's set design references Ostoja-Kotkowski's built set for the 1961 premiere. She has installed a two-level plywood construction connected by an angled staircase set against the upstage back wall. It has a wooden Victorian banister to mark the ageing decrepit house. The rooms upstairs are outlined in white painted wood with the scenes between the Young Man and Girl taking place in a darkened space in which his white shirt and her white dress are illuminated against a black background.

The Lusty's kitchen table dominates the stage below with the staircase rising behind it. Objects including the teapot, a loaf of bread, the glasses of stout, the grapes and the ham are all in shades of grey and dusty brown. The walls appear as if the painters have thrown buckets of black, grey and white paint at the wood panelled walls and it has dribbled down to floor level. The dusty black, grey and white set acknowledges the age of the text and the passing of time since its first production, while releasing its energy into a new theatrical environment. The gothic punk style seems to mock the Adelaide Festival Board and its overreactive sensibilities back in 1961.

This production announces in 2012, that the character of Mrs Lusty has overtaken the play, eclipsing the Young Man's journey towards self-discovery. In

Figure 3.3 Jacquy Phillips, Geoff Revell, Jonathan Mill and Jonathan Elsom as the Relatives in Patrick White's *The Ham Funeral*, directed by Adam Cook. Adelaide Festival of Arts, State Theatre Company of South Australia, 2012. Photo: Shane Reid.

this sense, Mrs Lusty has fulfilled her destiny as the Young Man's rival. Muggleton's dominance is marked by the voluptuous fat suit she wears under her costume that emphasises cartoonish breasts, cinched waist and padded bottom. Critics agree that she is "unfaltering in her energy" and "spectacular" as a woman who seeks passion in a stale life.[43] Her accent is as "authentically Cockney as jellied eel", returning the play to its London origins.[44] Will Lusty is a sullen presence and a dark counterpoint to Alma's exuberance, and bears the trace of Tasker's placement of the character at the table with his pipe. But he is now in white face with an iconic Edwardian moustache, charcoal pipe and dark grey all-in-one underwear. Jonathan Mills returns in Act Two as is the custom in productions of the play as one of the Relatives (see Figure 3.3).

---

43 Kelly Mildenhall, "The Ham Funeral", *Adelaide Theatre Guild*, 4 March 2012.
44 Rosemary Neill, "Sex and Alma Lusty, the Landlady of a Dangerous Age", *Australian*, 24 February 2012, 17.

Kate Gaul 2017 – the crumbling house dissolves

Kate Gaul has the distinction of being the first woman to direct *The Ham Funeral* although women performers, designers and musicians have played a critical artistic role in all performances of the plays from 1961 to the present. Gaul's production was for Siren Theatre Company and Griffin Independent at the Stables Theatre, Kings Cross in 2017. Lynne Lancaster described it as "a breathtaking production of a landmark play, riveting and humorous", while Jason Blake praised its "subversively exuberant spirit".[45] Ben Neutze is similarly beguiled, "Kate Gaul, one of Sydney's most insightful, confident and versatile directors, is entirely up to the challenges presented by the play, and has created a production that sings with all the music and poeticism of White's text".[46] The extent to which gender played a role in the production is inestimable; but the late arrival of the first woman director to the *mise-en-scène* of White's theatre helps to historicise the male tradition in which it is enmeshed. By extension, this gendered tradition is also revealed to exist within modern Australian theatre; Gaul's entry exposes this blind spot in the industry even if gender plays a minimal role in her approach to the play.

The set design by Jasmine Christie adapts the play to a small theatre space utilising lighting by Hartley T. A. Kemp and a soundscape by Nate Edmondson. The staging expands on the minimalist approach in the tradition of Armfield and Kantor by removing the built set in favour a bare and darkened space with only a kitchen table and a few chairs surviving as props. The house becomes a sonic memory of creaks and dripping taps created by Edmondson's soundscape. Objects such as the ham, stout bottles and rubbish bins for the street scene are carried on and off in a contemporary improvisational style of performance in which the emphasis is on the collaboration between cast and crew, and the transformational aspect of the stage world. Performers and objects are illuminated by Kemp's intense and atmospheric lights. The theatricality of the stage space imagined in the text, ["*The action of the play will also reveal that there is an invisible dressing table against the 'fourth wall', so that anybody making use of the mirror must expose themselves fully to the audience.*" (16)] is now fully realised with the audience's imagination playing a greater role in the performance making.

The production is eclectic in style with costuming, hair and make-up incorporating carnival clowns with bright punk hair and colourful make-up across male and female performers and characters. Costume is special occasion wear for Mrs Lusty's funeral outfit, and the iconic Australian shorts, blue singlet and thongs for Will Lusty. Hence, the Edwardian costume and period setting are abandoned. The gesture is towards adapting *The Ham Funeral* for contemporary Australia

---

45 Lynne Lancaster, "Patrick White's Play is Glowingly Brought to Life in this Siren Theatre Co Production for Griffin Theatre", *Arts Hub,* 22 May 2017; Jason Blake, "Tamed by Age, Patrick's First is Still in the Pink", *Sydney Morning Herald,* 22 May 2017, 26.
46 Ben Neutze, "The Ham Funeral Review (Griffin Theatre, Sydney)", *Daily Review,* 22 May 2017.

where themes of marital violence, poverty, rooming houses and idealistic artists can still be found amidst inner-city affluence and the housing boom.

According to *Time Out*, Eliza Logan creates an "achingly likeable and a little pitiable" Alma Lusty, who "suffers abuse on all fronts", from Will Lusty and the Young Man, who is "cold and cruel" to her.[47] Logan's Alma updates Kerry Walker's timid Mrs Lusty and tones down Amanda Muggleton's leading lady panache. Her Alma maintains the character's dominance of the stage but she is now more obviously constrained by the limitations of the text, meaning she is still unable to breach the norms of the Edwardian world she inhabits to walk free. In the same way, the limits of the text's sympathy for her, in so far as she ends the play "*at breaking point*" (73), cannot release her in the way of the Young Man. Logan's contemporary punkish Alma is still condemned to play out the tragi-comic human reality of her existence night after night rendering in the final analysis her stage dominance as a pyrrhic victory. Neutze refers to "the palpable sense of sadness" the audience feels for her confinement that resonates with the position of many women in the world of 2017.[48] *Time Out* notes that the sequence in which the Young Man chokes her "feels ugly but not gratuitous" – he inherits and does not question a gender hierarchy based in the violent assertion of male privilege.[49] Gaul is quoted referring to him as "a real dickhead" in a way that strips his poetic pretensions.[50] Expressing cognisance of the play's limitations in terms of Alma Lusty's prospects, the represented scenario is that Will Lusty has changed from the man Alma Lusty loved and as the marriage wore on, she was stuck with him, and the house. Interpreted by a female director in a social context in which violence against women is now recognised as a widespread social problem with fatal consequence, the scene is better understood as demonstrating that the means of escape that Alma calls for must be provided by the help of another.[51]

***

Gaul's interpretation brings the now substantial production history of *The Ham Funeral* into the second decade of the twenty-first century. It is remarkable given the early rejection of the play that leading theatre directors, designers and performers of the following decades have tested themselves on a Patrick White play, with *The Ham Funeral* as the choice of many. Gaul shows its expressionist

---

47   Cassie Tongue, "The Ham Funeral", *Time Out*, 22 May 2017.
48   Neutze, "The Ham Funeral Review".
49   Tongue, "The Ham Funeral".
50   Tongue, "The Ham Funeral".
51   "Between January 2014 and December 2016, CDWA [Counting Dead Women Australia] counted 234 femicides; approximating to one woman being violently murdered every 4.7 days in Australia across that time period." Patricia Cullen et. al., "Counting Dead Women in Australia: An In-Depth Case Review of Femicide", *Journal of Family Violence* 34 (2019): 2.

theatricality has contemporary appeal and relevance as its performativity is unleashed on new audiences curious about this work of Australian modernism.

4
Staging Suburbia: *The Season at Sarsaparilla*

The Season at Sarsaparilla is not widely recognised as a work of theatrical modernism. Chapter one argues, however, that the text's modernist intent displays itself in the technical innovation of its spatial framework, its condensed time frame and its focus on the minutiae of everyday life. It also suggests the play tends towards an absurdist view of human society without abandoning the idea that an existential consciousness can be found in all walks of life and places of residence, including much-maligned suburbia. The dialogue articulates awareness, often expressed as loss, of the sudden discontinuity of the present with the past and the approach of some new, not previously experienced reality that leads to uncharacteristic and comic behaviours. The dramatic characters are de-realised figurations that encode an ironic, theatricalist representation of typicalised behaviours in what audiences recognise as the suburbs of mid-century Australia. Despite the heightened representation, Staunton McNamara, writing in 1962, notes the "depth and power" of characters, in whom we "discern both the passions of the instinct and the nobilities of the human spirit".[1] In this view, *The Season at Sarsaparilla* is open to the performance of that which Graeme Davison calls the "deep pathos" that underlies suburban life.[2]

The local theatrical forerunner to Patrick White's suburban plays is Barry Humphries' development and performance of iconic suburban characters Edna Everage and Sandy Stone, both devised and played by the writer-performer himself. Edna, styled as a middle-class housewife from the Melbourne suburb of Moonee Ponds, first appeared in sketches at the University of Melbourne's Union Theatre in the 1950s and on television in 1956.[3] The full-length show, *A Nice Night's Entertainment with Barry Humphries,* was first performed in Melbourne in 1962.

---

1   Staunton McNamara, "Two Seasons of 'Sarsaparilla'", *Theatregoer* 2, no. 12 (December 1962): 21.
2   Graeme Davison, *City Dreamers: The Urban Imagination in Australia* (Sydney: New South Press, 2016).
3   Sue Turnbull, "Mapping the Vast Suburban Tundra: Australian Comedy from Dame Edna to Kath and Kim", *International Journal of Cultural Studies* 11, no. 1 (2008): n3 29.

Edna went on to become the global embodiment of anti-suburban satire, mocking house-proud female characters and their emasculated husbands. Materialism, snobbishness and cruelty towards others, especially those who were different, were the primary targets. Sue Turnbull writes of Humphries' 1956 show, which coincided with the Melbourne Olympic Games and the beginnings of television in Australia, "Not only did she [Edna] voice her pride in the details of her suburban home but also her suspicion of otherness in the form of the Olympic athlete who might be billeted upon her".[4] Traces of Edna and Sandy Stone are to be found in Clive and Girlie Pogson, whose suburban house is an all-consuming economic and moral asset. By the time Jim Sharman's revival was staged in 1976, in which Robyn Nevin plays Girlie, the character was said to have been over-shadowed by Humphries' Edna, who had become both more grotesque and more famous in the intervening years. Benedict Andrews would solve the problem of Girlie Pogson by casting Peter Carroll in the role in 2007, a move that arguably had the effect of incorporating Edna's history into the character.

In *The Season at Sarsaparilla,* White is concerned with everyday social life. Productions of the play tend to theatricalise the ordinariness of the dramatic action without tying the performance to realism or naturalism, nor to a life represented as hollow. This suggests that ordinary routine activities actually require a high degree of performative effort in their doing. As a satirical figure, Girlie Pogson's ordinary day is filled with the effort to enact or perform the daily movement of food and dishes from table to sink, and with dialogue, instructions, commands and commentary on her own household and that of her neighbours. Clive Pogson reads the newspaper avidly over breakfast and bursts forth from his front door fully dressed, ready for work and full of purpose. These ordinary acts are the substance of the action on stage and constitutive of the dramatic world. When Girlie watches with disapproval as Nola Boyle lies on the grass in her backyard of an evening, she is expressing an ordinary but normative bias against what she considers to be the other's indolence. In considering the investment of energy needed to maintain the ordinary, the spectator observes how enacting routines might also lead to rejecting, altering or abandoning them through inaction. This role falls to the teacher/narrator Roy Child, whose apparent inaction (during the school holidays) contrasts with the busyness of those around him. Roy, along with Nola and the little girl Pippy Pogson, show new observations are possible. In this way, the ordinariness of the action presents audiences with a more sympathetic and less deterministic view of Australian life than previously expressed in "The Prodigal Son". Ordinariness then is the key to understanding the substance of *The Season at Sarsaparilla* and what it presents to its audiences. As Paul Rae theorised recently after thinking about speech acts and the Austinian performative, "perhaps the theatrical enterprise more generally – can then be seen as the constant, if not

---

4   Turnbull, "Mapping the Vast Suburban Tundra", 19.

compulsive, rejoining of the ordinary, during which time it is made available for scrutiny, as it must serially and persistently be".[5] The "rejoining of the ordinary" in *The Season at Sarsaparilla* offers Australian suburbia as a subject for artistic interpretation and experimentation, and for scrutiny without fixing it to its original context. Theatrical realisations, as this chapter will show, retain the 1950s–1960s time frame of the play, while updating staging technology.

White imagines the play in the theatre as an ordinary modern streetscape of its time occupied by three suburban houses. At the beginning of Act One, the lights come up on "*the three homes in Mildred Street*", accompanied by audio of "*an outburst of barking from a pack of dogs somewhere in the distance*". Where *The Ham Funeral* features a great damp crumbling East London house filled with unseen lodgers in the grim aftermath of the Great War, *The Season at Sarsaparilla* features a suburban neighbourhood in which the house has become less gothic and more ordinary. It is a smaller single-storey home built from prefabricated materials for the postwar nuclear family. Other themes that cascade from the category of family and home are female confinement, social and existential alienation, and human endeavour. But it is the ordinariness of suburban life that is its central concern. Homely identities such as the housewife/home-maker and husband/breadwinner, and familial roles feature in commonplace scenarios around work, school, meals and child-rearing. White's dramatic insight is that ordinariness makes people vulnerable to discontent within the home or from the itinerant visitor or stranger – and that vulnerability is where the drama is located. The catalyst is the interruption of the barking dogs somewhere in the distance. The premiere performance emphasised these interruptions with thirty-second-long bursts of a barking dog audiotape.

The Season at Sarsaparilla had three different productions in quick succession. It was first performed at the Theatre Guild at the University of Adelaide on 14 September 1962 with John Tasker directing and design by Desmond Digby. The cover of the program featured a drawing of a young girl and a dog from a lithograph of the water colour by John Brack, "Girl with Dog". An introductory essay by Max Harris notes that with this play White turns to "the specific problems of embodying Australian life in Australian drama" and hopes that "White's powerful and febrile imagination, his poetic sensibility, and above all the magnificent originality of his language" will have an effect on dramatists and theatregoers.[6] Zoe Caldwell was the star attraction as Nola Boyle to Cliff Neate's Ernie Boyle and Leslie Dayman's Digger Masson.

A month later a new production directed by John Sumner with set design by Anne Fraser opened at the Union Theatre at the University of Melbourne. A commercial production followed in May 1963 at the Theatre Royal in Sydney co-produced by J.C. Williamson Theatres and the Elizabethan Trust, with Tasker

---

5 Paul Rae, *Real Theatre: Essays in Experience* (Cambridge: Cambridge University Press, 2019), 18.
6 Max Harris, "Introductory Essay", Theatre Program, *World Premiere of The Season at Sarsaparilla* (Theatre Guild, University of Adelaide 14–22 September 1962), Patrick White Collection, Series 1477, Barr Smith Library, University of Adelaide.

and Digby revising their Adelaide production. Zoe Caldwell, who had played Nola Boyle in Adelaide and Melbourne to great acclaim, left Australia to join the Tyrone Guthrie Theater and on to a distinguished career in theatre and film in the United States. The Sydney production went ahead "without Zoe" with Doreen Warburton as Nola.[7] Productions in three different theatres across three cities provided impetus for Patrick White's entry into the closed world of Australian theatre. Two different productions of a new Australian play within six months would be inconceivable in the economy of co-production prevalent in twenty-first century theatre. Despite the conservative wariness about the novelist turned playwright, the novelty of White's entry into the theatre in the early 1960s gave artists an opportunity to experiment, reflect and revise in a short period of concentrated time. This will become a pattern as Tasker and then Jim Sharman, Neil Armfield and Benedict Andrews' stage and restage the plays discovering new ways to solve old problems and identifying new difficulties and challenges. These include a large cast, multiple micro scenic spaces, and dialogue that ranges from monologue to intimate duologues and incidents involving larger groupings. The homes are set within an expanded scenography to accommodate the Australian backyard and the back lane, which facilitates the mobility of going to work, going shopping, and observing social life.

In Digby's original design, three identically shaped single-fronted weatherboard houses stand next to each other on raised platforms across the stage, each with steps leading down into a backyard. An invisible back gate leads onto a lane downstage. In choosing identical contemporary weatherboards, Digby relies on the cultural association of these low cost, poorly insulated houses with ordinary family life in the suburbs, and an imagined lower middle class. (The house is upgraded to brick veneer in Benedict Andrews' 2007 production.) The three detached houses are differentiated by minor variations in wrought-iron wire doors, pergolas, built-in cupboards and upright stoves. Hedley Cullen's photographs show the uniform box-like shape of modern housing design that can appear both egalitarian in its lack of class distinction and oppressive in its uniformity. The aesthetic conjures up a pulled apart and re-ordered version of a cubist painting in which the modern world is figured in geometric shapes, lines and planes. The audience sees fences and gates, and then the raised box houses, as it observes the daily lives of the neighbours. In this important respect, the modernist elements of the play's staging continue to replicate the optical privilege afforded the spectator by the naturalist stage. When the facades of the houses are raised, the spectator is offered a view into the kitchens of Mildred Street rendered "gaudy with ill-matched pastels and gleaming with plastic".[8] In this respect Digby's design foreshadows Pete

---

[7] Patrick White to Beryl Sheasby, 19 October 1962, Patrick White Collection, Series 1477, Barr Smith Library, University of Adelaide.
[8] Brek [Harry Kippax], "Razzle-Dazzle Over Dog Pack", *Nation*, 22 September 1962, 15.

Seeger's famous recording of Malvina Reynolds' song, "Little Boxes" released in 1963, which mocks the mass production of suburban houses in postwar America.[9]

Reynold's lyrics capture the irony of modernity that orients subjects towards the pleasures of consumption and choice at the same time as it confines them with ever more uniformity in regulated living spaces. Digby's stage reflects the sameness and prefabricated look of suburban modernity and picks up suggestions in the text in which younger family members compare the drabness of spending "the rest of our lives in boxes" to the joy of bursting out in "a shower of glorious fireworks" (90). Yet the design also subverts the structure of modernist order with quirky, cartoon-like details that highlight the production's satirical distance from any such street.

Director John Tasker's directorial notes indicate naturalistic actions such as Girlie Pogson preparing and serving breakfast consisting of "a boiled egg, toast, and tea, butter, jam, sugar, salt and pepper" and later two bottles of beer are taken from the fridge for Ernie and Digger Masson.[10] The interplay of character and objects, that Turnbull refers to elsewhere as "little suburban things",[11] are made into vital objects in the ritual performance of daily life. But it is also clear that conformity requires constant surveillance encapsulated in the opening moments when Girlie calls her daughter inside to sit down at the table to have breakfast. On stage, the iconic built-in cupboards, refrigerators, upright stoves and kitchenware appear in parentheses, signifiers of modernity writ large on the stage with heightened gestic qualities. Cooking is framed as a gendered practice regulated by appliances and commodities packaged and sold to aspirational housewives. More than mere background to the text, the objects are part of the story, speaking of new life possibilities, and the accompanying desires and lacks.

Harry Kippax writing as Brek praises the Adelaide Theatre Guild production for "its most valuable addition to our tiny corpus of plays of artistic worth" and one that should have "wide audience appeal" in words that appear contrived or forced.[12] His critique of the play's weaknesses is largely directed at the character of Roy Child, the outside eye or Chorus, and operator of the razzle-dazzle effect, for his priggish superiority to the neighbourhood's inhabitants, who "refuse to conform to the condemnation of his commentary".[13] The razzle-dazzle effect is simply a dappled rotating lighting effect that usually initiates a space in the narrative for reflection. Arthur Miller used it effectively in *Death of a Salesman* to capture Willy Loman's growing vulnerability and self-doubt at a time when the character's spoken word continued to exude confidence. May-Brit Akerholt finds the razzle-dazzle offers cover for an observer such as Roy to comment on Sarsaparilla at the same time as he is knowingly caught in the same spinning light.[14] Roy's existential

---

9   Pete Seeger, "Little Boxes", Schroder Music Company, 1963.
10 John Tasker, "Director's Script, Adelaide University Theatre Guild", John Tasker Collection 1961/2, Adelaide Festival Performing Arts Collection Archive.
11 Turnbull, "Mapping the Vast Suburban Tundra", 16.
12 Brek, "Razzle-Dazzle", 15.
13 Brek, "Razzle-Dazzle", 16.

dilemma remains unresolved but the attempt to represent the dilemma in the midst of an ordinary life that works against narrative closure attempts a new kind of anti-trajectory for the non-heroic dramatic character. But few critics were prepared to accommodate this possibility. Writing on the Sydney production in 1963, Kippax was still irritated by Roy, as well as other "redundant" marginal characters such as Julia, and the Alderman from the Town Hall. He also finds failure in the Knotts, who have "little to do except await their baby".[15] Yet he concedes that the actor playing Roy in Sydney presents more self-reflexivity in a way that improves a role that most critics consider unnecessary. Carmel Millhouse, once again playing Girlie Pogson, was said to bring out a more sympathetic aspect that meets with critical approval. Kippax sees the major virtues of the play as "the developing sense of place; the cumulative fascination of its people and their commonplace life" including the humour in the satire and the "comedy and pathos" of the Boyles.[16]

The scene of seduction between Nola Boyle and Digger Masson takes place against the backdrop of the howls and whines of the bitch in season who is under the house. Little Pippy Pogson is a witness peeping through the hole in the fence. Tasker understands the scene developing out of Masson's "half-drunkenness and randiness" as he tells her his most intimate memories of mateship in the desert; Nola is at first "static – not knowing what to think or feel" but is drawn in by the mesmerism of his revelations. The next morning, she makes no effort to conceal the infidelity and Masson will have to face Ernie.[17] Hedley Cullen's photograph shows the scene of reconciliation as Caldwell's Nola falls at Ernie's feet in the kitchen begging his forgiveness as Neate's Ernie, solid in his suit, looks down at her. To the contemporary eye, the melodrama of the scene stands out as Caldwell plays the fallen woman begging to be forgiven and accepted back into the jurisdiction of suburban values that she also holds dear. For Kippax the scene was further heightened when in the Sydney production, Dayman's performance as Digger Masson suggested more of "a certain type of shallow 'mateship'", that was said to embody "one of the most damaging of contemporary assaults on a cherished national assumption".[18] In raising the seduction of a mate's wife to the level of national significance, Kippax indicates the enduring power of the myth of mateship in the postwar years and its unravelling under the new conditions of peacetime prosperity.

Roger Covell finds the scene provides "its most warm and subtle interaction of character and emotion" and finds wider significance in the play's break overall with naturalism:

---

14   May-Brit Akerholt, *Patrick White* (Amsterdam: Rodopi Press, 1988), 58.
15   Harry Kippax (Brek), "Royal 'Season' – and Beyond", *Nation*, 1 June 1963, 17.
16   Kippax, "Royal 'Season'", 18.
17   Tasker, "Director's Script".
18   Kippax, "Royal 'Season'".

> The new play ... reconciles with great, if not consistent, success the two main achievements of Australian drama: the idiomatic fidelity of the "Doll" and "The One Day of the Year" and the lyrical realization of what is normally left unspoken that White first brought to the surface in "The Ham Funeral".[19]

Here Covell credits White with adding a layer of poetry to the vernacular that is especially present in Nola Boyle's monologue that speaks of the end of the day as "A time to loiter. The flowers are lolling ... I could eat the roses" (125). Here she picks up themes of longing previously expressed by Alma Lusty, "An' when I come out [of the theatre], the rain 'ad stopped, an' the blossom sticky on the chestnut trees. You could smell it, that strong and funny. It nearly bust me 'ead open ..." (17). These two prominent female characters are given expressive agency through lyrical dialogue that runs counter to their lack of agency in terms of the narratives in which they are both confined to predetermined gender roles. The action and effects such as infidelity, the razzle-dazzle and the silences that enclose a character such as Nola Boyle, indicate the pressure building in a confined social space not captured elsewhere for female characters in Australian drama at the time.

The *Herald Sun* notes that the play arrived for its second season at the Union Theatre at the University of Melbourne having received both "extravagant praise" in Adelaide and "the shocked reaction of others to its use of an analogy between the sexual behaviour of dogs and humans". The review goes on to attack its implausibility and the strain it places on all concerned from producers to audience:

> [White's] "charade of suburbia" with three sets of characters living next door to each other in an improbably varied cross-section of the community, sets difficult technical problems for writer and producer, and puts a big strain on the imagination and understanding of the audience.[20]

Geoffrey Hutton in *The Age* states emphatically that for all its dramatic flaws, including Roy, the play "is the work of a born playwright". He has praise for John Sumner's theatrically effective direction "particularly in its rapid changes of tempo".[21] Writing on both the Adelaide and Melbourne productions, Staunton McNamara declares that with the exception of Roy and the razzle-dazzle gimmick, the play "has considerable depth and power" in the way it "prises up the drab, monolithic rock of suburbia" to find "passion, instincts and nobilities in the human spirit".[22] Critics' rejection of White's use of the theatrical device is best understood as a rejection of the break with the closed world of naturalist drama. With the exception of the critique of Roy Child and the razzle-dazzle, the play seems to have inspired critics to rise to

---

19   Roger Covell, "Second Play by Patrick White", *Sydney Morning Herald*, 17 September 1962.
20   H. A. Standish, "'Sarsaparilla' Is Challenging", *Herald Sun*, 14 October 1962.
21   Geoffrey Hutton, "Patrick White Is a Born Playwright", *Age*, 17 October 1962.
22   McNamara, "Two Seasons of 'Sarsaparilla'".

the occasion of theatrical modernism with extended reviews. But Roy's direct address to the audience, like the Young Man's commentaries in *The Ham Funeral*, crosses a boundary by breaking the naturalist frame in a theatre culture that is resistant to it, quite apart from the quality of the performance.

The critical reception of the Sydney production was dramatically skewed towards outraged popular commentary. Ron Saw excoriated White's play for its sneering contempt for suburbia via actors who "hawked up those cusses like rotten oysters".[23] Norman Kessell in the *Sun* had already stirred up outrage at White's representation of Australian suburbia by asking rhetorically if Sydneysiders "agree with Mr White's obvious conviction that life in his homeland at the moment is just a robot-round of lust, love, the having of children, shopping for chain store specials, sweeping washing and cooking?"[24] Letters to the Editor duly followed decrying White, and Alan Seymour, for their grudges against Australians.

The popular uprising against *The Season at Sarsaparilla* in Sydney was largely manufactured by a few columnists inciting a phony class war between city elites and the battlers in the suburbs. It is also possible that in moving out from the protection of the university into the commercial theatre sector, the artist was exposed as a fraudster and trickster, like Plato's Ion. Nevertheless, the controversy manufactured in the Sydney press contributed to the view Patrick White was not one of us, those who did an honest day's work and raised a family.

The Season at Sarsaparilla, 1976

Thirteen years later Jim Sharman staged a revival of *The Season at Sarsaparilla* for Sydney's Old Tote Theatre at the Sydney Opera House. Sharman was the first Australian theatre director to gain international recognition for his London, New York and Australian productions of the rock musicals *Hair* (Metro, Sydney 1969–71), *Jesus Christ Superstar* (Adelaide Festival 1972) and *The Rocky Horror Show* (Royal Court Theatre, London 1973 and Roxy Theatre, Hollywood, 1974). These high energy, taboo-breaking musicals played provocatively with socially conservative sensibilities around rebellious youth, religion, and sexuality. But Sharman also committed to new and experimental drama having directed the Old Tote production of Alex Buzo's play about racial violence in Australia, *Norm and Ahmed*, in 1969. Whereas a relatively unknown and inexperienced John Tasker was invited by White to direct the premier performances of his plays in the early 1960s, Sharman approached White for permission to "disturb the dust" that time had deposited on *The Season at Sarsaparilla* with a new production. He had a cast and crew in mind including scenographer Wendy Dickson, who had designed *Night on Bald Mountain* in Adelaide in 1964, and had worked with Sharman on

---

23 Ron Saw, "Everything But the Kitchen Sink", *Daily Mirror*, 23 May 1963.
24 Norman Kessell, "Could This Really Be Us?", *Sun*, 15 May 1963.

The Threepenny Opera for the first Opera House season in 1973. Hence Sharman's vision for the revival was animated by a new generation of actors, including NIDA graduate Kate Fitzpatrick, who had performed the role of Pirate Jenny in *The Threepenny Opera* and Magenta in *The Rocky Horror Show*. She was to play Nola Boyle to Max Cullen's Ernie Boyle and Bill Hunter's Digger Masson; Robyn Nevin would be Girlie Pogson.[25]

Sharman's production has historical and theatrical significance for the way it marks the Australian chapter of the international movement in modern Western theatre in which the director becomes the primary creative force behind the theatrical realisation of the dramatic text. The "rise of the director" recognises the collaborative process in which the theatre director leads a team of creative artists including dramaturgs, scenographers and designers in the interpretation, adaptation and remediation of texts for performance, a shift increasingly reflected in theatre scholarship.[26] Sharman's theatrical presence as early as 1968, while still at NIDA, together with Rex Cramphorn and the older John Tasker, led Katharine Brisbane to reflect they were the leaders of "a new kind of directors' theatre" that was emerging in modern European theatre.[27] In Europe, director's theatre is principally associated with the displacement of the pre-eminence of the play text in the theatrical experience and its replacement with a more visual and later intermedial scenography, featuring strong images, lighting and sound effects, and in many cases a collective approach to the creative re-interpretation of the original play.[28] Sharman represented this figure in the Australian context and brought with it a disruption of the divisions between art and popular culture that suited the playful mixture of the metaphysical, the political and vaudeville found in White's plays.

Sharman's revival brought the 1960s play into an encounter with the changed cultural conditions of production and reception that gave its creative energy a more adventurous outlet than had previously been possible in Australia. The nation's capital cities now hosted small subsidised theatres that rejected the English repertory tradition in favour of locally made vernacular Australian theatre that arose from the cultural transformations of the radical movements of the 1960s.[29] Patrick White's plays pre-dated the New Wave of Australian drama and without Sharman's interest, may have been forgotten and the last four plays never written. Fortunately, White was impressed with Sharman, who was uniquely capable of moving between art house theatre and the commercial sector without falling victim

---

25 Jim Sharman, *Blood and Tinsel: A Memoir,* (Melbourne: Miegunyah Press, 2008). Quote attributed by Sharman to Patrick White, 257.
26 David Bradby and David Williams, *Directors' Theatre* (New York: St Martin's Press, 1988).
27 Katharine Brisbane, *Not Wrong – Just Different: Observations on the Rise of Contemporary Australian Theatre* (Sydney: Currency Press, 2005), 54.
28 Maria M. Delgado and Dan Rebellato, "Introduction", in *Contemporary European Theatre Directors: A Companion,* eds Maria M. Delgado and Dan Rebellato (New York: Routledge, 2010), 1–11.
29 Denise Varney, *Radical Visions 1968–2008: The Impact of the Sixties on Australian Drama* (Amsterdam: Rodopi, 2011), 16–39.

to prejudices attached to both sides of the artistic divide in Australia. David Marr reflects that Sharman was perfect for White's plays: "He knew the traditions that Patrick was writing out of, and instead of being troubled by the mix, because Patrick's plays are an odd mix, he was inspired".[30]

The revival of *The Season at Sarsaparilla* was in Sharman's words "rigorously faithful to the text", but he shifts the period to the 1950s, and aims for a "stark, bright, Brechtian" style.[31] Fresh from directing *The Threepenny Opera* at the Opera House, Sharman saw how Sarsaparilla, like Victorian London, presented an indicative social milieu that informed and transformed people's lives while pointing out the failings of the "system" whether it be the age of steam in imperial London or modernity in capitalist suburbia. Marr described opening night as "electrifying", while Neil Armfield, still a student, recalled it being "a staggeringly fresh experience … I'd never seen anything like it".[32] Katharine Brisbane noted that for its "brilliance" Patrick White's text "contains structural and technical problems" which Sharman's production did not resolve but that "developmental work is by its nature continuous and changing, and essential to authors, actors and audience in a wide variety of ways. The alternative to change and variety is stagnation and monotony".[33]

Wendy Dickson installed three raised platforms, each with a short flight of stairs down to the stage. Each of the platforms had a partial upstage wall and spaces that suggested doorways into the rest of the house but actually opened into a void. The set was built in such a way that the stage was visible as an outer frame covered in black curtains. The audience viewed three outlines of a kitchen, with linoleum on the floor and a mixture of naturalistic objects and props, such as the chrome and laminex kitchen tables and chairs. Other stage objects were mimed, foregrounding the theatricality of the dramatic world. Further stylisations included a basic colour for each family – brown for the Knotts, blue for the Pogsons and pink for the Boyles, also picked up in costumes for Mavis, Girlie and Nola.

John Tasker, who had directed Zoe Caldwell in the original production, wrote that Fitzpatrick's performance as Nola in Act Two was "raw, exposed, vulnerable yet still with an enormous rage for life".[34] Robert McFarlane's photographs of Bill Hunter's Digger Masson show a slightly balding middle-aged man, who styles himself as a Humphrey Bogart type with a grey trilby hat worn at a slant, sleeves rolled up to reveal thick biceps, and a jaunty brown and yellow tie hanging loosely over a matching brown shirt. He holds his roll-your-own cigarette in a cupped hand and stands sideways to look out into the auditorium. This Digger Masson is a narcissistic figure, who sees himself admirably reflected in the audiences' gaze, unlike Leslie Dayman's 1962 Digger who was too "full of yearning reminiscences"[35]

---

30 David Marr, interviewed by Sandra D'Urso, 25 October 2017.
31 Sharman, *Blood and Tinsel*, 260.
32 Marr, interview; Neil Armfield, interviewed by Sandra D'Urso, 9 January 2018.
33 Brisbane, *Not Wrong – Just Different*, 255.
34 John Tasker, "Review: 'The Season at Sarsaparilla'", *Theatre-Australia* (Nov–Dec 1976): 17.
35 Covell, "Second Play".

to be considered fully present on stage. Later sitting at the chrome and laminex table, he tells tales of foxholes and mateship at Sidi Haneish in the Western Desert, a prelapsarian paradise where diggers swam naked in the sea and feasted on figs and melons, in the thrall of homoerotic desire. His gaze is directed at the audience with only occasional glances at Nola. Nola, who distrusts Digger, is gradually drawn in by the exotic tales and the smoke. Even as he nominally addresses Nola, the story of "the juice running out of our mouths", and bodies drying on desert sand, is about men. Fitzpatrick's Nola is blond and pig-tailed, an open-faced ingénue, dressed in a yellow sundress, most unlike the slattern she is taken for in the 1962/63 productions. Fitzpatrick presents a girl-woman of limited opportunities attracted by the worldliness Digger invokes to impress others. As Fitzpatrick recalls:

> She is a sinner; the ordinary, open, kind-hearted, uncomplicated, sad, lonely, barren "as an old coot", bored, warm, flawed, possibly oversexed, bowed but not broken wife of Ernie Boyle, the sanitary (night-cart/dunny) man, brilliantly played by Max Cullen.[36]

These words and the photographic images emphasise the ways in which Digger Masson performs for an impressionable Nola, knowing she is under the influence of alcohol and is angry enough with her husband to betray him. In Sharman's production, the scene establishes Digger's hold over both Nola and Ernie. Asked recently about the scene with Digger Masson, Fitzpatrick recalls that the scene was not just between the man and the woman but between the two men. In the aftermath of war, the terrible betrayal was that of a mate sleeping with his friend's wife. Of Ernie's response she says:

> I always felt it was more because his friend had slept with me rather than I had betrayed him. When Nola delivers the line, "I was always this kind of a bitch", she understands that she's not the important part of the triangle, but decides to go through with it because she's so listless.[37]

In Scene Two as the aftermath plays out, Ernie's interior state is expressed in a series of costume changes. At first, he is dressed as the cuckold in maroon striped pyjamas sitting at the table where Digger has charmed his wife. Then he dresses in a suit to go into the city on a bender to re-assert his dignity[38] and then after he is reconciled with Nola, he changes back into his work clothes to begin another shift. Fitzpatrick recalls that Nola's redemption is secured when the audience forgives her. This occurs when she delivers her line addressed to them: "Might as well get undressed

---

36   Kate Fitzpatrick, *Name Dropping: The Life and Loves of Kate Fitzpatrick* (Sydney: Harper Collins, 2004). Kindle Edition. Chap 9 Loc. 3784.
37   Kate Fitzpatrick, interviewed by Sandra D'Urso, 23 August 2018.
38   Like Stan Parker in *The Tree of Man*.

meself. Don't know whatever persuaded me I could wear a yella frock".[39] This scene stands out in Sharman's production as one in which a new understanding of Nola Boyle's character as vulnerable, easily led and hungry for love, takes precedence over her performed identity as "sexy, blowsy and overripe",[40] or her neglect.

Tasker describes Nevin's Girlie Pogson as achieving the character's "fussiness, the small-minded values and the accent of 'daintiness' the role requires" while also presenting the character's loneliness.[41] He notes that Barry Humphries' Edna Everage had risen to fame in the intervening years between the first performance and its revival with the effect it is "is an uphill battle for Miss Nevin to banish Mrs Everage from the stage".[42]

Sharman's revival of *The Season at Sarsaparilla*, 1976, was notable for several reasons. In addition to the fame attached to Jim Sharman, it was the first time a Patrick White play had been staged against the backdrop of the New Wave of Australian drama. The idea of Australian accents, vernacular, character types and places were no longer startling to a largely Anglophone theatre culture. The Australian-authored plays and devised works that issued out of new companies such as the Australian Performing Group and venues such as La Mama, Jane St and La Boite had rejected stage naturalism in favour of Brechtian and Artaudian techniques of episodic action and theatre of cruelty. In this context, *The Season at Sarsaparilla* with its lower middle class, ordinary Australians is an anti-bourgeois drama and thus compatible with the leftist politics that circulated in the theatre. A new generation of actors trained at NIDA were better equipped to work with White's anti-naturalism and discover the theatricality of character and situation.

Neil Armfield Playhouse Adelaide, 1984

Neil Armfield recalls Jim Sharman's *Season at Sarsaparilla* and was especially impressed by Wendy Dickson's set, which "cleaned the stage" to show "the thrilling way in which a bare stage can be monumentally powerful".[43] The minimalist aesthetic was suggestive for Armfield of a theatre of human marionettes in all manner of gradations from playful, to imaginative, to the act of coming alive and the struggle to do so. Sharman, who was Artistic Director from 1982 to 1983 of the Lighthouse Theatre Adelaide, later to become the State Theatre Company of South Australia, invited Armfield to direct a new production just over twenty years after its Adelaide premiere.

Armfield drew on the precedent of the three box-like adjoining houses set on raised platforms as seen in Digby's design for the premiere and updated in

---

39 Fitzpatrick, *Name Dropping*. (Note in the original script it was an orange blouse).
40 Frank Harris, "It's a Good Season – At Last", *Daily Mirror*, 10 November 1976.
41 Tasker, "Review".
42 Tasker, "Review".
43 Neil Armfield, interviewed by Sandra D'Urso, 9 January 2018.

minimalist style by Wendy Dickson for Sharman's 1976 production. Stephen Curtis and Amanda Lovejoy co-designed the set. Curtis had recently designed Armfield's premiere of *Signal Driver* at the Lighthouse Theatre in 1982. The design sets the platforms side by side each with a rear wall located upstage. The space in front is occupied by the kitchens with steps leading down to the three yards downstage. These were divided by low wood paling fences. The kitchens were without side walls and featured tables and chairs, a fridge, sink or a stove. A Mixmaster took pride of place on top of the fridge in the Boyle's kitchen, like a decorative Grecian urn in an aristocratic Athenian house. The irony of the object lies in its futility in a kitchen where the lady of the house, Nola Boyle, has little if any interest in baking; she favours fried eggs, meat and "termaters" (146). Significantly a photograph of the production shows Ernie (Russell Kiefel) and Digger Masson (Stuart McCreery) sitting opposite each other at the kitchen table arguing about war and peace with the Mixmaster and the fridge in full view:

> MASSON: (*sitting forward, intent, glass between his hands*) Remember those bloody fox-holes in the old Des? Remember 'ow we lay there waitin'? An' the snipers up on the bloody escarpment? We used to lie and talk about what we was goin' ter eat. An' the sheilas we was goin' ter do. An' the sky, Ern. I never seen such an open sky. As we layed there talkin' into each other's ears. Blokes were close to each other then.
> An' you'd wake up with your hair full of dew and spiders ...
> *There is a silence.*
> (*Looks straight at* ERN) I reckon you forgot all that. You got sold on the bloody Mixmasters.
>
> ERN: (*unhappy*) Nao! I didn't forget none of that. But 'oo wants to go on harpin'? I've had a crook back ever since. Lyin' in bloody fox-'oles in the dew! (111)

Digger Masson considers the appliance a sign of Ernie's emasculation at the altar of domesticity and a consuming life. With the Mixmaster sitting as it does on top of the fridge, another coveted white good, Masson views suburban life as a sign of Ernie's submission to the domestic realm, traditionally a female space, and a betrayal of masculine values. Nola (Jacquy Phillips) making up the third point of the triangle leans against the doorway with arms folded during this dialogue looking down at the men with disdain. She is notably excluded from the discussion but maintains a proud stance that suggests Ernie should not tempt fate by inviting the stranger into a lonely house.

Armfield's construction of the scene between the two former diggers sees each of the characters negotiate a much larger reality than the short visit that reunites and then separates them. They stumble through the new conditions of consuming life in which the mind and not the body is called to account. It is not simply that a "consuming life" is an inauthentic life, as Masson implies; nor does Digger Masson's scorn fatally dent Ernie's self-regard. As Zygmunt Bauman observes, "the 'society of consumers' … stands for the kind of society that promotes, encourages or enforces the choice of a consumerist lifestyle and life strategy and dislikes all alternative cultural options".[44] On this view, the two men represent alternative cultural options in which Ernie stands for the emerging consumerist lifestyle and Masson a kind of idealised other in which men are "close", women are available, and danger provides an existential experience. Masson will further assert an itinerant, promiscuous cultural option by turning Nola into one of the "sheilas we was goin' ter do", sleeping with her while Ernie empties the town's sanitary bins. At the same time, making love to his mate's wife severs the code of mateship and enacts his view of Ernie's emasculated domestic status. That Nola is so willingly seduced and follows up with a melodramatic performance full of self-loathing and self-pity turns the focus away from Masson and back onto the Mildred Street couple.

In this sense, Masson becomes a non-subject, a mere catalyst, and a consumer object used and discarded by Nola. Despite his scepticism towards modern suburban life, he is a character who represents an unexamined life that fails to see that his position is also, a "life strategy" in the new social formation of postwar modernity. His discrediting repositions Ernie as the man of his times. White's sympathetic shaping of Ernie shows he is neither a man for whom "the mind is the least of possessions" nor a man who behaves "without thinking about what they consider to be their life purpose".[45] What we see in Ernie is the dialectical power and appeal of consuming life.

Critic Peter Ward finds the return of *The Season at Sarsaparilla* to the Adelaide stage twenty years after its premiere sheds new light on the play:

> And what seemed new and a little daring then, some placed White among the great suburb-knockers, turns out now to be an amusing period piece about what one might describe as the intricate and tedious business of being human.[46]

This humanist view distinguishes White's play from Barry Humphries' and Robin Boyd's anti-suburban sentiments and finds a significant role for the previously maligned narrator/Chorus figure Roy Child. No longer upset with the non-dramatic character of Roy, Ward finds sympathy in the character's dual yearnings to see the world and to retain his connection to the familiar. He finds the simple happiness of Mavis and Harry Knott action enough for characters earlier critics found under-developed. This commentary suggests that Armfield did not intervene in the play, indeed he has stated he did not adapt it.

---

44 Zygmunt Bauman, *Liquid Times: Living in an Age of Uncertainty* (London: Scribe, 2007), 53.
45 Bauman, *Liquid Times*, 52.
46 Peter Ward, "White's Suburban Rituals Withstand Time", *Australian*, 26 November 1984, 12.

4 Staging Suburbia

Benedict Andrews' Production, 2007

The 2007 Sydney Theatre Company production of the play directed by Benedict Andrews represented the iconic status of the suburban home in Australian society with a hyperrealist set in which a single cream brick veneer house was built and placed on a revolving stage. The production was remounted for the Melbourne Theatre Company in early 2008.

Audiences peered through doors and windows for views of the characters inside the house while the doors allowed entrances and exits to and from a narrow strip of stage floor downstage that stood in for the back lane. Robert Cousins' ingenious design was then lit by Nick Schlieper in vibrant hues that marked the passing of day, the interludes with the razzle-dazzle, and ended in a golden confetti shower of summer rain as the house spun. The effect was one of the Australian 1960s house writ large upon the stage and presented as a work of theatrical art.

In raising the house to a work of art, the design quoted the widely-known painting by Howard Arkley, *Triple Fronted* (1987), featuring a proud brick veneer house rising from a flawless lime-coloured lawn and bound by a driveway leading to an adjoining garage. Arkley's image was a monument to the everyday in a way that erased the cultural cringe perpetrated by Robin Boyd and others in the 1960s. At the Drama Theatre at the Sydney Opera House, the iconic revolving house was accordingly double coded for both the dominant suburban architectural style of the 1960s, described elsewhere by Brigid Rooney as "modernist or vernacular", and the recognition of its iconic status within representations of Australian modernity.[47] The production made a further pitch that by 2007 *The Season of Sarsaparilla* both belongs to the "canon" of artistic representations of the Australian suburb and has contributed to its mythic status within the nation's cultural memory. Décor, objects and costume were similarly styled as realist representations of iconic sixties-ness. The key advance of this production, compared to previous stagings, was the co-location of the three families in the one house. This adaptation turned the singular iconic house into a provisional space in which lives flow across each other, presence is temporary and rights to urban space are negotiated.

The great theme of the ordinariness of the suburb and its co-mingling of entrapment and desire were given renewed emphasis in Andrews and Cousins' design. The proscenium stage was the first frame that trapped people and place frozen in space and time, resisting progress and anxious about the minutiae of daily life, while the walls of the house acted as a second frame enclosing characters, especially the females, in the interior spaces of the home. With most of the action located indoors, spectators viewed the characters as fragments – heads, upper torsos and silhouettes – through the windows and doors of the house. Bodies were no longer whole, solid and enduring but moved across spaces and openings,

---

47 Brigid Rooney, *Suburban Space, the Novel and Australian Modernity* (London: Anthem Press, 2018), 1.

disappearing and reappearing from view in fluid, mobile and fleeting glimpses suggesting that subjects are not so much fixed in unchanging time but passing through it while still attached to lifecycles, objects and habits.

The final frame was provided by the use of CCTV and two large screens on either side of the house. Cameras placed inside the house captured private images of ordinary people at home projected, larger than life, onto the screens. The effect was an ultra-heightened anti-naturalism. Spectators, and at times, characters in the play, observed the action, now remediated as soap opera, playing out on screens.

The enchantment of the characters with their screen images was consistent with the observation that "In recent years, 'ordinary people' have themselves enthusiastically endorsed and greedily bought into the surveillance society with home security camera systems" and embraced reality TV programs such as *Big Brother*.[48] Keith Gallasch wrote "the perversity of our curiosity (and its reality TV correlative) is brought lovingly home by the cameras installed within".[49]

Benedict Andrews makes no attempt to subvert the Orwellian and Foucauldian elements of the art of surveillance, merely noting its ordinary presence in daily life and perhaps capturing the narcissism that will explode in the following decade through Instagram and Facebook. In 2007, this technical innovation, unavailable in previous productions, alters perception with a two-way vision of past and present. Modernity's past is re-processed to accord with contemporary modes of viewing and reception, and themes of surveillance; mediated images and the loss of privacy come into view for the twenty-first century audience. Organ music composed and played by Alan John (who also plays Deedree and Mr Erbage), added an early TV sound to the overall effect of the past in the present.

Cross-gender casting extended to Girlie Pogson, played by Peter Carroll, who had earlier played one of the Sundown Home ladies in *A Cheery Soul* and Theo Vokes in *Signal Driver*. Carroll's Girlie was coupled with the highly regarded John Gaden as Clive Pogson, in a pairing that added to the theatrical pleasure of the performance. The casting speaks to the greater gender fluidity of contemporary theatre as well as in society and culture more generally, while the queering of the middle-class couple through the combination of Carroll and Gaden offers a diversity-conscious perspective. Carroll cleverly extracts the camp sensibility of Girlie Pogson's obsession with surfaces and appearance, and references White's view of masculinity's inner feminine self that features in *The Ham Funeral*. The production presents the 1960s housewife as an embodiment of a pragmatic materialist approach to life that is essentially masculine, rational and authoritarian, while her female identity is denied, repressed and comically sublimated into the fetishised cleanliness of her kitchen. She waits on her husband like a well-dressed

---

48 Steve Dixon, *Digital Performance: A History of New Media in Theater, Dance, Performance Art, and Installation* (Cambridge: MIT Press, 2007), 439.
49 Keith Gallasch, "Keith Gallasch in the Worlds of Patrick White and Ronnie Burkett", *RealTime* 78 (April–May 2007), 11.

4 Staging Suburbia

Figure 4.1 Emily Russell as Mavis, Peter Carroll as Girlie and Pamela Rabe as Nola in Patrick White's *The Season at Sarsaparilla*, directed by Benedict Andrews, Sydney Theatre Company, 2007. Photo: Tania Kelley © Tania Kelley/Copyright Agency, 2020.

maître d'hôtel and scolds her children like a governess. The extent to which the pathos of Girlie's girlhood memories is made palpable in Carroll's performance softens the harsh critique of the female character and averts gender bias. By occupying the sign of her own ordinariness, Carroll's Girlie, as Gallasch notes, "is the downside of 50s optimism" and appears as an indictment of the cultural imposition of a docile subjectivity on modern femininity.[50]

Girlie is the foil to her nemeses, the languid and generously figured Nola Boyle (Pamela Rabe) and hungry, pregnant Mavis Knott (Emily Russell) (see Figure 4.1). Rabe's tall and husky-voiced Nola spends much of her day in a petticoat and light dressing-gown, options not available to Zoe Caldwell in 1962, or chosen for Fitzpatrick whose costume was a yellow frock in 1976, nor Jacquy Phillips, who wore a floral print sleeveless frock in 1984. Rabe's Nola generates a powerful theatrical presence as she pads around her kitchen and garden. She is warm-hearted and kind to Pippy Pogson, aware of prissy Girlie Pogson's prying eyes and is a desiring and affectionate woman to her husband Ernie. The monologue at sunset in the garden begins with a sensuous fantasy about roses, skin and perfume and then shifts towards an expression of the isolation of a woman at home waiting for

---

50 Gallasch, "Keith Gallasch in the Worlds of Patrick White and Ronnie Burkett".

the men to return from work, from bars and from war. Alison Croggon sees in Rabe's performance an expression of "appalling loneliness".[51] The scene is a prelude to the loveless sex she has with her husband's Digger mate, Rowley Masson, that Croggon notes perceptively is portrayed as a kind of rape. Here the tables are turned in favour of Nola, who is no longer perceived as the slattern of old. Digger on the other hand is manipulative and persistent in forcing himself on a vulnerable woman. After Masson leaves, Nola is left to draw on her capacity to absorb and overcome the suffering and recrimination that follows.

Nola and Girlie offer a critique of 1960s modernity that frees women from the excessive drudgery of housework but denies them an alternative life in the world of work outside the home. On Cousins' set the women's lives are absurdly meaningless. The audience sees Girlie's arms through the window of her kitchen going through the motions of cleaning and re-cleaning surfaces that are not visible to the spectator. Modern medical technology is now likely to find the source of the couple's childlessness in Ernie's sterility, reversing Nola's self-image and self-recrimination as "barren as an old boot" (166). And before her, Alma Lusty. The production offers a composite image of the feminine as decorative, respectable and useless, desexualised or over-sexualised, living vicariously through the experiences of husbands and children. Pregnant Mavis Knott is rendered a maternal body passively content before the drama of childbirth.

Each production of the play tends to highlight a different aspect of the drama. In most productions, the triangle comprised of Nola, Ernie and Digger Masson, under Pippy's horrified gaze, is central to the overall mood of the play. In Andrews' production the triangle comprised of the younger generation – Roy Child, Judy Pogson and Ron Suddards, a post-office clerk – activates a parallel romance. Luke Mullins's Roy Child spends much stage time kissing Judy Pogson as they contemplate escaping the drudgery of suburban life. But Judy prefers the kindness and decency of Ron to the dreams and eloquence of Roy. In this production, Dan Spielman's Ron represents a more attractive option than previously, with the effect that Judy acquires more rather than less credit for her decision in a further updating of the feminine roles in the play.

Prior to *The Season at Sarsaparilla*, Andrews had directed *Netherwood* for his graduation piece at Flinders University in Adelaide, and assisted Neil Armfield in his production of *Night on Bald Mountain*. This gave him a sense of closeness to Patrick White the playwright and an admiration for the writer's sense of the theatrical. Of Sarsaparilla as a time and place he notes "that particular suburbia was built upon certain political notions of domesticity and protecting your quarter acre"[52] that still apply in the twentieth century in debates about home ownership.

---

51 Alison Croggon, "Review: The Season at Sarsaparilla", *Theatre Notes* (blog), 26 March 2007, https://theatrenotes.blogspot.com/2007/03/review-season-at-sarsaparilla.html.
52 Andrew Taylor, "Audacious Director Benedict Andrews Stamps his Style on a Literary Giant", *Sydney Morning Herald,* 27 February 2007.

The overall effect of the theatricalist staging is a gesture of appreciation for the modernity that underpins contemporary Australian life, despite its problems. Andrews is not "blowing off" about Australia, as White had, but speaks from a generation born ten years after the play was first staged, to audiences forty years later, with some nostalgia for the past.

From the point of view of contemporary design aesthetics, Desmond Digby's early staging was an attempt to represent ordinary life in a schematic way but it appears overly busy and cluttered to the contemporary eye. Proxemic relations were not the only restriction imposed by the quantity of objects in the space – there was little room for physical work, for performers to embody characters walking, moving, and doing things. The clutter represents the accumulation of material objects in a claustrophobic world in which human subjects are hemmed in and restricted by the very modern life that was supposed to free them from inner-city overcrowding. The clutter nevertheless functioned as a self-conscious assertion of the object world into which human subjects were placed, and around which and in relation to which they acclimatised self to a mode of modern life.

The historical significance of Sharman's highly successful revival of *Season*, backed up with the revival of *A Cheery Soul* in 1979, featuring Nevin as Girlie Pogson and then Miss Docker, is that it inaugurated the practice in which ambitious directors, including Neil Armfield, Michael Kantor, Benedict Andrews, Kate Gaul and Kip Williams, have flagged a commitment to the art form of theatre by directing a Patrick White play. Kate Gaul has said of her production of *The Ham Funeral* in 2018: "Patrick White is a great Australian playwright and as an Australian theatre director I wanted to do one of his plays. I am drawn to text based, non-naturalist theatre and Patrick White is unique in Australia for that style".[53] After Sharman, working on a Patrick White play is the equivalent of British directors presenting a Shakespeare or Brechtian revival on the London stage. Sharman's international and mainstream reputation raised the profile of Patrick White as a significant Australian playwright, and accorded legitimacy to anti-naturalist theatricality as a genuine alternative to mainstream naturalism. White's theatre arguably becomes canonical and career-making.

In Armfield's production emphasis is given to the dramatic character as a marionette performing on a minimalist stage through a series of awakenings, becomings, repetitions and struggles. The Mixmaster becomes an object designating peacetime, marriage and domesticity and how these social practices conspire to make a man go soft. Ernie's rejoinder is that his position as husband, homeowner and provider is preferable to "lyin in bloody fox-'oles". With that, he gestures towards the emergence of a new code of masculinity based in property ownership and assets. The dialogic exchange with Masson brings to the surface a previously unseen degree of self-reflexivity in Ernie who shows he is well aware of

---

53   Kate Gaul, Interview with the author, 26 September, 2019.

emerging codes of postwar masculinity vested in the possession and consumption of consumer goods.

Benedict Andrew's extensive use of the intrusive camera updates White's theatrical modernism by drawing on contemporary intermedial performance. The double vision of modernity's pasts and its presents frames a past where female life is staged as absurd realism and remediated as soap opera. The final frame is the present of the performance where audiences attuned to lifestyle and reality TV accept the intrusion of the camera into daily life while contemplating the overlapping instances of theatre as live and mediated performance. The interrelationship between the screens and the materiality of the iconic set points to the ongoing drama of Australian theatrical modernism in which screen-based scenography represents the latest phase of innovation at war with tradition. On this reading, the sheer size of the house, its seeming unassailable dominance of the stage, tells the story of the enduring power of representational systems based on iconicity in Australian theatre. The screens draw the audience's attention away from the house into a new interface with theatre as the relationship between stage and screen, and the destabilisation of mimetic drama by its remediation. Benedict Andrew's production can be read therefore as a challenge to the dominant representational systems of Australian theatre based in iconic sets and live action. That the challenge is mounted via a revivified production of Patrick White's theatre is indicative of the enduring richness of the work.

5
Performing Militant Virtue and Loneliness: *A Cheery Soul*

A Cheery Soul was first performed by the Union Theatre Repertory Company (UTRC) at the Union Theatre, University of Melbourne on 19 November 1963 in one of only two non-Adelaide premieres of a Patrick White play. After some hesitation, John Sumner, resident director at UTRC, agreed to stage the premiere in Melbourne in a four-week season.[1] Desmond Digby was called on once more for set design and the relatively unknown Nita Pannell performed the central role of Miss Docker.[2] The production history of the play in performance suggests that this larger-than-life character develops over time as a caricature of assertive, militant Christian virtue, of a kind that can heckle and badger a vicar to death, but that barely conceals the lifelong loneliness of a now ageing woman. Critic Roger Covell recognised the enduring solitary life of the character when he wrote: "White makes it clear that she is loveless because she has never been loved", as a child, as a young woman in domestic service and now as an eccentric do-gooder.[3] By the twenty-first century, when the question of endemic loneliness in Australian life is under investigation, Kip William's production for the Sydney Theatre Company (STC) in 2018 captures the theme of loneliness, described in social theory as an "ambiguous and little understood emotion", one that is barely visible or talked about, but has emerged with greater clarity.[4]

---

1 Julian Meyrick offers a detailed account of the correspondence between White and Sumner in the lead up to the premiere in Meyrick, "Modernist Drama Decried: Patrick White, Spoiled Identity" *Australasian Drama Studies* 71 (October 2017), 50–66.
2 Patrick White had insisted to Sumner that there was no "other actress in Australia" with the right voice for the role having previously seen her in Alan Seymour's *The One Day of the Year* at the Palace Theatre Sydney in 1961. Patrick White, to Harry Medlin, 3 October 1962, Patrick White Collection, Series 1477, Barr Smith Library, University of Adelaide. Sadly, the only record of Pannell's Miss Docker is a BBC1 Wednesday Play series from 1966 that is not available in Australia.
3 Roger Covell, "Patrick White's Plays", *Quadrant* 8, no. 1 (April–May 1964): 11.
4 Adrian Franklin, "A Lonely Society? Loneliness and Liquid Modernity in Australia" in *Australian Journal of Social Issues* 47 no. 1, 2012: 11–28, 12.

As indicated in chapter one, *A Cheery Soul* is set in the fictional suburb of Sarsaparilla in the 1960s but is spatially more complex than both *The Ham Funeral* and *The Season at Sarsaparilla* in so far as each of its three acts follows the homeless lead character across different locations. Act One begins with Miss Docker moving into the little veranda room of a middle-class suburban home, with an emphasis on its status as temporary accommodation. As Act Two begins she has been moved into the Sundown Home for Old People, and in Act Three, she is on the move to the local church, and the surrounding town and country roads. Scenes set in gardens and moving cars extend the physical action beyond the boundaries of the two earlier plays, introducing a cinematic flexibility into the previously fixed sets of naturalist theatre. These spaces within spaces also facilitate temporal shifts that accommodate memory, fantasy and dreamscapes. These performative aspects of the dramatic text disrupt the conventional three-act structure and enact White's early break with the unities of time and space in and for Australian theatre.

The performative mode is comic absurdist drama with expressionist aspects that link its visual effects and themes to *The Ham Funeral*, including the presence of female isolation hidden beneath banter and cheeriness. These expressionist aspects play out as Miss Docker increasingly presents audiences with a mask-like face, heavily made-up with exaggerated features and with her bodily form shaped more and more by interior states of mind and emotion.

In the premiere production, Digby designs the Custance's middle-class home along similar lines to the houses in *The Season at Sarsaparilla*. In Act Two a shift to open staging supports temporal and scenic shifts between the present and interludes set in the past: White wrote in a letter to Digby that he was thinking about "scrims and gauzes" for scenic fluidity.[5] In Act Three the church appears behind a full-length scrim that rises to reveal the dramatic scene of the Vicar's death. The unity of Act Three is segmented into eight scenes incorporating choral recitals, the rituals of religious ceremony, and transitory moments featuring Miss Docker alone on streets and roads. The use of flexible stage props such as rostra, lighting and sound effects, and bodily elements of movement and stillness, provide the premiere with innovative theatrical solutions to the fluidity imagined in White's stage directions.

In his program notes "About the Play", Sumner attempts to persuade audience members that the play is a comedy, while warning at the same time that the character of Miss Docker is "of near-epic proportions … and her decline, although outwardly self-inflicted and at times ludicrous, has an underlying chill, which cannot fail to arouse uneasiness and perhaps compassion in observers".[6] Alluding

---

5   Patrick White to Desmond Digby, 15 March 1963, Patrick White Collection, Series 1477, Barr Smith Library, University of Adelaide.
6   John Sumner, "About the Play", *A Cheery Soul*, (Union Theatre Repertory Company, Union Theatre Melbourne University, 19 November 1963), theatre program, MTC Archive, University of Melbourne Library.

cautiously to the expressionist and Brechtian elements, and allowing that the play might startle audiences, Sumner attempts to conjure empathy as a pleasing response that might give rise to a transformative experience. He also frames the season as a rare opportunity to see a new work by a novelist of "international repute", who chooses to live and work in Australia.[7] None of these strategies seem to work. *A Cheery Soul* is neither a critical nor a financial success and attracts only meagre audiences and poor reviews. Geoffrey Hutton's review in *The Age* concedes that the play is a comedy in Moliere's sense of the "merciless exposure of human egotism and folly", but he finds Miss Docker an eternal bore, who is incapable of undergoing any desirable epiphany or anagnorisis. Although he admires Nita Pannell's "remarkable non-stop performance", the play withholds the aesthetic means of transformation by "pounding and hammering idea after idea, and style after style into the compass of the evening".[8] In other words, White's drama disappoints because it withholds the expected satisfactions and pleasures that attend a night at the theatre for audiences.

In a similar vein, Keith Macartney in *Meanjin*, praises Pannell's performance but thinks the play is a mess:

> I feel reasonably certain that, if *A Cheery Soul* had been offered by an unknown playwright, it would have been rejected out of hand. One hopes that Mr White, whose talents are undeniable, will realize that as a writer for the theatre he has much to learn, and that he will be content to simplify and strengthen his material.[9]

Roger Covell, on the other hand, acknowledges the disorderly structure of White's theatre, but finds the stage naturalism of the first act surprisingly less satisfying than the "fluid mingling of memory and reality and nightmare in the second and third acts". He likes the play ("faults not withstanding") for the way it is "illuminated by White's characteristic humour and finely focused observation" and finds the overall mood reflects the playwright at his "darkest".[10] This latter point concedes a degree of gravity in the work that warrants further attention, as if the form itself is taken as a sign that something new is underway in Australian theatre.

Covell's review provides further detail about the production, such that Pannell's "magnificently greedy" Miss Docker gains sympathy "more quickly than she was meant to" in Act One and that the blackouts in the last act were too long! In a longer essay published in *Quadrant*, Covell refers to the key scenes involving Miss Docker and Mr and Mrs Lillie in Act Two as a "dramatic fantasia in which present and past, fact and nightmare, mingle freely".[11] Helmut Newton's photographs provide

---

7   Sumner, "About the Play".
8   Geoffrey Hutton, "Bitter Satire of A Cheery Soul", *Age,* 21 November 1963, 5.
9   Keith Macartney, "Patrick White's 'A Cheery Soul'", *Meanjin Quarterly* 23, no. 1 (March 1964): 95.
10 Roger Covell, "White Play Opens in Melbourne", *Sydney Morning Herald,* 20 November 1963, 14.

additional insights. We see Pannell's Miss Docker in a moment of stillness as a woman with a melancholy expression, the ladies at the Sundown Home behind her. Her hair is secured into a bun at the nape of her neck and her face is make-up free in a naturalist look that inspires compassion – her ordinary dress, broad Anglo-Celtic face and sad eyes lack the marks of caricature and show an unconcealed sadness. White's preference for Pannell, who appears to have played the role with more pathos than militancy, suggests the production presented a Miss Docker who ends the play, as Covell put it, "old and shattered but not entirely defeated".[12]

Pannell was joined in the cast by Elspeth Ballantyne, who played a maid at the Sundown Home and Baby Porteous, an elderly spinster, Sheila Florance as Mrs Lillie and Doreen Warburton, who had played Nola Boyle in Sydney, as Mrs Custance. The play's stylistic changes from naturalism in Act One to non-naturalistic expressionism in Acts Two and Three placed new demands on the actors. In a recent interview with Anne Pender, Ballantyne recalled that the actors found the text "unusual" and "demanding" with abrupt shifts between an alien "presentational and expressionistic" style and the more familiar naturalism.[13] The new style of acting recalls Bertolt Brecht's experiments with Epic Theatre at the Berlin Ensemble where the company had the resources to employ a resident ensemble, which would spend up to a year in rehearsal, trying out approaches to a new kind of performance grounded in anti-naturalist techniques such as short episodic scenes, the creation of tableaux, the distancing effect and dialectical choices. Sumner's cast had no such time or guidance, and it would take decades before Robyn Nevin and Jim Sharman, skilled in both Brechtian modernism and non-naturalist forms (including musicals), were equipped to realise the theatricalist potential of the play. Neil Armfield later took a long view of the production of Patrick White's plays to distinguish between the premiere production, when everything had to be tried for the first time, and its subsequent revivals. The later productions were able to benefit from the "cycle", in which a performance history gradually builds around a play and acts as a guide and point of departure for each new cast and crew.[14]

Returning to the grainy photographs of the production, Act Three presents rows of pews facing the vicar in his pulpit from which he is seen leaning forward preaching with his arms raised. Miss Docker sits apart in her Sunday best. Upstage, a painted scrim shows swirling white clouds. Covell writes that the death of the clergyman was the "climax of a scene of quite horrifying power" that continued to haunt with its vividness.[15]

---

11 Roger Covell, "Patrick White's Plays", 11.
12 Roger Covell, "Patrick White's Plays", 11.
13 Anne Pender, "Robyn Nevin, Patrick White and the Art of the Modern in Australian Theatre", *Australasian Drama Studies: Special Issue, Patrick White and Australian Theatrical Modernism* 71, no. 2 (2017): 79.
14 Neil Armfield, Interview with Sandra D'Urso, 9 January 2018.
15 Covell, "Patrick White's Plays", 11.

In his recent review of the archival records of the production, Andrew Fuhrman suggests that Sumner and Digby "were struggling toward the expression of something new" but did not have the budget, or more critically, the background in modernist theatre to achieve the "transformational artistic vision" necessary for the realisation of the text.[16] He concludes that the production was trapped in naturalism, "a style that proved inadequate" to the play. Subsequent productions were better able to release the theatricality of the play, presenting rich opportunities for Miss Docker to express both insight and reflection through silence, bodily expressivity, wordless action and other scenic stage elements such as music, lighting and atmosphere.

A Cheery Soul: Jim Sharman Revival 1979

The case for *A Cheery Soul* as having a place in the history of Australian modernist theatre was advanced through Robyn Nevin's performance as Miss Docker in the 1979 revival of *A Cheery Soul*, directed by Jim Sharman at the Sydney Opera House Drama Theatre with design by Brian Thomson. The key moment is her affectation of a silent scream. Those in the audience who know their Brecht recognise the quotation of Helene Weigel's Mother Courage in the contradictory act of giving expression to and suppressing grief. The silent scream also quotes the scream of the grieving mother in Pablo Picasso's Spanish Civil War painting *Guernica* (1937) and the expressionist painting *The Scream* (1893) by Norwegian artist Edvard Munch. Miss Docker's antipodean scream reveals the deeply anguished interiority of the character, locked in as she is to a continual performance of cheeriness. On the DVD of the restored video recording of the performance the scream is also a masterly harnessing of theatrical presence through enhanced projection and physicality.[17] These Brechtian references throughout Sharman's production invite questions, to which I return, about the history and politics that drive the performance.

The performance was described at the time as "dazzling".[18] Metatheatrical elements add a new layer to the play's experiments with dramaturgical form. Actors play multiple parts and remain on stage throughout to sit and watch the play in full view of the audience, bringing the act of spectatorship into the frame. Anne Pender writes that "the constellation of White as playwright, Sharman as director and Nevin as lead actor in *A Cheery Soul* brought the elements of aesthetic modernism and Australian acting together in one extraordinary production".[19]

---

16   Andrew Fuhrmann, "Making Room for Modernism: The 1979 Sydney Theatre Company Production of Patrick White's *A Cheery Soul*", *Australasian Drama Studies: Special Issue Patrick White and Australian Theatrical Modernism* 71, no. 2 (2017): 95.
17   *A Cheery Soul* by Patrick White, directed by Jim Sharman, Sydney Theatre Company, 1979. DVD version of restored video recording, STC Archives, Sydney.
18   Harry Kippax, "A Cheery Soul – To Cheer Us Up", *Sydney Morning Herald*, 19 January 1979.
19   Pender, "Robyn Nevin, Patrick White", 72.

Katharine Brisbane's review considered it the "finest production Jim Sharman has ever done".[20] Gone were the cautious apologies for White's cumbersome play of 1963. Scenes are staged in open spaces rather than located in rooms or houses. Signs fly in and out – "Kitchen at the Custances" or "Sundown Home for Old People" (98–9) – to literalise Thomson's tribute to White's theatricalist stage directions. Thomson explains:

> I just loved … how Patrick would write in the stage-directions … 'The kitchen at the Custances'. Then there were things like – 'On the way to church' – and I just thought they were striking phrases.[21]

Elizabeth Schafer credits Thomson's previous collaborations with Sharman on *Hair*, *The Rocky Horror Show* and *Jesus Christ Superstar* as the key to the production's assertion of theatricality over textual sobriety.[22] It is noteworthy that in praising the production, while also acknowledging that the play text is "difficult", Brisbane is one of the few critics to understand the productive challenge involved in staging White's expressionist anti-naturalist theatre.[23] Most critics expected the play text to be complete in itself and not in need of creative development in the move from page to stage, especially for a new work.

The restored video recording suggests that the elements of aesthetic modernism most on show are a selective use of Brechtian techniques, although Nevin's technique, as I will argue, draws on Artaudian cruelty as well. Thomson took a minimalist approach to staging, focusing on crisp theatrical image-making, often in the form of tableaux staged before a curtain or half-curtain or on a lit rostrum. The program was projected onto the Drama Theatre's fire curtain and again on the upstage curtain in a way that adapts Brecht's notion of the "primitive attempt at literarizing the theatre"[24] to punctuate its representational apparatus. The device works to split the spectator's attention between the dramatic world of the play and representation in a mode of "complex seeing"[25] that was encouraged throughout the performance.

Sharman establishes the theatricality of the performance with the addition of a prologue that I describe in detail here. It takes the form of a silent onstage tableau in which Miss Docker stands centre stage bathed in blue light. She wears a purple floral dress underneath a black coat and carries black gloves, a handbag and her

---

20 Katharine Brisbane, *Not Wrong – Just Different: Observations on the Rise of Contemporary Australian Theatre* (Sydney: Currency Press, 2005), 288.
21 Brian Thomson, interviewed by Sandra D'Urso, 18 May 2018.
22 Elizabeth Schafer, "A Ham Funeral, Patrick White, Collaboration and Neil Armfield", *Australian Studies* 3 (2011), 1–24, 16.
23 Brisbane, *Not Wrong – Just Different*, 290.
24 Bertolt Brecht, "The Literarization of the Theatre", in *Brecht on Theatre: The Development of an Aesthetic*, ed. and trans. John Willett (London: Methuen, 1984), 43.
25 Brecht, "The Literarization of the Theatre", 44.

hat. Her face is overlaid with a second skin of white mask-like make-up and her lips are bright red. She appears to be monumentalised as a subject in time and space and as an object of the spectator's gaze. Around her in front of the billowing upstage curtain stand other cast members in costume. Mrs Custance is identifiable as a young woman in a print frock with a yellow apron; Mr Custance is in a dark suit. Both stand on either side of Miss Docker watching her with a slightly unsettled demeanour. There is a long pause after which a slow piano begins to play. Then in a sudden dramatic move, Miss Docker turns sideways, slides her right foot forward and tilts backwards while looking at the audience. Still holding onto her hat, she opens her mouth wide, to affect a silent scream. The other actors exit as the light fades on Miss Docker. The tableau finishes while also anticipating the final scene in which she walks alone in the opposite direction across the stage, bent over against the wind.

Miss Docker's open-mouthed red-rimmed scream occurs twice more in the performance. Andrew Fuhrmann interprets the scream in psychological terms as a response to the repressive force of cheeriness, the dissipating effect of "cheerful materialism and shallowness", which he equates with a recurring theme in White's critique of Australian society and culture.[26] In emotional terms, I suggest the scream is also an expression of the silent epidemic of loneliness in modern societies related to the break-up of families and communities, and to gender- and age-related isolation in utilitarian societies. This is especially the case for Miss Docker whose scream is not a cry of grief for a lost loved one, but a solitary expression of the self. This prologue has the effect of situating Miss Docker centre stage as a figure before she enters the play via the Custance's front door.

For Act One at the Custances, the stage is bare, with merely a table and a stove to represent the kitchen, while Miss Docker's room is located behind a half-curtain on which the sign "Verandah Room" is painted. The spectator is invited to see comedy in the way the characters cling to naturalism on a bare stage with minimal props. The Custances in their minimalist kitchen defamiliarise suburbia as "foundational" to Australian modernity, revealing an imposed "settler society" making its "home" on alien land.[27] In this domain, Mrs Custance is an alienated anxious wife cooking English food at a stove which Mr Custance then eats quickly, before pushing his plate into the middle of the table and moving his cup and saucer into place. The satiric distillation of the English ritual of dinner displays the small ways in which a husband exercises entitlement and a wife obeys, both robotic in their predetermined roles. Absent from the suburban scene is the presence of children, the explanation for which – Mrs Custance was wrongly sterilised by a surgeon – remains a strictly guarded secret.

---

26 Fuhrmann, "Making Room for Modernism", 105.
27 Brigid Rooney, *Suburban Space, the Novel and Australian Modernity* (London: Anthem Press, 2018), 1.

The arrival of the laughing, talkative and assertive Miss Docker in a red coat and hat occurs as a major interruption of the "exclusive domicile of marriage".[28] In a key moment of splendid disruption, she sit in her rocking chair, laughing, with her knees apart, as her shadow is projected larger than life onto the half-curtain behind her. Nevin's exultant Miss Docker wickedly celebrates her escape from marriage and domesticity and the magnetic force she represents.

Act Two begins on a darkened stage with the sign for the Sundown Home printed on the upstage curtain. There is an elegant side table with flowers in matching vases and some armchairs. The stage is otherwise bare. Old Ladies dressed in black enter followed by Miss Docker in a red cardigan, her broad Australian accent standing out against the reserved tones of the others. Sharman places groups of women together as a Chorus centre stage. Peter Carroll, who played Mr Custance, is now Mrs Webb. Once again, the stage is bathed in blue light that illuminates the ladies' white faces and hair. Their eyes are darkened and their cheeks look sunken like expressionist images of hollowness in the face of death. Mrs Lillie sits to the side on her own, mourning for a husband that she loved and whose death was overtaken by the unwanted ministrations of Miss Docker. Played by Maggie Kirkpatrick, she assumes a dignified aristocratic demeanour. Miss Docker's gossipy account of Tom Lillie's death is humiliating and cruel as she laughs while describing his failing body. The funeral re-enactment takes place on a rostrum with simple wooden chairs depicting the car taking the mourners – Mrs Lillie, the two well-bred Porteous sisters, Mrs Pinfold and Miss Docker – to the funeral. The switch to narrative is accompanied by rising intensity as the sound of a car speeding away leaves Miss Docker behind on a dark stage. The Chorus' careful enunciation works in unison against her singular cries. When Miss Docker stumbles onto her knees and announces she has "mucked up my best nylongs" (230), the audience laughs at the voice, and at her downfall. Here Miss Docker turns to the laughing audience and opens her mouth in a second silent scream. Meanwhile the Chorus roll words around their tongues while the piano plays gently. The scene then switches back to the present and Miss Docker's photos.

In the final moments of Act Three, the wind blows the upstage curtains and Miss Docker is in the wilderness, delusional, and is urinated on by the invisible dog amidst laughter from some boys. She has entered the land of the damned but is still bargaining with her god/dog. She weeps walks on into the howling wind, bent over in silhouette as a tramp laughs loudly.

Neil Armfield recalled the performance as one of "monumental simplicity" as in a composed, rather than cold or brutalist modern, aesthetic.[29] He went on to recall how stunning it was to see the bare elements of the stage revealed: "a wooden floor and a curtain basically, and essential props and that kind of thrilling sense of

---

28   Judith Barbour, "Cheery Souls and Lost Souls: The Outsiders in Patrick White's Plays", *Southerly* 42, no. 2 (1982): 140.
29   Armfield, interview.

the human puppet, which was very much how White conceived the marionettes of the stage".³⁰ Armfield's insight into White's conceptual approach to character offers a guide to the gestic qualities of the representation of not only Miss Docker but of each of the characters. It is as if they find their feet on Sharman and Thomson's stage in a theatre better positioned aesthetically to realise the anti-realist character.

Brisbane writes that Nevin's Miss Docker commanded attention from the moment she entered to her final moment, "when she twists in our direction, emitting a [Brechtian] silent scream".³¹ Pender vividly recalls Miss Docker's "clown-like makeup revealing a grotesque and comic mask – the grin of red, oversized mouth".³² This visceral description provides a rich example of how performative acts on stage do more than express a pre-existing identity as stipulated by a text but "engender identity through those very acts".³³ In demonstrating the overall fluidity of texts and interpretations over time, and from revival to revival, Nevin's Miss Docker is among the performances that challenge the hegemony of text and playwright over theatrical performance. The relationship with the audience is also given a higher profile than imagined in the text or achieved by Sumner in the premiere production. Fuhrmann likens the curtain to an "enormous vaudeville playbill", an inclusive larger than life acknowledgement of the audience's presence at the theatrical event.³⁴

In evoking the Brechtian method, the wider social context for the silent scream comes into play. It becomes visible in contexts in which Miss Docker is prevented from expressing a point of view in a world in which her social superiors control the emotional atmosphere of a room or even a theatre, such as the Sydney Opera House. Where Mother Courage's silent scream is a *gestus* signifying the control of emotional space by the victor in a war zone, Miss Docker's scream is that of an orphan, now a woman without social connections, who is enraged but powerless to do more than indulge in minor subversive acts, some with unintended consequences, such as the vicar's death. The production's political point is that the modern suburb reproduces bourgeois values and liberal democratic ideology. In 1979, the Western world is already beginning its retreat from the achievement of greater social equality through its steady contraction of the nineteenth-century gap between rich and poor. Miss Docker's social status will continue to decline.

---

30   Armfield, interview.
31   Brisbane, *Not Wrong – Just Different*, 290.
32   Pender, "Robyn Nevin, Patrick White", 82.
33   Erika Fischer-Lichte, *The Transformative Power of Performance*, trans. Saskya Jain (New York: Routledge, 2008), 27.
34   Fuhrmann, "Making Room for Modernism", 97.

Neil Armfield directs *A Cheery Soul*

A decade later, Neil Armfield revived *A Cheery Soul* and staged it three more times, taking it into the twenty-first century. His first production for the Queensland Theatre Company in 1992 featured Carol Skinner as Miss Docker with design by Bill Haycock. Armfield acknowledged Sharman's production as a major influence on the revival, in particular, the thrilling way in which a bare stage can be so "powerful".[35] Adrian Kiernander tells us the stage included a revolve, was framed by an upstage curtain and was otherwise bare.[36] The audience could observe both actors and props waiting in the wings for entrances, extending the idea of spectatorship embedded in Sharman's Brechtian-influenced stage. The *Brisbane Review* gave more details of Armfield and Haycock's staging effects as quoted by Schafer:

> The kitchen is a *Women's Weekly* dream of the late fifties ... But by placing it all on a revolve and exposing the lights and props at the sides of the huge Suncorp stage, we are in a world of alienation, where we observe from afar and are therefore allowed to judge.[37]

Sue Gough writing for the *Bulletin* describes Armfield as "the perfect guide, a director who understands White's theatricality like no other", with Haycock, a designer "who understands exactly the effects he wants to achieve." She was particularly drawn to the heightened "David Lynch-style 1960s interiors".[38] In the face of previous criticism of the play's stylistic disunity, Sharman's and then Armfield's revivals, which focus on the theatrical potential of the play, begin to discover the depth and range of its critical intent. Making the scenographic effects speak rather than merely provide the background for the performers' actions, they set a signifying system in motion that audiences can read and experience alongside or in contradiction to character, dialogue and action. Brecht theorised that scenic writing, now referred to as "scenographic dramaturgy", which accounts for the visual world of the production including the performers, encouraged an audience to view history in relative terms.[39] Hence the distinguishing marks of a 1950s or '60s suburban kitchen are revealed thirty years later as impermanent at the same time as they remind audiences of the social conditions of the era, such as Mrs Custance's anxious subservience to her breadwinner husband. In this Brechtian view, the potential and indeed the reception of a revival is the extent to which it reveals the past while recognising new variations of the same themes in the present.

---

35 Armfield, interview.
36 Adrian Kiernander, "Chain-Saw Voice Rips into Society", *Australian*, 8 June 1992.
37 Schafer, "A Ham Funeral", 13.
38 Sue Gough, "Driving Miss Docker", *Bulletin*, 22 June, 1992, 103.
39 Melissa Poll, *Robert Lepage's Scenographic Dramaturg: The Aesthetic Signature at Work* (London: Palgrave, 2018), 3.

In Act Two, Armfield and Haycock fill the Sundown Home with swirling mists against a background of unrelieved darkness, velour sofas and dusty chinoiserie. Here Miss Docker appears, dressed "in a foul shade of brown", to sit among the ladies "like some monstrous lump of excrement". They recoil from her endless talk and lumpen body before they try to expel the abject figure in their midst in a scene of "commedia, Greek tragedy and the absurd all rolled into one."[40]

In spite of his misgivings about Patrick White as a playwright, Leonard Radic praises Armfield's eye for detail and Carole Skinner's Miss Docker for her "unquenching cheerfulness, and also energy". Still complaining about White's "abrupt shifts of style and tone" and resenting its eclectic influences and stylistic impurities, Radic admits that Armfield manages "these stylistic shifts with ease".[41] Skinner's Miss Docker is filled with "mindless energy" and "an idiot grin and cackle",[42] with "a chain-saw voice which carves its way out through her reddened mouth and flattens all before it".[43]

Schafer notes the production continues Sharman's non-naturalistic style but takes it further by compressing the three acts into two. She draws attention to additional innovations such as the representation of a newlywed Millicent Lillie, who appears bare-breasted in a scene representing old Mrs Lillie's memory, in what was said to be "a hair-tingling moment".[44] In 1989 in *Call of the Wild* and later works, writer-director Jenny Kemp drew on modernist representations of full or partial female nudity, inspired by the paintings of Belgian surrealist artist Paul Delvaux, to express the "intelligent, meditative and inward-looking" female psyche.[45] Armfield's partially nude Millicent Lillie can be understood in light of this theatrical tradition as a figment of Mrs Lillie's meditation on the idea of youth, love and adventure. The contrast between the elderly body that trembles with palsy and the young woman's ideal beauty makes a powerful statement about the relation between the bodily self, the unconscious and the everyday social self. Miss Docker's manic cackling adds to the cruelty latent in her kindness. Armfield does not repeat this scene when the production goes to the Adelaide Festival of Arts in 1994.

Armfield directed a new production in 1996 for the Melbourne Theatre Company at the Playhouse with designer Dale Ferguson and a cast led by Robyn Nevin returning to perform as Miss Docker. Nevin's Miss Docker, as Helen Thomson wrote, was "simply superb" in showing the multiple shades of the character:

---

40 Sue Gough, "Driving Miss Docker", 103–4.
41 Leonard Radic, "White Makes Cheery Return", *Age*, 3 March 1994, 15.
42 Gough, "Driving Miss Docker".
43 Kiernander, "Chain-Saw Voice Rips into Society".
44 Schafer, "A Ham Funeral", 14.
45 Rachel Fensham and Denise Varney, *The Dolls' Revolution: Australian Theatre and the Cultural Imagination* (Melbourne: Australian Scholarly Publishing, 2005), 74.

Every tiny gesture, every chuckle and laugh, is used to devastating effect, thinly masking the aggression, envy, desire, and hunger for love and power, all of which underlie Miss Docker's monstrous goodness.[46]

Nevin was joined by well-known comedian Sue Ingleton, whose Mrs Lillie was "a decayed gothic heroine", and with Ross Williams and Margaret Mills as the "highly strung but mannered" Custances.[47] Ian Scott and Melita Jurisic played the Reverend and Mrs Wakeman, the former handsome in his robes but ineffective as a preacher, the latter nervously attentive to his vulnerability. Others in the strong cast included Julie Forsyth, Monica Maughan, and Bob Hornery. By the mid-1990s, Australian theatre had produced a generation of actors whose early careers were immersed in non-naturalist, symbolist, and introspective theatre. Forsyth began her career at Anthill Theatre in South Melbourne working with Jean-Pierre Mignon on a series of New Wave French pieces for theatre including Raymond Cousse's *Kid's Stuff* (1988) and would perform the role of Miss Quodling in Matthew Lutton's *Night on Bald Mountain* in 2016. Jurisic worked with Jim Sharman at the Lighthouse Theatre, Adelaide, where she appeared in the premiere production of *Netherwood* in 1983. She was in Lucian Savron's salon-style production of *The Ham Funeral* in 1995 and played the alcoholic Miriam Sword in Lutton's *Night on Bald Mountain* with Forsyth. In the meantime, she worked with Grotowski-influenced director Nico Lathouris in Melbourne, and Jean-Pierre Mignon at Anthill Theatre in South Melbourne. Margaret Mills and Ian Scott have worked extensively with writer-director Jenny Kemp, whose introspective surrealist theatre works constitute a significant feminist trajectory within Australian modernist theatre.[48] Others in the cast, such as Maughan and Hornery, were gifted comics as well suggesting a deliberate emphasis on comedy that was applauded by critics.

Nevin's Miss Docker enters through the front rows of the audience assuming its complicity with her world view:

> MISS DOCKER: (OFF) Isn't it lovely to be amongst friends! What would we do without them! (*Pause*) Neat place they've got. (*Pause*) As a matter of personal taste, I'd have painted it cream and green. (188)

Seamless transitions in the production are assisted by the installation of a travelator or moving walkway that spans the width of the stage. John Preston writes that the device emphasises the passing parade of the "various landscapes laid waste by Miss Docker's deadly sorties".[49] Photographic records show a moment in Act One

---

46 Helen Thomson, "Rare Level of Quality", *Age*, 9 May 1996, 17.
47 Thomson, "Rare Level of Quality".
48 Rachel Fensham, "Modernity and the White Imaginary in Australian Feminist Theatre", *Hecate* 29, no. 1 (2003), 7–18. See also Fensham and Varney, *The Dolls' Revolution*.

with Mr and Mrs Custance seated on vinyl chairs at either end of a laminex and chrome kitchen table with Miss Docker in the middle facing the audience, like a child between its parents. The tomato plants, a minor textual reference, now rise up in the background, oversized and looming, portending the threat unfolding in the household. The placement of the tomatoes in such a prominent line of vision for the audience frames the dramatic action in a particularly unexpected but logical way in terms of the complementarity it offers to action and dialogue. As theorist Joslin McKinney writes, the "spatial, material and temporal nature of scenography" acts in a similar way to how environments act on human perception.[50] The spatial placement of the tomatoes offers or affords the audience a glimpse of the underlying tensions rising to the surface in the Custance household: Miss Docker berates Mr Custance, who looks straight ahead fuming, while Mrs Custance stares down at her plate. Mr Custance's beloved tomatoes cue the pall of dread descending on the house while mocking the well-meaning, now stricken couple. Later the traumatised Custances cling to each other like survivors of a tempest. The tomato plants have been pruned and rendered docile. Used in this surrealist, satirical, and anti-naturalist manner, the elements of space, materiality and time create the theatricality through which the play comes to life for the audience in ways that could not be foreseen from an historical perspective.

The production is simultaneously enhanced by an older Robyn Nevin reprising the role. Bryce Hallett observes that she gives a "flawlessly nuanced" performance that "reveals much about contradictory human nature and frailty; the delicate line between good and evil and loneliness manifest as righteous charity".[51] The idea that Miss Docker's behaviour is driven by loneliness introduces a new interpretation of the character for the twenty-first century, one that is not necessarily more sympathetic to the character so much as it links her to a social condition on the rise in the modern era. White has previously referenced social alienation and isolation in *The Ham Funeral*, through the Young Man, as well as the unseen lodgers and Mrs Lusty. But Miss Docker's loneliness is repressed in social contexts only to be revealed in desolate spaces such as the road outside the town. These scenes have become more pronounced in recent productions that situate Miss Docker on a bare stage. Helen Thomson also sees in Nevin's 1996 performance the realisation that Miss Docker is "the inevitable real victim" in the play because she is shown to be unable to destroy the love that binds her victims to each other: the Custances clinging to each other at the end of Act One, the Lillies and their romantic youth, and Mrs Wakeman's devotion to her fragile husband.[52]

---

49 John Preston, "Disaster Turns into Triumph", *Australian Financial Review: Weekend Review*, 17 May 1996, 15.
50 Joslin McKinney, "Scenographic Materialism, Affordance and Extended Cognition in Kris Verdonck's ACTOR #1", *Theatre and Performance Design*, 1, nos. 1–2 (2015): 81.
51 Bryce Hallett, "A Cheery Soul", *Australian*, 10 May 1996.
52 Thomson, "Rare Level of Quality".

Armfield and Ferguson revived the play for an STC/Belvoir co-production at the Sydney Opera House in 2000 with Robyn Nevin once more in her role as Miss Docker. Otherwise there was a new cast. The walkway returns and is well-suited to the width of the Drama Theatre stage. The play begins with the theatre's red curtains half open to reveal a clothesline rotating centre stage with the three giant tomato plants behind it. The tomato plants are now affording important cues for the audience's perception of how Miss Docker's threat to prune them activates castration anxiety in Mr Custance.

Nevin's Miss Docker enters once again through the auditorium, resplendent in her now iconic coat and hat, floral dress, white face, and bright lipstick. The frequency of the revivals allow Armfield and Nevin to express an evolving understanding of the character over time, finding new elements or changes in emphasis. In Act Two, armchairs and sofas indicate the Nursing Home but the ladies' accents have become less English and more vernacular Australian. For the scene in which the young Mr and Mrs Lillie appear, she is in white and he is now bare chested in pyjama pants. There is violin music and the couple embrace. The moving walkway is used for the journey to Tom Lillie's funeral, leaving Miss Docker alone on stage, walking the wrong way against the direction of the moving platform. Running back and forwards, she calls out before falling and picking herself up. The funeral scene has evolved into a key measure of the scale of the event in Miss Docker's unconscious.

At the end of Act Three, Nevin reprises her stylised stance from 1979 but now she staggers on the mechanical travelator moving backwards and forwards with her handbag buffeted by the wind (Figure 5.1).

As the violin raises the tension, the Tramp enters but does not see the imaginary dog that wets Miss Docker's stockings. She begins walking once more to the sound of the music that is now low, and tailored for pathos as the tramp laughs: "Every man to 'is his own poison" (264). This final scene depicting Nevin's older more fragile Miss Docker, shadowed by the mocking figure of the Tramp, and subject to the stigma of loneliness (materialised by the dog), draws attention to the lack of belonging as a condition of modern industrial societies in which individual life paths are detached from "specific and relatively fixed social and cultural contexts."[53]

STC *A Cheery Soul* 2018

Kip Williams' revival in 2018 for the Sydney Theatre Company sees *A Cheery Soul* return to the Drama Theatre at the Sydney Opera House. It has become evident over the history of the play in production that advances in performance techniques and stage technology have changed the audience's experience of the play from

---

53 Franklin, "A lonely society?", 17.

Figure 5.1 Robyn Nevin as Miss Docker in Patrick White's *A Cheery Soul*, directed by Neil Armfield, Sydney Theatre Company, 2000. Photo: Heidrun Lohr.

dislike to transformative aesthetic pleasure. An increasing emphasis on the moving body, space, sound and light offers an increasingly multi-sensorial engagement with the dramatic material. In this production, scenographic design is critical to Williams' vision of the play. An expanded design team realises this vision with Elizabeth Gadsby designing the set, Alice Babidge the costumes, Nick Schlieper the lighting and David Bergman co-ordinating video and sound. Music is composed by Clemence Williams. The performance space becomes a platform on which the multimedia performance unfolds. Its base is a shiny black floor into which a revolving stage is set, reminiscent of Armfield's 1992 production, with a black upstage wall providing a void space and a large screen for projections. Drawing on Christopher Baugh's study of contemporary scenography, in this production as in others in this period, scenography is not simply a series of "illustrative effects", but is integral to the construction of the narrative and its unfolding in the plot so that it integrates "the material and structural component of performance" making.[54] This enhanced structural and semiotic role is especially evident in the beginning of Act One and the extended memory sequence in Act Two, which concerns Miss Docker's experience of Tom Lillie's funeral.

---

54 Christopher Baugh, *Theatre, Performance and Technology: The Development and Transformation of Scenography* (Basingstoke: Palgrave, 2013), 240.

Act One highlights narrative elements that have not previously been marked for special attention, such as a car crash Mrs Custance has witnessed and her surgery, both of which have taken place outside the timeframe of the play. These events have explanatory power in relation to the altercation with Miss Docker giving the scene greater significance in the work as a whole. The stage lights come up on a blond Mrs Custance (Anita Hegh) on a darkened stage. She wears a pink frock and is hanging out her washing on an iconic Hills Hoist clothesline in a yard that is graced with a dozen identical pots of tall tomato plants set neatly on a square of brown carpet. The red tomatoes contrast with the bright green leaves but look too neat and plastic to belong to the natural world. As Mrs Custance turns to a door stage right, she looks up at a black and white projection of herself high up on the upstage wall of the space. The picture dissolves into the scene of a car crash, that may involve Mrs Custance or another person in the present or the past, and she covers her face in horror. The sounds of screeching tyres and sirens blare across the space before fading into a Hollywood movie soundtrack. A kitchen is brought on stage by stagehands, as the screen shows Mrs Custance weeping as she enters the house at the same time as the stage revolves to reveal the inside of the house. The kitchen is decorated in 1950s pastel and she begins to prepare a meal. Mr Custance (Anthony Taufa) enters. The sirens, the darkened stage, the fragile woman, a Hitchcock-like soundtrack introduces a performative state of hysteria to underscore the domestic scene.

The production's visual representation of the car crash, previously lost in the expository dialogue at the beginning of the play, exploits the symbolic lines it casts. When the dialogue turns later to the children the Custances did not have after her botched operation by an absent-minded surgeon, the implication is that Mrs Custance was once the victim of a car crash, the outcome of which was the loss of her womb. We now hear better the lines that Mr Custance had wanted to sue the surgeon, but his wife was too afraid to pursue it through the courts. This adds explanatory power to Mrs Custance's fragile mental state and her husband's desire to protect her from further upset in the form of Miss Docker's car crash–like disruption of the privacy of their married life. In this symbolic system, Miss Docker is imagined as the child, albeit an elderly one, that Mrs Custance wants to help, but the self-centred and needy Miss Docker, who as a child wet her bed, exhausts their resources. Of cultural significance in this production is that Mrs Custance continues to be less English but more anxious than her predecessors. This anxiety is assisted by Williams' directing which keeps up a fast pace and with effective use of light to highlight and downplay the spoken word to great effect.

Miss Docker is performed by Sarah Peirse, who is as petite and wiry as Nevin, but imbues the character with a subdued demeanour overall. She is more naturalistic thereby and less the manic white-faced, red-lipped clown that Nevin spawned over repeated performances. Miss Docker has once again become more ordinary, even banal – her voice is lower but faster, talking ceaselessly up close to people's faces, intruding into their personal space and activating their desire to recoil from her. Critic Steve Dow found Peirse's Miss Docker "comically exasperating", but capable of also "eliciting" sympathy.[55] Another writes that Peirse balances Miss Docker's "manipulative, covetous, emotionally stunted" self with moments of pathos that arouse sympathy for the "sadness and loneliness" beneath her cheery goodness.[56] Cassie Tongue praises "a knock-out leading performance bent and shuffling, with restless hands, unflagging energy".[57] In losing the clown, Miss Docker has become more human and therefore sympathetic, but her banality reminds audiences that her goodness is not far from evil.

In an amusing reprisal of a role he played thirty years ago in another play – David Williamson's early New Wave drama *The Removalists* at La Mama Theatre Melbourne in 1974 – actor Bruce Spence enters as one of the furniture removal men, hired to move Miss Docker's cumbersome bits of furniture including the tall boy and the eponymous rocking chair into the Custance's small veranda room. (Spence plays several roles including one of the old ladies at the Sundowner Home, and the Tramp.) He places the rocker centre stage in the kitchen in an emphatic pronouncement of Miss Docker's arrival as Mrs Custance runs around with tiny footsteps breathlessly.

On the first evening, Miss Docker talks all the way through dinner leading Mr Custance to sullenly retreat to his beloved tomato plants. A projection high above the kitchen scene shows him first caressing a ripe tomato and then squashing it in his hand, snuffing the life out of it, and letting the juices run down his arm. On stage, the women are clearing up after dinner, Miss Docker replacing Mr Custance who had earlier helped his wife in a scene that ends in intimacy. The crushing of the tomato is comic grotesque but it also enacts both a fantasy of male violence and an act of self-castration. Here the tomatoes as stage objects and projected bloody vision contain the threat to the compact of love and lust between the heterosexual couple. When Mrs Custance inevitably tells Miss Docker she will have to leave and is to go to the Sundown Home, Miss Docker weeps out loud and sobs like a baby, distressing her hostess and making her miserable with guilt. Act One ends with the Custances guilty but happy as a projection of one of Miss Docker's abandoned trinkets is seen on the screen catapulting into space.

In Act Two, the Sundown Home is bathed in red light with armchairs on either side and double doors in the upstage wall. The wall doubles as a small screen for Miss Docker's slide shows of her past and for grainy black and white home movie reels of the Lillie's romantic trip to Egypt for their honeymoon. Tara Morice's Miss Lillie is less English and less aristocratic than her stage predecessors. She sits on her own lost in melancholy. Of the other old ladies, Bruce Spence re-enters as a very tall Mrs Penfold with upswept white hair. When Mrs Lillie makes herself known to

---

55 Steve Dow, "STC's A Cheery Soul", *Saturday Paper*, 17 November 2018.
56 John Shand, "A Cheery Soul Review: Surrealism, Anglicanism, Carnal Desire and Satire", *Sydney Morning Herald*, 11 November 2018.
57 Cassie Tongue, "A Cheery Soul Review", *Time Out*, 11 November 2018.

Miss Docker, the latter finds a slide of poor Mr Lillie on his sick bed and projects it onto the wall to the widow's great distress. She then retreats into memory as the lights dim and young actors enter as the glamorous Mr and Mrs Lillie dancing. Miss Docker is running her own show off to the side dancing a few steps of the Charleston with the ladies, desperate to bring the attention back to herself.

Mrs Lillie's memories of her husband and his death now merge with Miss Docker's recollections of nursing the dying man in an act of goodness. Mr Lillie's bed is wheeled in and Miss Docker and Mrs Lillie stand either side. Each directs her speech to the audience with the other hearing. Miss Docker reveals how annoyed she was that Tom Lillie died without thanking her. The bed is removed as Miss Docker continues to express her annoyance as she then recounts the events that occurred at the funeral, which were the worst of all.

For this scene, the Sundown Home is removed to leave a bare stage. The lights come up on four women dressed in black dresses and furs, sitting at a table centre stage.[58] A car horn sounds and a pale blue Morris Minor is driven onto the revolving stage behind the seated ladies. Miss Docker enters talking loudly and gets into the tiny car with the other four ladies squashing into the middle of the front seat. She is intent on restoring her stature by assuming the role of a significant mourner. A camera person enters with a movie camera on a stand to capture the interior of the car, which is projected in close-up on the screen above. As the car moves on the revolve, violin and plucked cello chords accompany the women's chatter. An image of Miss Docker is then centre stage with her 1950s glasses and lipstick in the middle of the front seat. She is happy to be there right in the moment, assuming a dominant role, instructing, advising and criticising the driver. The Chorus of ladies from the Sundown Home enter in black dresses to narrate the scene. When the car stops, and Miss Docker clambers out of the car to direct everyone, the women shut the door quickly and instruct the driver to drive on. The car exits leaving Miss Docker alone and distraught on the stage. She runs this way and that before falling on all fours weeping, evoking sympathy for her plight. When she gets to her feet, she turns to walk back in the direction of Sarsaparilla. The screen shows her anguished face as she opens and closes her mouth.

Then unexpectedly, singers enter to the soundtrack of Judy Garland's "Get Happy", spliced into another song, the Depression era "Happy Days" (are here again). They accompany Miss Docker on her walk back to town, offering friendship and a helping hand. An upsurge of solidarity and connection is staged as Miss Docker smiles and sings with her mysterious friends, becoming for a moment, a trooper in the Hollywood sense, against adversity. When the Interlude dissolves, the singers exit and the action returns to the present, whereby the audience realises Miss Docker's experience of solidarity has been fleeting. Mrs Lillie is still sad and

---

58 Angus McPherson, "A Cheery Soul", *Limelight*, 10 November 2018.

goes to bed; Miss Docker is back to being "Little Me" (232). She lurches around the stage her voice and laughter echoing. End of Act Two.

For Act Three's pivotal scene at All Saints Sunday service, two rows of pews separated by a central aisle lead to the upstage pulpit above which a projection of Miss Docker's stern disapproving face is visible. The scene is bathed in red light. Dressed in her hat and coat, Miss Docker has already mowed with manic intent a square of green carpet, signifying the rectory garden, with Wakeman's tormented face projected behind her. She has argued with Mrs Wakeman about her pruning style, a source of discord also found in the Custance garden.

In the final scene, Miss Docker is a lonely figure on a darkened, empty stage walking metaphorically into winds blowing in a different direction. She sees the dog and calls it over by patting her knee. The boys enter, young and vibrant. They laugh when the dog wets Miss Docker as she squats to pat it. Recovering, she turns and bends into the wind, walking off slowly. Her voice falters on the word "pray" as lights fade on her face (Figure 5.2).

Looking back, we can see White's dramaturgical experimentation in this play unravels the horizon of expectations surrounding and perpetrating the dominance of stage naturalism. Later productions of *A Cheery Soul* were historically and stylistically better equipped than Sumner and Digby's premiere production, to present the play's visionary drama about militant virtue and loneliness in a modern secular community. Jim Sharman's revival at the Sydney Opera House Drama Theatre with designer Brian Thomson, and Robyn Nevin as Miss Docker, made the breakthrough into theatricality realising the stylistic innovations embedded in the play text. In addition to contemporary reviews of the production, and essays by Elizabeth Schafer, Andrew Fuhrmann and Anne Pender, the restored video recording of the performance is doubly significant for this production is among the first in Australian theatre to have such archival footage. It was not until the 1980s that video recordings of live production became available and even now researchers have trouble accessing them. For Pender, who saw the production, Nevin's performance offered audiences a "lonely woman of gargantuan bitterness and anger" with an "overpowering presence" that was "frightening, hilarious and pitiful".[59]

A decade later in 1992, Neil Armfield revived *A Cheery Soul* in Brisbane and staged it three more times, taking it into the twenty-first century. A new production in 1996 for the Melbourne Theatre Company at the Playhouse with designer Dale Ferguson saw Robyn Nevin return as Miss Docker. And again Robyn Nevin performed the role for the STC/Belvoir co-production at the Sydney Opera House for the Sydney Festival in 2000–01. Kip Williams' revival in 2018 for the Sydney Theatre Company saw *A Cheery Soul* return to the Drama Theatre at the Sydney Opera House, almost forty years after Jim Sharman's dazzling 1979 production rescued the play from its unhappy past.

---

59 Pender, "Robyn Nevin, Patrick White", 82.

Figure 5.2 Sarah Peirse as Miss Docker in Patrick White's *A Cheery Soul*, directed by Kip Williams, Sydney Theatre Company, 2018. Photo: Daniel Boud.

6
Country Retreat: *Night on Bald Mountain* and *Netherwood*

The theatrical worlds of *Night on Bald Mountain* and *Netherwood* are paired for their treatments of the outsider figure in non-urban settings. Shared themes of the country retreat and a turn to the natural world see the environment become a spatial presence in the human dramas that unfold. Exterior and interior spaces such as a mountain, a country house and indeterminate vistas are structurally and thematically woven into the narrative, offering promise, refuge or danger for modernity's others, or those that are either othered or choose to be so. These othered individuals include fragile identities, and those abandoned in childhood or who have been sexually abused in institutional care and workplace locations.

Night on Bald Mountain is the final work of White's 1960s quartet. As indicated in the summary in chapter two, the play is a densely interwoven dramatic text set in two spaces in the Blue Mountains in New South Wales. As indicated, the text bears the most resemblance of the four early plays to modern psychological realism. It thus represents a change of mood and style from the comic satire of the three earlier plays to a more serious drama on the theme of domestic coercion and sexual violence. The change of style reworks the modernist theme of the unhappy marriage, a Strindbergian influence, in the form of Hugo and Miriam Sword.

The play was first directed by John Tasker at Union Hall, Adelaide University in 1964, in a production that pointed to the growing importance of creative collaboration amongst playwright, director, and designer in the stage realisation of dramatic texts. Neil Armfield restaged the play in 1996 for Company B Belvoir and the State Theatre of South Australia with Anna Borghesi as designer and Benedict Andrews as assistant director. (Andrews as discussed in chapter four went on to direct the ground-breaking production of *The Season at Sarsaparilla* in 2007.) A new production in 2014 at the Malthouse Theatre in Melbourne, directed by Matthew Lutton and designed by Dale Ferguson, provides the trans-temporal comparison.

Netherwood is a further instance of the pivotal role of the director and designer in realising White's theatricalist vision. This large cast play was directed by Jim Sharman for the Lighthouse State Theatre of South Australia in 1983 with Kerry

Walker as Mog, Alan John performing a cross-gender role as Dora Pilbeam, and Geoffrey Rush as the supercilious Dr Eberhard. Design was by Ken Wilby. The production was restaged at the Festival of Sydney the following year. There was a reading of the play in Canberra in 1994 under the umbrella of "Readings of Patrick White's Plays" at The Street Theatre, Acton, directed by Catherine Mann with three actors. *Netherwood* is a play that is ready for revival especially for its critical commentary on the social stigmatism of disability, sexual abuse in institutional care and the mistreatment or neglect of mental illness.

Night on Bald Mountain 1964

The premiere of *Night on Bald Mountain* took place against the Board of Governors controversial and acrimonious rejection of the play for its 1964 Adelaide Festival of Arts.[1] After refusing to hand over the Union Hall Theatre for an alternative festival production, the University of Adelaide's Theatre Guild held its ground and staged the third Adelaide premiere of a Patrick White play in as many years. Under pressure, the governors reluctantly awarded the play festival fringe status, thereby providing limited funding and programming. Back in June 1963, John Tasker had agreed to direct the play and White had been actively considering casting, unaware the play would be rejected by the Festival. His first choice for Miss Quodling was Nita Pannell, who had received praise for her performance as Miss Docker in *A Cheery Soul* in Melbourne, despite criticism of the play itself. For Hugo Sword, White at first hoped Michael Redgrave, Peter Coe or Peter Finch could be invited to play the part, but rejection by the "philistine Adelaide Establishment" meant funds would not be available for such an international enterprise.[2] Harry Medlin, Chair of the Theatre Guild, suggested a budget of 3,500 pounds, which was three times more than each of *The Ham Funeral* and *The Season at Sarsaparilla* but not enough to pay extensive travel and salary costs for non-Adelaide based actors.[3]

White's letters to Medlin about casting provide important insights into his conception of the characters. He insisted, for example, that Professor Sword had to be played by an actor with "presence and looks" in order to present the character as "something of a god, even though an eroded one".[4] Around this time, White was quoted in *The Times* of London as being conscious of the need "to overcome the doubts and suspicions which attend the professional production of a play by an

---

1 Denise Varney and Sandra D'Urso, *Australian Theatre, Modernism and Patrick White: Governing Culture*. London: Anthem Books, 2018. See especially chapter 3, *Night on Bald Mountain* and the Adelaide Festival.
2 Patrick White to Harry Medlin, 17 July 1963. Patrick White Collection, Series 1477, Barr Smith Library, University of Adelaide.
3 Harry Medlin to Patrick White, 27 July 1963. Patrick White Collection, Series 1477, Barr Smith Library, University of Adelaide.
4 White to Medlin, 17 July 1963.

Australian, both in Australia and anywhere else".[5] He notes that London theatre is far more liberal than the Adelaide Establishment could imagine:

> For instance – <u>Oh What a Lovely War</u> (in which the 'fucks' and the 'bollocks' have taken over from the 'bloodies'), <u>The Bed Sitting Room</u> (the Royal family sent up every quarter of an hour), and after the national anthem is played on a tin-whistle, the audience is told: "well, if you stand for that, you can stand for anything" [6] (Underlining in the original)

He wants to suggest that his "innocent 19th century plays come in for a bashing from the Australian puritans".[7] With its depiction of middle-class alcoholism and sexual abuse, White is anticipating a backlash against *Night on Bald Mountain*, and is intent on reassuring Medlin that the play's themes are in line with London standards, although his references are to the transgressions of comedy and satire rather than serious drama.[8]

On the production side, White was satisfied that the Guild's Union Theatre production could accommodate the play's complicated staging and lighting requirements, but there was tension between White and his director. Tasker wanted more changes than White was prepared to make, including re-setting the narrative to 1925 instead of the present. White had shifted *The Ham Funeral* from 1947 to 1919, but this time he argued such a time frame would upset the plausibility of the dramatic world.[9] Dickson reported slow progress on the set commenting that White's detailed staging notes were "extremely difficult" to design and posed considerable technical difficulties. Her solution included an ambitious and expensive design with a revolving stage and visual projections. White remained deeply involved in many aspects of the production, noting for example that in Dickson's drawings, "a conservatory had crept into the Sword's house just where I had wanted a large unobstructed window, through which one might see distance and the atmospheric changes on Bald Mountain".[10] We learn from the archive that there was only one fog machine in Australia in 1963 so that the mists that circulated around the mountain would have to be created with lighting effects. Casting was finalised in January with Nita Pannell as Miss Quodling and Alexander Archdale as

---

5   *Times* (London), "Putting the Theatre Across in Australia", 15 July 1963.
6   Patrick White to Harry Medlin, 10 August 1963. Patrick White Collection, Series 1477, Barr Smith Library, University of Adelaide.
7   White to Medlin, 10 August 1963.
8   Much to White's disappointment, London theatres had declined to stage his plays. He claimed he was determined to "fight until my four plays are done in London. Otherwise I am going back to novels, which depend solely on myself and which are a dignified and peaceful act of creation". Patrick White Letter to Desmond Digby, 15 August 1963. MS 10056/1, National Library Australia.
9   Patrick White to Beryl Sheasby, 10 February 1964. Patrick White Collection, Series 1477, Barr Smith Library, University of Adelaide.
10 White to Sheasby, 10 February 1964.

Hugo Sword, with Joan Bruce as Miriam, Barbara West as Stella and Bob Leach as Denis Craig.

The goat yard and ramshackle hut were built on the revolving stage, the other side of which was the house occupied by the Swords. Archival images of Miss Quodling's ramshackle hut show an effect of dilapidation with random uneven and crooked wooden palings nailed to flimsy cross beams.[11] A piece of hessian was tied to the top of the hut to provide a doorway. The scenic image is of a temporary shelter requiring constant repair work but that has become permanent, as in a structure that is not so much fixed but in danger of collapsing or being reclaimed by the mountain. Large sculpturally shaped objects in front of the hut are suggestive of the permanence of the rocks that Miss Quodling admires. Critic Madeleine Armstrong's review in the *Bulletin* offers some more detail:

> The curtain rises on the shack of Miss Quodling, the goat keeper, on Bald Mountain. In the dawn light this extraordinarily ramshackle structure, made of old palings, rusty iron and tattered hessian, has a surprising beauty. The biblical simplicity of the setting (designed by Wendy Dickson) is matched by Miss Quodling herself who is busy milking her goats, alternately cursing and wooing them before she sets them free to leap about the mountainside.[12]

The emphasis on the materiality of old palings and rusty iron, and the vibrancy of the dawn light, suggest the set achieved an effect of human labour and industry in close proximity to nature. So described the scenographic design begins to suggest an ecological integration of the human and non-human, in terms of Miss Quodling, the goats, and the mountainside that together generate affects such as "a surprising beauty". This scenographic integration of bodies, objects, space and light enhances the audience's experience of the performance by elevating perception of non-textual signification and its affects in ways that mark the theatrical innovation and ambition of *Night on Bald Mountain* for its time on the Australian stage. Where White insists that Dickson's interior design of the house serves the dialogue, the external scenes on the mountain, are more open to visual and kinesic elements. In other words, once outside the living room of naturalist theatre, White's theatre opens itself to the world of theatricality with advances in scenography in Western theatre in the twentieth century making it possible. As the scenographer, Dickson and her team of set builders become important collaborators. In doing so, this production allows for the communicative capacities of scenography to break away from the old hierarchies of text and performance.

---

11 *Miss Quodling's Shack and Goat Yards*, photo, *Night on Bald Mountain* (Union Theatre, University of Adelaide, 9 March, 1964), Barr Smith Library, University of Adelaide. Photographer: Sheridan Photography.
12 Madeleine Armstrong, "The Professor's Tragedy", *Bulletin*, 28 March 1964.

6 Country Retreat

Photographs of Nita Pannell's Miss Quodling show a rough-living character, an outsider in the eyes of the house dwelling people, whose presentation appears to be a bodily extension of her ramshackle hut.[13] She could be a female version of Estragon or Vladimir in Beckett's *Waiting for Godot*, surviving outdoors in the elements, but she is a loner and has given up on God. As indicated in the text, she wears layers of clothes, beginning with a worn-out dirt-laden checked skirt and a woollen cardigan, over which is a grubby jacket with large pockets and finally a hessian cape tied at the front. The body looks sturdy enough to withstand the elements. Thick stockings, lace-up boots and an old brimmed hat complete the look of a female goat keeper.

The country house further up the mountain is a place for "the crippled spirits" of culture and civilisation, as Armstrong put it, and Dickson presents here, on the other side of the revolving stage, a rural retreat complete with details such as wood panelling and the large windows with views, as requested by the playwright.[14] Compared to Miss Quodling's shack, images of the interior show the inherited privilege of Professor Sword, as well as the naturalist interior in which he assumes the role of patriarch. Details include a stage floor level study and a dining room with bookshelves, a solid desk with papers, a linen-covered table, woven rugs and vases with flowers.[15] Upstairs is a mezzanine-level master bedroom and a right-angled staircase leading up to a front door and more bedrooms. Tasker wrote that the attention to detail in the set had caused headaches but agreed overall that the "magnitude of the show and the challenge it presented to us all" made it the most exciting production he had been connected with so far in his short career.[16]

Another photograph depicts Joan Bruce as Miriam Sword dressed in a nightgown with her hair loose confronting Alexander Archdale's Hugo Sword on the staircase. This liminal setting and costume – she occupies neither upstairs nor downstairs and is dressed for bedroom rather than living room, night instead of day – lends itself to melodrama. She is seen lunging at Sword as Stella holds her back.[17] According to Armstrong, Archdale's Sword was petty and absurd, a far cry from White's idea of the character as "something of a god, even though an eroded one".[18] The image is nevertheless suggestive of the confrontational marital scenes depicted in 1960s theatre such as Edward Albee's *Who's Afraid of Virginia Woolf*, first staged in 1962 with German-American actor and teacher Uta Hagen in the role of Martha, and later a film starring Richard Burton and Elizabeth Taylor as the warring couple.

---

13 Nita Pannell as Miss Quodling, photo, *Night on Bald Mountain*, Union Theatre, University of Adelaide, 9 March, 1964, Barr Smith Library, University of Adelaide, Photographer: Sheridan Photography.
14 Armstrong, "The Professor's Tragedy".
15 Interior, photo, *Night on Bald Mountain*, Union Theatre, University of Adelaide, 9 March, 1964, Barr Smith Library, University of Adelaide, Photographer: Sheridan Photography.
16 John Tasker to George Mayo, Deputy Chairman Guild Theatre, 16 April 1964, Patrick White Collection, Series 1477, Barr Smith Library, University of Adelaide.
17 Interior, photo, *Night on Bald Mountain*, 1964.
18 White to Medlin, 17 July 1963.

In this context, the production engages with the rising critique in postwar European and American theatre of the middle-class home as a psychologically repressive space and a regime that was oppressive for women. Here, as in *Virginia Woolf*, the ruined heart of the marriage revolves around the loss of a child; the phantom in Albee's play in White's becomes the adult daughter who has escaped the stifling effects of home, and perhaps the threat of the father. The complexity and scale of the premiere of *Night in Bald Mountain* took White deeper into psychological themes and tormented characters, who were plagued by failure and inflicted cruelty on others, and into scenographies that challenged the long-standing hierarchy of text and performance.

Acting the Goat: Neil Armfield's *Night on Bald Mountain* (1996)

Thirty-two years later, in 1996, Neil Armfield directed the first revival of *Night on Bald Mountain*:

> Five years after Patrick died, I received the blessing of his agent Barbara Mobbs to direct the revival of this play for State Theatre SA and Belvoir. A play about goats and people, innocence and the corrupting blight of human will, it played brilliantly with a cast including Barry Otto, Gillian Jones, Essie Davis and Carole Skinner, extraordinary as the indomitable Miss Quodling. I have directed ten productions of Patrick's plays – five of them since his death – and this is the one I really wish he could have seen. That is the thing about his plays – they only work in wonderful productions. Patrick knew this, and that is why he was so selective about his directors. And it's not a case of bad writing needing to be rescued, or papered over; rather the plays present great challenges that need to be overcome.[19]

Much had changed theatrically, aesthetically and philosophically since 1964, when critics such as Kippax struggled with the seeming contradictions and ambiguities of the play while obsessing over a thing called dramatic conflict that had to be properly explicated and resolved. Critic John Edge wrote:

> Watching the revival after 32 years of Patrick White's *Night on Bald Mountain*, one is surprised at the fuss it occasioned in 1964. There is nothing unfamiliar in White's mixing of structural and linguistic modes, with its echoes of Ibsen, Strindberg, O'Neill and Pirandello, among others. Nor can anything in the play's content enrage …[20]

---

19   Neil Armfield, "Patrick White: A Centenary Tribute", *Meanjin* 71, no. 2 (2012): 18.
20   John Edge, "New Growth on Bald Mountain", *Bulletin*, 25 June 1996, 84.

Not all critics agreed. Those who preferred pure genre, such as Kippax and Peter Ward, argued that the death of Stella Summerhayes did not constitute an Australian tragedy as White had (allegedly) intended because the essential oppositions between "good and evil, freedom and necessity, truth and deceit, malicious fate and elusive justice – are not to be found in Bald Mountain"; hence the play is "relentlessly bleak" and an "emotional muddle".[21] As many critics have and continue to do, Ward reserves his praise for the valiant efforts of the cast who work hard to compensate for the problem of White's flawed dramaturgy. Ward's critique is arguably shaped by a strong disapproval of the "glowering presence of White" over productions of the plays, even posthumously, as with Armfield's production. Introducing a more measured approach, John McCallum makes the point that the question is not the equivocal – "is this a good play or not" – but with each production – the question is – "is this a good show or not?"[22] To which he answers it is.

As noted in critically acclaimed revivals of *The Season at Sarsaparilla* and *A Cheery Soul*, Armfield's revival of *Night on Bald Mountain* was enhanced by changing practices which saw directors, designers and actors more fully engaged in the creative process so that the dramatic text was no longer treated as a finished product that stood alone on the stage. McCallum agrees that the text presents problems but rejects the view that there were inherent dramaturgical flaws to do with White's mixing of genre. On the contrary, he argues, Armfield's cast and crew turn past difficulties into strengths by emphasising the anti-realist aspects of the play. In doing so they turn to the mythic rather than psychological aspects of narrative, character and place.[23] For Armfield, the setting was one of the keys to the dramatic world. Bald Mountain was a vulnerable world, where like Prospero and his island, or Hiroshima, one could be ground to dust.

Armfield's 1996 revival featured leading Australian stage designers and composers Anna Borghesi and Carl Vine. According to accounts, Vine's score began with a sombre symphonic work which moved onto a light chamber music piece that ran counter to Mussorgsky's orchestral composition on the theme of the Witches' Sabbath. Borghesi's set was a constructivist design in which the two-storey house, including its internal staircase and balcony, was exposed to the audience through a wall of windowless rusty iron window frames giving the impression of the bars of a prison rather than a middle-class household. The overall constructivist aesthetic echoes the modernist turn to scenography and architecture on the modern stage, as proposed by Russian architect, artist and critic El Lissitzky, who placed special importance on the transition from painted sets to three-dimensional architecture. This design principle was to allow for the new physicalisation of the body of the actor and to create the illusion of reality without attempting to fill in the whole picture. Borghesi's functional use of wood to frame, support and situate

---

21 Peter Ward, "No Human Grandeur in White's Bleak Night", *Australian*, 11 June 1996, 12.
22 John McCallum, "Night Chillingly Excites", *Australian*, 13 July 1996.
23 McCallum, "Night Chillingly Excites".

actors on stage enhanced the modernist dimensions of White's text at the same time as it added a contemporary understanding of theatre space as "'art space' … distinct from reality and immune to attempts at naturalistic imitation".[24]

In addition to the cast of leading actors listed above, Ralph Cotterill played the housekeeper Mrs Sibley in a sign of the increasing gender fluidity in the casting of White's plays in recognition, perhaps, that female stereotypes operate as a masquerade of patriarchal expectations of feminine servitude. These cross-gender cast figures include the Chorus of Old Ladies in both Jim Sharman's 1979 and Armfield's 1992 revivals of *A Cheery Soul*, Alan John's Dora in *Netherwood* (1983), and Peter Carroll's Girlie Pogson in Benedict Andrews' *The Season at Sarsaparilla* in 2007, among others. Cotterill's Mrs Sibley appears with crimped white curls and a fluffy lilac cardigan, suggesting parodic femininity at odds with the no-nonsense portrayal of character prescribed in the text. Mrs Sibley's "terminally banal" interpretation contributes to the lightness of touch that Armfield's production projects.[25]

The opening moments of the production, in which Miss Quodling tends her goats, is radically anthropomorphised in Armfield's production with the cast positioned on stage "acting the goat", that is, playing the goats with bells around their necks. Elizabeth Schafer adds that each goat foreshadows the character the actor will go on to play.[26] As Armfield recalls:

> The idea of those actors coming on stage and crumpling down to their knees and starting to bray like goats was risky, it felt kind of wonderfully on the edge of ridiculous … It felt like a great way of lifting the curtain and exposing your actors all at once, and in the boldest way possible. A sort of an outrageous idea in a sense, which then kind of really helps to amplify the movement of the text. And give great strength to Miss Quodling as this kind of earth god, which she is.[27]

The presentation of actors as Miss Quodling's goats raises the level of comedy in the opening scene and unsettles the rigid hierarchy between the human occupants of the house and the goatherd at the same time as it undercuts the psychological realism later played out by these same human actors as dramatic characters. Armfield's production contributes to a growing sense that theatre makers and audiences are developing a familiarity and playfulness with White's plays. Gone is the sententious criticism of the early years. Armfield boldly clears away Tasker's melodrama, especially in relation to the occupants of the house, to work with the idea of characters as marionettes engaged in enacting a story rather than characters in themselves. Critics were receptive with John Edge in the *Bulletin* making special

---

24 Thea Brejzek, "The Scenographic (Re-)Turn: Figures of Surface, Space and Spectator in Theatre and Architecture Theory 1680–1980", *Theatre & Performance Design* 1, nos. 1–2 (2015): 24.
25 Vicky Roach, "Night on a Precipice", *Daily Telegraph*, 12 July 1996, 45.
26 Elizabeth Schafer, "A Ham Funeral, Patrick White, Collaboration and Neil Armfield", *Australian Studies* 3 (2011): 18.
27 Neil Armfield, interviewed by Sandra D'Urso, 9 January 2018.

note of the "superb opening, where the actors appear as 'the flock' of the goat woman" to remind us of White's sense of "bitter comedy".[28]

While praising Armfield's directing, James Waites found Barry Otto's "tremolo voice and blinking eyelids" unoriginal in terms of the character but agreed that his delivery of "poisonous barbs" and expressions of self-loathing combined with bitter passion were frightening in a way that gave credence to Stella's terror.[29] Carrie Kablean found, on the other hand, that Otto delivered his lines with "withering, desiccated crispness" in a production that included allegory, enchantment and humour as well as the devasting loss of the "gentle goodness" in Essie Davis' Stella.[30] Kelly Burke seemed distracted by the similarity she perceived between Gillian Jones' Miriam and the television character, Morticia Addams, with her pale face and long black hair flowing down over a long oriental gown. But Jones' gothic Miriam draws on the text in which she mocks her husband's poetry and religious beliefs while sharing a drunken joke with Miss Quodling about Hugo's "Gothic soul" (314). Elizabeth Schafer cautions against the effort to render the drama entirely playful. The realist psychological dimension of White's drama does not go away, she argues, especially in relation to Stella's death. The passing of time between 1964 and 1996, when child sexual abuse enters public discourse, makes Stella's death compelling for reasons other than the clumsy advances of Professor Sword. Schafer argues the possibility of child sexual abuse carries the force of tragedy; McCallum agrees describing her final scene with its hint of "real abuse" as "deeply disturbing".[31] The merging of the patriarchal Sword with the incestuous father fuses into an imaginary in which Stella identifies as victim of the tyranny of civilisation, just as Miss Quodling had feared. On balance the final word on Armfield's 1996 production is given to David Marr:

> Reading Bald Mountain, I'd never seen how it could hang together: all the outdoor stuff with Miss Quodling, the wise goat woman of the mountain, and her mob of invisible goats, and the indoor stuff with the barren professor and his alcoholic wife. But it does hang together, in part because the director, Neil Armfield, who so often served the old man well by disobeying him, has put the goats on stage. They are, of course, the folk from the big house on the hill.[32]

The operative words here are that the theatre offers audiences, critics and scholars the opportunity to "see how it could hang together" in acknowledgement that the play text is only part of the whole event.

---

28 Edge, "New Growth on Bald Mountain", 84.
29 James Waites, "Armfield Glows with White Magic", *Sydney Morning Herald*, 12 July 1996, 12.
30 Carrie Kablean, "Goats, Bells and All", *Sunday Telegraph*, 14 July 1996, 156.
31 McCallum, "Night Chillingly Excites".
32 David Marr, "Quite a Night on Bald Mountain", *Sydney Morning Herald*, 9 July 1996, 14.

Night on a Ziggurat: Matthew Lutton's *Night on Bald Mountain* (2014)

Matthew Lutton's *Night on Bald Mountain* for the Malthouse Theatre in 2014 was the first Melbourne production of the play, fifty years after its Adelaide premiere. Lutton's creative team included set design and costume by Dale Ferguson, composer and musician Ida Duelund Hansen, and Paul Jackson for lighting. The cast included performers with past experience in White's theatre with Julie Forsyth as Miss Quodling, Peter Carroll as Hugo Sword, Melita Jurisic as Miriam Sword and Luke Mullins as Denis Craig. New to White's theatre were Nikki Shiels as Stella Summerhayes, Sue Jones as Mrs Sibley and Syd Brisbane as Mr Cantwell and the hiker. Lutton's approach to the alleged inconsistencies and weaknesses of the play was to view the text as a refusal to "adhere to a consistent style" and the naturalist values contained therein. In his view, stylistic modes "mutate" in a way that recognises the adaptive capacities of texts, while also acknowledging "how difficult the play is".[33] Yet Lutton manages to integrate the alleged inconsistencies by means of a stunning set.

Dale Ferguson's set design triggers a powerful signifying presence that puts scenography at the heart of the audience's experience of the play. The design exploits the shifting hierarchies of theatre over the period in which White's plays are written and performed – the change in emphasis from text to *mise-en-scène* and from playwright to director and designer, and from character to performer. With this production, direction, design, and performance play a determining role in the interpretation and realisation of the text, re-affirming the dramaturgical shift in which contemporary scenography is no longer considered background but an integrated component of performance.

Ferguson's scenography both resonated with contemporary multifunctional theatre design and referenced the 1964 and 1996 productions by Wendy Dickson and Anna Borghesi without reproducing them. The built set filled the stage from floor to ceiling and was a structure rather than a representation of the mountain, house and goat yard. It consisted of four receding terraces or stages each with a room-sized upright back wall so that the structure looked like a giant's staircase or a ziggurat. The structure was a flexible space providing provisional locations for the interior rooms of the house and the open spaces. Built with raw untreated plywood, the material spoke to the transience of the theatrical set over time and the contingent illusion of place (Figure 6.1).

---

33 Matthew Lutton, "Gasping at Great Truths" in Program Notes, Malthouse Prompt Pack, 2014, 6–7.

6 Country Retreat

Figure 6.1 Dale Ferguson's set for Patrick White's *Night on Bald Mountain*, directed by Matthew Lutton, Malthouse Theatre, Melbourne, 2014. Photo: Pia Johnson.

In practical staging terms, doors concealed in the upright walls opened and closed for entrances and exits replacing the lateral wings of a conventional theatre. Items of furniture such as Hugo Sword's desk and Miriam's dressing table were carried on and removed through the doorways as required. Design challenges previously attached to White's detailed set design and his insistence that windows look onto the mountain as the right lines are spoken, were simply and effectively met. Jackson's lighting bathed the structure in blue mist for the mountain, a yellow wash for dawn, and soft interior stage lighting for the house. The levels encouraged simultaneous views of Professor Sword and Denis Craig at breakfast on the ground floor level, and Miriam in an oriental dressing-gown slumped in an armchair in her first floor bedroom, attended by Stella Summerhayes. Miriam's bedroom was located above Miss Quodling's goat yard, seen in the beginning and end of the play, reinforcing the link between the two older women (see Figure 6.2). Co-location of spaces and scenes solved the problems of cohesion that was said to be a weakness of the written text.

In this production the staging acquires its own language and presence, confident that audiences will imagine the scenes as they are lit according to place, time and mood. Multiple symbolic referents come to life. In addition to the religious overtones of the ancient ziggurat, critic Ben Packer notes that the size of the structure "dramatically dwarfs the actors who often teeter perilously on its higher level".[34] This observation points to the mythical dimension of the drama in which the particular story of these characters is less significant than the thematic forces that flow through them. These include the fate of outsider figures, the vulnerability of the young, the turn to nature and the tyranny of civilised man.

As the performance begins, the lights come up on the second level while simultaneously the outline of a cellist becomes visible on the upper level providing an eerie soundscape to complement the intriguing physical structure. Alison Croggon acknowledges the crucial importance of Vine's score when she describes Lutton's production as "lucid and symphonic" as if the text itself is a score with Ida Dueluend's double bass punctuating the action.[35] An unseen door opens for Miss Quodling's entrance. As she begins her dawn monologue, one-dimensional cute goats made from plywood rise up one after the other on several floor levels. Comic bleating sounds are heard so that the stage begins to resemble a children's pop-up picture book. Julie Forsyth's Miss Quodling's voice is amplified so that her broad Australian accent, delivered in musical phrasings, fills the theatre. She gives special emphasis to particular words – she is "sentimental" about the nanny goats, mindful of the buck's "nature", and identifies with the "barren" rocks (270–72). The period is timeless although this Miss Quodling is the first to wear trousers. The overall effect of the staging and Miss Quodling's speech to the morning on Bald Mountain is magical and utterly absorbing.[36]

Stella and later Denis Craig appear through concealed doors and the inner story within the overall frame narrative of Bald Mountain begins. All characters wear microphones which enhance the spoken word so that individual words and phrases are foregrounded. For Stella repetition of the word "Dad" (277ff) and later "My father" (283ff) stand out. The emphasis on the word Melbourne as her birthplace and home contrasts a sheltered past with the hardness of the mountain. Nikki Shiels' Stella is wide-eyed, enthusiastic and modest, a fitting embodiment of what Miss Quodling worries is her vulnerability, those aspects of goodness and kindness that the Swords will cannibalise. A game of hide-and-seek with Denis along the levels of the set and in and out of door openings prefigures the predatory moves of Professor Sword on the sleeping beauty in Act Three.

Lutton's production sustains dramatic tension with seamless transitions between Miss Quodling's goat yard and the house, supported by lighting and cello. In Act Two in the house, Peter Carroll's Hugo Sword does not quite embody the fallen god White imagined but presents a resonant voice that emanates from an elderly, thin and empty body. The voice is all that remains of his controlling influence and its utterance of White's dialogue gives it a coldly calculating force. Carroll's Sword is nevertheless troubled and at times angry that his universe has not

---

34   Ben Packer, "Night on Bald Mountain (Malthouse Theatre)", *Limelight*, 23 May 2014.
35   Alison Croggon, "Night on Bald Mountain Review – Scathing Satire and Sensual Tragedy", *Guardian*, 9 May 2014.
36   Author's notes, based on viewing of live performance in 2014 and digital recording in 2019.

Figure 6.2 Julie Forsyth as the Goat Keeper and Melita Jurisic as Miriam in Patrick White's *Night on Bald Mountain*, directed by Matthew Lutton, Malthouse Theatre, Melbourne, 2014. Photo: Pia Johnson.

acted as he had ordained. The key moment for this interpretation is his perplexed account of how his intellectual power and Miriam's artistic sensibilities failed to fit together in an alchemical union.

Miriam's version of the failed marriage is revealed in the sad and hilarious scene with Miss Quodling. This scene follows the frenetically paced sequence in which Miriam conspires to take delivery of a whisky order from Mr Cantwell, the grocer, in exchange for her agate ring. When Miss Quodling arrives, looking for an escaped goat, Miriam invites her in for a drink and asks her a key question about how she "broke free?" (312) This question initiates a scene of cross-class female identification and solidarity. Jurisic's Miriam has transformed herself into a middle-class woman in neat black skirt, white embroidered blouse and black high heels to take delivery of the cheap Australian whisky but this exterior is only a temporary cover for a more desperate performance of physical and vocal drunkenness. Miss Quodling meanwhile reveals more about her escape from lower middle-class respectability to Bald Mountain, while understanding her host is a sick woman. The gender solidarity between the two women is established by means of shared space as well as whisky. They sit side by side at a table looking out into the audience as they talk and laugh together. Their focus is a shared vision of the world in which freedom is grossly restricted for women of all classes. These spatial arrangements present a powerful onstage empathy between the two performers and the audience.

The scene that follows between Sword and Stella is choreographed in a way that exposes the cruelty of Hugo's manipulative behaviour. Stella's placement in relation to Sword is important. She is asleep as he enters her bedroom; she is woken but still sleepy; she thinks her employer wants her to attend to his wife; and is then confused to discover it is she he wants to see, and touch. The starkness of Sword's presumption that he could have sex with his employee is a clear demonstration of intent based on his view of Stella not as a fellow human and young employee but a young fertile body that is his to take. Set on the third level of the stepped stage, in soft lighting, with music and vocals that repeat his words, the theatrical elements magnify the audience's view of the paradigmatic scene of sexual harassment leading to sexual abuse. The victim's experience of the unwanted encounter is made clear. She pushes him away after which he continues to force himself on her and then breaks her will by insinuating the return of the repressed in the form of the father/lover figure. The level of intensity is raised further as the audience begins to wonder about the Sword's daughter, who escaped her father as her mother fell into the haze of alcoholism. Nikki Shiels' Stella evokes total sympathy and horror as the audience finds itself bearing witness to a criminal act in a secluded house late at night while the household sleeps.

In the aftermath, Stella can be seen in eerie blue light climbing desperately up the ziggurat structure to the top level to get away. Here she is an embodiment of female terror, of flight, and of the desire to escape. She finds and opens the final upper door for her exit. Simultaneous action lights up Miss Quodling's shack, where Miriam enters in a ball gown seeking refuge from the house to sit with the Goat Keeper. In the next scene, the incongruity of the white gown in the early morning light, set against the tragedy of Stella's death, acknowledges the operatic quality of the drama, its melodrama and its pathos. The gothic mood does not reduce the tragedy of Stella's death, rather it acknowledges that theatre is "The place of Crime" as Hélène Cixous memorably called it, and the female suicide is one of its horrors.[37] When Hugo Sword enters, he is clothed in the costume of the perpetrator, despite his self-absorbed confession: "Miriam, I killed Stella Summerhayes" (354).

In the final sequence Miss Quodling is once again alone on the mountain in the early morning. Forsyth addresses the audience in slow measured tones allowing time for Stella's death and Sword's moral culpability to be absorbed. The final twist of fate, when it occurs, takes Forsyth's breath away opening a lacuna in the theatrical world. If Stella's death is tragic, then the fall down the side of the mountain of Miss Quodling's beloved goat, Dolores, is the comic, even parodic, denouement. But when Miss Quodling howls, her loss has gravitas and is an epic rendering of the loss of the innocents to the corrosive state of the world. The final lines refer to there being nothing left but dust, after which the silence itself would breed again, are delivered into a silent but thoroughly absorbed theatre.[38]

In the aftermath, Alison Croggon concludes that she is not sure if *Night on Bald Mountain* with its "structural awkwardness and unruliness" is a "good" play, but grants that perhaps for that "very reason" it makes "great theatre".[39] This ambivalent conclusion is sustainable in the light of contemporary thinking about theatre. In its theatrical realisation of the dramatic text, the mimetic character of performance "requires", as Christopher Balme puts it, the "transformation" of written dialogue by an actor, and the whole apparatus of the theatre.[40] Added to this transformation, as many theorists such as Erika Fischer-Lichte understand, is the embodiment of the text for the spectator. Theatre is variously transformational, transformative, affective, intentional and uplifting. The transformative relationship between text and performance can mean that "great" theatre is not necessarily tied to a "good" play. Croggon's astute conclusion about Lutton's production of *Night on Bald Mountain* accords with the question John McCallum asked of Armfield's production in 1996. Was his production of *Night on Bald Mountain* not so much good drama but a good show?

---

37 Hélène Cixous, "From the Place of Crime, the Place of Pardon (1986–7)" in *Twentieth Century Theatre: A Sourcebook* ed. Richard Drain (London: Routledge, 1995), 340–344.
38 These comments on the delivery and the audience response are the author's, based on live viewing of the performance in 2014 and reviewings of the digital recording at the Malthouse Theatre, Melbourne, in 2019.
39 Croggon, "Night on Bald Mountain Review".
40 Christopher Balme, *The Cambridge Introduction to Theatre Studies* (Cambridge: Cambridge University Press, 2008), 70.

The distinction between the text and its stage realisation can work both ways. There remain critics who have blasted Patrick White's plays since the 1960s, while commiserating with the brave directors who have tackled them. Norman Kessel in *The Sun* excoriated the Sydney production of *The Season at Sarsaparilla* because Patrick White appeared to look down on suburbia. In the case of Lutton's *Night on Bald Mountain* fifty years later, freelance critic Byron Bache, writing for the *Herald Sun*, continues the tradition. According to Bache, Patrick White is not even a great novelist, let alone a playwright and *Night on Bald Mountain* (erroneously referred to as the writer's last play) is "terrible", as "illuminating as a tea light, and about half as warm".[41] Yet he goes on to write that the design is tremendous, the lighting and sound are perfect, the cast is stellar and Lutton's direction of "White's crabbed little nullodrama" is inspired. The invective finishes with the rhetorical flourish: "there's a reason nobody remembers White as a playwright", but it is not clear if Bache understands that plays live and die on being performed, and performed well.

Netherwood: Massacre at Bowral

Netherwood was written for South Australia's Lighthouse Theatre Company and premiered in 1983 under the direction of Jim Sharman. The play is written in one act with a *lights fade* and *lights up* note in italics leaving open the option of having an interval or running it in one act. While seemingly a minor structural point, the effective loosening of the two-act convention marks an increasing recognition by White of the contingency of the text in relation to its stage realisation. More broadly, the minor staging note is indicative of a more radical international shift underway in the relationship between the written text and its performance as both move further away from realism towards increasingly imaginative scenarios. The writer of these kinds of poetic and symbolic scenarios does so on the understanding that directors, designers and performers expect to solve challenging staging problems. Patrick White remains conservatively attached to the idea of drama as enacted by named characters in time and place, but how a performance weaves the narrative, or the gaps in the narrative into a whole performance, is left to the creative production team.

For this radical renegotiation of text and performance, we need look no further than the company White kept. Having observed and befriended directors Jim Sharman and Neil Armfield during the rehearsals of *The Season at Sarsaparilla* (1976) and *A Cheery Soul* (1979), and in the lead up to the premieres of new plays *Big Toys* (1981) and *Signal Driver* (1982), White was up to date with new developments in theatre. Sharman and Armfield's revivals of the early plays participate in the continuous renewal of aesthetic modernism in Australian theatre;

---

41 Byron Bache, "Theatre Review: Night on Bald Mountain, Malthouse Theatre", *Herald Sun*, 12 May 2014.

the later works, *Netherwood* and *Shepherd on the Rocks*, are written with these directors in mind. These plays broke new ground by unwinding the strict conventions of dramatic narrative, especially in relation to the unities of time and place, and with that, notions of rationality, motivation, plausibility and predictive behaviour. In this process dramatic characters became more consciously theatrical, performative and self-regarding than introspective, psychologically motivated, semi-autonomous subjects. White's theatre had since *The Ham Funeral* tended towards the theatricalist, that is, the multiplication of dramatic complexity through competing realities; now it extends the range of character and situation well beyond the real and the plausible into the realm of irony and farce.

The trend towards a greater emphasis on theatricality and the theatricalist play contributed in Western theatre scholarship to the emergence of categories such as postmodern, postdramatic and late modernist theatres. Hans-Thies Lehmann's theory of postdramatic theatre arose from observations of the changing of the guard at the Berliner Ensemble in Berlin as the Brechtian legacy was challenged by dissidents such as playwright and director Heiner Müller. Rather than drawing on a method such as epic theatre, he claimed his play texts were not devised with intentionality but were a step into "absolute darkness, the absolutely unfamiliar" without which the theatre as an art form cannot continue.[42] But postdramatic theatre has a longer history going back to "the 'no longer dramatic' forms of theatre that have emerged since the 1970s".[43] Taking a longer view, changes in technology including television interrupted by advertisements, have led to a "simultaneous and multi-perspectival form of perceiving" that replaces "the linear-successive" approach.[44] Literary modernists, including Patrick White, expanded on this new perspective, but theatre with its complex material apparatus, its reliance on human subjects, its liveness and the constant imperative to balance commercial and artistic considerations was slow to adapt. By the 1980s, non-narrative, non-text-based, devised and unruly performance events created by companies such as Forced Entertainment, with the self-described piece *Bloody Mess* (2004), performed a metatheatrical refusal to get on with the show. Stages of the shift to non-narrative theatre coincided with the rise of the director, as previously discussed in relation to Jim Sharman in chapter five. Sharman, along with directors such as Rex Cramphorn in Sydney, and writer directors Richard Murphet and Jenny Kemp in Melbourne and others, including Michael Kantor at the Malthouse Melbourne, introduced 'no longer dramatic' theatre to Australia.

Sharman directed Patrick White's *Netherwood* under the mantle of the artistically ambitious Lighthouse Theatre and its ensemble of actors. As set out in

---

42 Heiner Müller, *A Heiner Müller Reader*, ed. and trans. Carl Weber (Baltimore, MD: Johns Hopkins University Press, 2001), 228–9.
43 Karen Jürs-Munby, "Introduction", in *Postdramatic Theatre*, by Hans-Thies Lehmann, trans. Karen Jürs-Munby (London: Routledge, 2006), 1.
44 Hans-Thies Lehmann, *Postdramatic Theatre*, trans. Karen Jürs-Munby (London: Routledge, 2006), 16.

the discussion of the text in chapter two, *Netherwood* is play about fragile identities and institutional violence. It concerns three groups of characters – marginalised outsider figures, those who would care for or contain them, such as carers and doctors, and those who threaten them, such as the police and right-wing nationalists. The drama is nominally set within the context of reforms to the mental health system initiated in the 1970s and the shift from institutional to community care, but White broadens the theme to consider the boundaries between sanity and insanity, rational and irrational behaviour, and a period of change in farming communities that pits old-timers against city folk escaping the rat race. In this respect the play articulates a turning point between old money and modern wealth, newcomers and old grazing families, and conflicting ideologies around land use. There is drama and conflict between and across the three sides, but things get postdramatic and highly theatrical when the carers join forces with the cared-for in games of masquerade and identity subversion. The final massacre is in line with the irrational theatricalist turn of the play.

The play begins conventionally in the living room of a large dilapidated Australian country house, known as Netherwood in its better days, in the lush Southern Highlands north west of Sydney. The period is the 1970s. In a long note to describe the setting, White writes that the living room has glass doors upstage left and right opening onto a terrace. Beyond that is an "indeterminate vista, blue to smokey grey, darkening on either side of the house from the presence of conifers" (99). The room retains features of its former elegance with family relics, an alcove lined with books, a grand piano, an oval dining table with mis-matched chairs and a large but worn Turkish carpet. A large gilt framed mirror is the main feature of the upstage wall between the two large doors but it "has a smeary, silvered, non-reflecting surface" (99). Antiques are mixed with cheap modern items and certain objects are singled out in White's description for special attention, notably a baby's high chair and a ramshackle day bed. Doors in the walls, right and left, lead to kitchens and bedrooms.

The dilapidated style is reminiscent of Chekhov's turn of the century *mise-en-scène* for the tragi-comedies that capture the declining fortunes of the Russian aristocracy. The allusion to *The Cherry Orchard* is reinforced through the recent history of the house in which the tragic drowning of a little boy in the lake led to the family selling the property and leaving the district. The Chekhovian elements of the text offer a clue to the presence of latent emotions connected to past tragedies, although in the case of Mog and Harry, the events took place outside the family home in institutional frameworks. Repressed memories and emotions manifest in characters' various attachments to objects, in particular, Mog and the baby highchair, Dora and the piano, and Harry's wheelchair and guns.

Images of the Adelaide production include a photograph by David Wilson of the final moments of the play in which the living and the dead occupy the living room.[45] The design could be the set for *The Cherry Orchard* which makes the fallen bodies look comically out of place against the conventional space of dramatic realism in a way that is suggestive of a dramaturgy which confidently changes style between beginning and end. The room adheres to White's description to feature four upstage long windows that open onto a terrace with trees leading into the distance. Critic Peter Ward thought the encroaching pine forest created "a sense of the world closing in, as indeed it does at the end".[46] The downstage area features the dining table, now overturned, and the daybed across which lies the body, mobster-style, of the slain policeman, on his back, having been shot in the chest with his head facing the audience and arms outstretched. Gillian Jones' Miss Gelbart kneels between Alice and Royce, who are sitting on the floor in shock. Gelbart's arms are outstretched with her hands resting on their shoulders in an attitude of blessing. The religiously themed composition extends to Alice, who sits in a Pietà-like pose cradling Mog's dead body. Harry's body rests on Royce's outstretched leg as if sleeping. Flo Stubbs' body lies on its back off to the side at the foot of the daybed while Fred Stubbs is slumped against the railing of a raised platform leading to the front door of the house. Upstage centre is the grand piano on which Sergeant Bell leans as if he is at a bar after a day's work. Rolf Eberhard is standing further upstage near the glass doors, his white suit spotless under the lights. The bodies lie where they have fallen, as David Marr puts it, "like a Jacobean tragedy",[47] or a spaghetti western. Sharman has the living remain still, frozen in time, looking out into the audience, feigning innocence. The stage picture constitutes a message about the "sanity in insanity and the insanity in sanity" that White considered to be central to the incompatibility of old and new Australia, of progressive city and conservative country folk.[48]

Harry Kippax writes of Sharman's premiere at the Playhouse, Adelaide, that *Netherwood* is "faithfully presented by Mr Sharman" but like *Signal Driver*, it was a "disappointment".[49] He rejects the new Patrick White play, but deftly refrains from blaming Sharman for its faults. Kippax spares Ken Wilby's set because it is "evocative" and "real", as is the acting, especially "Miss Phillips" as Alice and "Miss Walker" as Mog. The formality of Kippax review is distinctly old school. He compares the new play unfavourably with *Signal Driver*, which began "tenuously and garrulously" but improved as it went on to gain "stature and significance", whereas *Netherwood* does the opposite. It begins well by introducing interesting and provocative characters in a mysterious country household, of which Kerry Walker's Mog, performed as an aggressive working-class waif, is the most interesting. Alan John's Dora is similarly interesting for his depiction of a "deranged

---

45   Image is published in May-Brit Akerholt, *Patrick White* (Amsterdam: Rodopi Press, 1988), Fig. 16.
46   Peter Ward, "Netherwood is White Magic", *Australian*, 13 June 1983, 8.
47   David Marr, *Patrick White: A Life* (Milsons Point: Vintage Books, 1992), 611.
48   Marr, *Patrick White*, 611.
49   Harry Kippax, "White Play Still Disappoints Under Sharman Direction", *Sydney Morning Herald*, 23 January 1984, 10. All other references in this section, unless otherwise stated, are from this review.

ex-pianist who may be a transvestite". Despite these promising attributes, Kippax finds the play, meaning the text and not the performance, is a thesis rather than a play. Critical values can be discerned once again through words coded for good and bad theatre – authentic, convincing, conflict, dramatic development – all considered lacking in White's drama. First, Kippax wants the dramatic tension between the characters to develop into an authentic or believable conflict, presumably on the model of rising tension leading to a climax and denouement as in the well-made play, or in some variation of that structure. Second, the drama is paramount and must be convincing and subservient to a theme, and not a manifesto, a lecture or dogma. The conflict must arise out of differences of temperament, personality or customs and the enduring conflict between idealism and vitalism that he first conceived in relation to *The Ham Funeral* in 1965.[50] Finally, dramatic development must take place within the humanist subject and not supernatural beings or minor characters. Dora's transvestism, for example, is "decorative" rather than "functional"; her on-stage musical accompaniment helped create "atmosphere" as a background to the central drama but could not in itself influence the narrative.

Kippax approves of how the audience "gets to know" the characters over the first hour of the play because it coheres to the necessary exposition of the well-made play. But in the second hour, and without an interval, the play's progress "bogs down" in fantasy. Role-swapping charades from the past do not work to expose the inner reality of the main characters Royce and Alice. He recognises that charade exposes the sexual ambivalence of both characters, and helps explain their sterile marriage and escape from their past lives, but where White is able to explore these themes "masterfully" in *A Twyborn Affair* in prose, he fails in the medium of drama. That is to say, he fails to turn it into conflict. The result is White lectures rather than dramatises. As for the shootout at the end, Kippax dismisses it. John Moses discovers that White had been thinking about shootouts since writing melodramas for the school magazine, one of which "The Mexican Bandits", involved the entire cast dying under gunfire in the final scene.[51] Even so, Kippax objects to the incursion of popular forms of charade and B-grade movies into modern theatre, whereas White and Sharman had no objection to this at all.

But the bloodshed is not just B-grade arbitrary brutality. The image described above of the play's end makes it clear that the most vulnerable have been killed by the most powerful. In other words, an orchestrated act of cruelty towards the outsider has taken place. Beyond the bloodshed stands class distinction and fear of the outsider. Artaud's writings on cruelty shed light on the final scene:

> Cruelty is not, essentially, synonymous with bloodshed, martyred flesh, a crucified enemy ... Above all, cruelty is lucid, a kind of rigid direction,

---

50 Harry Kippax, "The Novelist as Dramatist", *Sydney Morning Herald*, 23 October 1965, 19.
51 John Moses, "Ship of Fools Becalmed by Odd Lack of Mystery", *Australian*, 23 January 1984, 8.

submission to necessity. There's no cruelty without consciousness, without some kind of applied consciousness. This is the consciousness that gives to the exercise of all life's acts its colour of blood, its cruel nuance, since it is understood that life is always someone's death.[52]

The point of cruelty is not the spectacle of bloodshed itself but the expression of political power. Brecht would agree and add that the gestures constituted by the Sergeant *"sitting on the edge of the table, swinging a leg, preparing to make his cigarette"* (168) as he surveys the carnage directs the audience's attention towards the power of the state.

On viewing the remounted production at the Seymour Centre in Sydney in January 1984, Kippax still found the play disappointing. Of interest is how he distinguished between the play and the production, about which he "feels more warmly".[53] He finds Ken Wilby's set, for example, which featured "the decayed country house, with its big panels of glass, its veranda and its background of green pines" to be "convincing and evocative". But once again, Kippax holds to his view of the performance as a "novelist's text", which he intends as a measure of its shortcomings. The acting is good and "a paean to ensembles" despite the text.

There are so many questions that might have engaged a less bigoted critic. Might the play in performance be experimenting with ways for theatre to explore the characters' inner realities outside the realm of modern psychological realism? Might it be evoking the absurd in order to explore new conditions emerging around late capitalism and the mental health crisis that are still barely recognised or understood? Kippax's refusal to expand the boundaries of what he assumes to be a universally acknowledged definition of drama as Aristotelian is perplexing.

If he had considered the charade as masquerade then he might have considered the non-expository, non-discursive work that it performs. Nunley and co-authors argue that masquerade performances do many things. They "entertain, distract, provoke, inspire fear, and instruct audiences both descriptively and non-discursively" and are "embedded in memory and ritual".[54] Masking also helps reconstruct social memory.

John Moses at *The Australian* was more willing to be puzzled. But he found a detail to work on, taking issue with the set for its lack of the necessary state of dilapidation that White had stipulated. He found the living room too bourgeois, the effects of which he claims "irreparably damages" the playwright's intentions.[55] Of special note is that the mirror that should have a smeary, silvered non-reflecting surface was instead bright and clear. The review is illustrated by a production

---

52 Antonin Artaud, *The Theatre and Its Double*, trans. Mary Caroline Richards (New York: Grove Press, 1958) 102.
53 Kippax, "White Play Still Disappoints", 10.
54 John Nunley, Cara McCarty, John Emigh and Lesley Ferris, *Masks: Faces of Culture* (New York: Harry N. Abrams, 1999), 15–17.
55 Moses, "Ship of Fools".

shot of a close-up of Jacquy Phillips as Alice looking into the upstage mirror as Geoffrey Rush's Eberhard looks on smoking a cigar. Her image is clearly reflected. The effect is that the stage fails to create the magic and mystery, which haunt the narrative. Moses argues that the play wants to present the dark areas of the soul as a personal hell in a world where nothing is at it seems, as signified by the non-reflecting mirror. This theatre literate critique works from a set of vastly different values from Kippax. Where Kippax is focused on the flaws in White's text as the paramount issue, Moses accepts the play's intentions and questions the theatrical (mis)interpretation of a crucial signifying object.

In the spaces of refuge or exile from the pressures and disappointments of city and suburb, the dramatic narratives in *Night on Bald Mountain* and *Netherwood* follow the ways cultural custodians, both public and private, encroach on the outsider figure. Failure to uphold the normative codes of civilised man or woman is shown to have consequences, many of which involve cruelty and tyranny. The police massacre the weak and vulnerable inhabitants of Netherwood. In *Night on Bald Mountain*, a young woman is driven to suicide. These ultra-theatricalist outcomes are powerfully suggestive of a theatre that drives home a point about the impossibility of living a life deemed to be unconventional. By linking theatrical realisations of *Night on Bald Mountain* and *Netherwood*, first performed twenty years apart in 1964 and 1983 respectively, this chapter has explored theatricalist stagings of White's dramatic representations of the forces of oppression, tyranny and cruelty of culture and civilisation within the prosperous democracy of modern Australia.

7

Sydney, Sexuality and Uranium: *Big Toys* and *Signal Driver*

One of the many questions for Patrick White as he became increasingly active in the anti-nuclear movement, is "how we may develop the moral strength, not so much to face as to call off the nuclear war with which the world is threatened".[1] His public opposition to uranium mining and nuclear power generation emanated from a post-World War Two and Cold War perspective on Hiroshima and the nuclear arms race. The prospect of nuclear war was first raised in White's theatre in *A Cheery Soul* when close to the end of the play, Sunday worshippers enter a reflective space during which a vision of the great mushroom cloud is beheld, bringing together Hiroshima, recent British nuclear testing at Maralinga and future scenarios. Australian uranium, already being extracted in mines in South Australia (Radium Hill 1954–62), the Northern Territory (Rum Jungle 1954–71) and Queensland (Mary Kathleen 1958–63), would potentially be a supplier of the raw materials for such a war.[2]

In *Big Toys* and *Signal Driver* uranium is represented as an immanent existential threat and a generator of conflict and contradiction at the social and political level. White reflects that in *Big Toys* he was "glad I've had my say about hypocritical, plutocratic, contemporary Sydney society. I've also been able to say what I think about uranium and atomic weapons".[3] Uranium is introduced early in Act One and interwoven with the plot line involving the law, the trade unions and the chairmanship of a powerful mining operation. In *Signal Driver*, the everyday life of ordinary folk runs its course against a wider frame, introduced by two metaphysical Beings, who narrate how "Whitey" is digging up "yellow cake" (58) in the Northern Territory that will "blow us all to bits" (95). Put together the plays

---

[1] Patrick White and Australian National University, "Role of the Australian Citizen in a Nuclear War" (Centre for Continuing Education, 1983) Manuscript. Patrick White Papers MS9982, National Library of Australia.
[2] Paul Kay, "Australia's Uranium Mines: Past and Present" Science, Technology, Environment and Resource Group, Parliamentary Library, Parliament of Australia.
[3] David Marr, *Patrick White: A Life* (Milsons Point: Vintage Books, 1992), 576.

present the bleak fatalistic view that the nation lacks the moral strength to stop the rich and powerful leading us to self-destruction.

Big Toys: "A Play of the '70s"

Big Toys has to date had five professional productions between 1977 and 1994. It was first performed by the Old Tote Theatre Company at the Parade Theatre, Sydney in July 1977 with Jim Sharman directing and stage design by Brian Thomson. The production toured to the Comedy Theatre, Melbourne in conjunction with J.C. Williamson Productions Ltd in October and to Canberra by arrangement with the Canberra Theatre Trust in November. These commercial arrangements enabled the premiere of a new Patrick White play to take place for the first time outside the semi-professional university theatre sector. This was no doubt facilitated by Sharman's successful revival of *The Season at Sarsaparilla* at the Drama Theatre at the Sydney Opera House in 1976 and was followed by a similarly landmark revival of *A Cheery Soul* in 1979, offering a period of concentrated attention on Patrick White's new and old plays in the mainstream commercial sector. This enhanced profile did not mean that critics were ready to reconsider their views of White's non-naturalist theatre.

White claimed to have written *Big Toys* for Kate Fitzpatrick in the role of Double Bay socialite Mag Bosanquet. According to Fitzpatrick:

> At the end of a great run (of *Season at Sarsaparilla*) Patrick threw a New Year's Eve party at his house in Martin Road, Centennial Park. Around midnight he stood on a chair and made a speech. He said he'd been so happy with *Sarsaparilla's* reception he'd written a new play for me during the run. He wished me happy New Year, kissed me and presented me with a hand-typed, hand corrected manuscript on onion-skin paper in a mottled dark-blue folder. It was called *Big Toys* and my character's name was Mag. I was transported.[4]

As indicated in chapter two, the agency of social class, the intrigues of capital, and the politics and economics of uranium mining are central to the unfolding story. While the text appears to foreground Sydney as a place of glamour, corporate power and wealth, the play is wholly set in the confined space of a penthouse bedroom with glass doors opening onto a terrace with views of the "rhinestone city" that twinkled in the distance from Bald Mountain, and which Miss Quodling described as a constellation of "glitter" not to be trusted (272). Brian Thomson's set uses new technology to represent the city's glitter, producing the signs but not the space itself that remains an imagined place. The audience sees the characters

---

[4] Kate Fitzpatrick, *Name Dropping: The Life and Loves of Kate Fitzpatrick* (Sydney: Harper Collins, 2004). Kindle. Loc. 3784.

in an idiosyncratic microworld, comically enhanced by the eccentric design of the penthouse. For Ritchie Bosanquet QC, played by tall and lean Arthur Dignam, a satirical representation of the city's lack of moral character, and the sociopathic indifference of wealth and power, the penthouse is a space for business by social means. Ritchie's wife Mag, and Terry Legge, the Communist Trade Unionist, played by Max Cullen, appear as more human-bodied characters with the weaknesses and entrapments of mortal flesh.

As the framing element in the play, the city encompasses the natural and built environment that interlocks with narrative, character and place in the drama. As this chapter will discover, changes in photographic technology make it possible for characters to physically interact with the iconic presence of the environment, its weather and light changes and its effects on mood.

Photographs of Dignam as Ritchie Bosanquet and Fitzpatrick as Mag in the program for the Sydney production show each in a posed still in character in front of a floor to ceiling window. Max Cullen's Terry Legge, the union man, is similarly posed and framed. A quote from each character is chosen to accompany the photographic image. Dignam and Fitzpatrick are both captured in business wear. As the QC Dignam wears a navy three-piece pinstriped suit with fob watch, a blue shirt and a navy old school tie. He wears large dark rimmed spectacles, and stands with one hand in his trouser pocket and the other holding a cigarette at shoulder height with his fingers self-consciously arranged. Smoke rises. His chin is raised, mouth pursed and his eyes look down at the camera. The play is set in 1976 but Ritchie's hair is brushed back from his high forehead, short at the back and with just a hint of a fashionable side burn. He looks too young for the tenor of the pinstriped suit and the formal stance, with the effect that there is a slightly parodic estrangement effect. Dignam creates the image that gives truth to Mag's line: "you've never ever been a human being – although you're dressed as one" (7). The quote cited is: "At heart we all admire sincerity. It's what we all long for", adding to the theatricality of the waxwork-like figure and his characteristic hypocrisy.

Kate Fitzpatrick's Mag is similarly dressed in a dark suit with an open-necked blouse, black stockings and high-heeled strappy shoes. She could be dressed for business except her business will be lunch. She stands for the camera with both hands in her pockets and her face turned for a profile. One knee is slightly bent in a mannequin stance so that she appears half-way between demure and alluring. Her blond hair is pulled back in a chignon and her lips dark red. The camera catches the strong line of her jaw and perfect pale skin. Her quote is: "Lives go different ways, that's all – even the lives of old friends. They always come together again". She looks away from the viewer as if parodically presenting herself for the other's gaze. Cullen's Terry Legge is an image of scepticism. In a more relaxed stance, he leans on the window frame and looks quizzically at the camera. His costume is light-coloured check trousers, a woollen polo neck jumper and brown leather jacket for the Sydney winter of 1976. His quote is "Whatever becomes of you afterwards, the past matters".[5] The costumes by Victoria Alexander clearly delineate character and class, while also offering insight into the provisional but incomplete or unconvincing integration of social role-playing and identity.

Brian Thomson's set is designed to signify the contemporary opulence of the penthouse apartment enjoyed by the rich with views of Sydney Harbour, the iconic Opera House, the Bridge and glittering high rise towers. The Bosanquets' bedroom and sitting room are spacious, occupying most of the stage. But the realist depiction of an interior domestic space is offset by the comical repetition of circular shapes and the theatrical layers that underpin the whole effect. The room is in-the-round on a circular buff-coloured shag pile carpet, itself set on a revolving stage. The layers thicken the stage suggesting the embeddedness of wealth and the wealthy into the geophysical make-up of the city. The ground and the earth are a long way below and also far away on secret mining leases up north. The interior décor continues the circular theme with a large round bed, a circular wardrobe attached to a dressing table, a circular mirror, a circular glass-topped coffee and drinks table and a circular bedside table and lamp in tones of oatmeal, orange and brown. The furnishings include chunky sofas and a decorative bonsai plant.

The back wall of the stage opens to let Sydney in as the fifth element, its vista changing with the mood of the play and temporal shifts. As indicated new technologies enable large-scale photographic enlargement of harbour views. There are four alternating backdrops: two floor-to-ceiling panels on rollers when closed reveal large size letters spelling out the words BIG TOYS in capitals; the panels open to reveal glass windows and doors, behind which is a cyclorama featuring Sydney Harbour by day; another panorama features the harbour by night with coloured lights all around; and a final vista is a threatening dark sky moving into a black void. The images were photographed and enlarged by Brett Hilder in nine vertical sections. Two sections can be removed to provide access to the terrace through the sliding glass door. The impression is one of modern luxury in a sexualised bedroom and lounge space.

The performance begins with the panels closed and the words Big Toys visible. Mag is relaxing on the bed in a short white monographed silk robe chatting on a red phone while playing with an oversized red balloon. Images show how she looks at the balloon while talking and pushing it upwards towards the ceiling with a hand and then a bare toe. Finally, as it falls and lolls against her on the bed, she pricks it with a fingernail. The accompanying sound cuts through the languor and the audience watches the balloon sags around her like "like some ugly old wrinkled scrotum" (5). The random conversation, the balloon, and the capricious action, present an opening image of beauty, idleness and privilege. But the spectator might also notice that Mag does not like the feel of the balloon lolling against her bare leg. Moments later the telephone rings again and the balloon is forgotten. Mag tells her husband she is off to give a talk at the Town Hall on her current interest: "The

---

5   *Big Toys* (The Old Tote Company, Sydney. Photographs by Brett Hilder, 1977), theatre program. NIDA Archive.

Hegemony of the Nuclear Family" (7). In her frivolous register, described by White as "*Eastern suburbs rich*", Mag explains that the meeting is about "the anti-uranium thing", rendering her talk on the nuclear family comically off the point.

After an interval in which excerpts from Mozart's *The Marriage of Figaro* are played, Ritchie enters to discover Terry in his violet and green floral kimono, worn over a white t-shirt. The comic allusion to Mozart's opera embeds another semiotic frame in the performance that carries "pre-given references".[6] In this case, Mozart's opera references both the age of aristocracy, soon to collapse, and eighteenth-century games of sexual intrigue and power. It frames each act implicating modern day Ritchie and Mag Bosanquet in its aristocratic worldview. The staging undermines their sovereign selves while exposing corruption and engaging the audience in critique of the characters' words and deeds. Furthermore, by hailing the operatic, the music further undermines the self-importance of the characters.

The audience and Ritchie see that the bedclothes are disarranged, whereupon he exits to return in something less formal, a comical red raw silk jumpsuit that Mag has bought him. It is afternoon, and the view of Sydney is both witness and player in the scene that follows in which Ritchie entices Terry with Mag's emerald necklace. This occurs as the lights darken on the harbour and in the absence of Mag, Ritchie and Terry engage in a whisky fuelled exchange that eventually culminates in the moment with the emeralds. Extracting information from Terry about Stannard back when they were work mates and comrades, Ritchie wryly notes: "Two forceful men – you were both unfortunate in your wives…" (32). It is also the most explicit evocation of Ritchie's sexuality, which comes in the form of a confession to Terry, "Mag tells me I'm cold. I see myself as a rather warm character. In fact, I'm frequently embarrassed by my own sexuality" (34). All the while the two men continue to drink and converse in the bedroom. At one point Terry sits at Mag's dressing table looking into the mirror. All the while Ritchie has been intimating the sexual undertones of Terry and Stannard's matey relationship. Images of the scene show Terry still dishevelled from the sexual encounter with Mag, but by now looking utterly miserable. Ritchie stands behind him bending over to hold the emerald necklace around Terry's neck while also checking the mirror in a studied performance of manipulation and power over the other man. Terry's expression is resigned as he gives in to his own weakness, not in bitterness but self-pity. His eyebrows are raised, there is a slight frown of mis-recognition and his bottom lip protrudes. He sees himself in drag, and is the victim and the perpetrator of his newly discovered self. Sydney Harbour promises discretion – although it illuminates and frames the forbidden scene, it guarantees that there are no witnesses. It is as if they inhabit a world of their own making, away from prying eyes. The spell is broken only when Ritchie suddenly fastens the clasp and Mag enters.

---

6   John Frow, *Genre* (London: Routledge, 2005), 19.

The scene presents heterosexuality as an emblem of lawfulness and white sovereignty, while requiring an abiding homoeroticism to lie ready to surface. Key symbols such as the penthouse, an emerald necklace with "superb stones", a fur coat and the keys to a Ferrari are objects of desire and discord. Material surfaces such as glass windows, mirrors, jewellery, minerals (uranium, plutonium), the metallic shine of the Ferrari are counterposed with soft objects such as fur, flesh, sexuality, identity and an unstable idea of "humanity" in the context of economic development and investment in the post-Whitlam years. There is sustained tension between the tendency towards realism – the objects on stage – and the discontinuities between character and object, including the shifting sands of identification and loyalty.

In Act Three, Mag registers her distress as the westerlies blow across the harbour. The glass doors provide some shelter but as Sydney disappears behind a blackened cloud, the glass is like a prison wall as Mag presses the palms of her hands against it.

Jim Sharman wrote in a director's introduction in the Old Tote program of *Big Toys*:

> Comic, tragic, cruelly baited and barbed, this is a play of the 70s, displaying a sophisticated and elegant overlay but revealing the corruption and confusion which arises in a society unsure of its direction and ambitious people unsure of themselves.[7]

These elements led Katharine Brisbane to refer to the drama as a "comedy of manners" and May-Brit Akerholt as "a drama of bitter irony".[8] Axel Kruse refers to the production at the Parade Theatre as a "masterpiece" in terms of text, direction and design but notes that its critical reception mostly returned to the old wariness about theatre's poetic intensity and its departure from realism.[9] The expectation that drama must be true to life and plausible has marked the adverse reception of White's theatre from the beginning in a critical mindset that Kruse identifies as antagonist to modernist theatre. *Big Toys*, he argues, "makes a show of art" in three characteristic ways: the art deco lettering of the title on the back wall of the stage/bedroom that rolls back to the accompaniment of loud stage machinery noise to reveal the view of Sydney; Mag in her fur coat at the end of the play as she mimes driving the Ferrari and before turning to utter the lines "Christ … Christ …" (52) and weeping silently; and the use of arias from Mozart's *The Marriage of Figaro* between acts to underscore the sex games among the three characters. White's approach to the novel and to theatre, he argues, favours "a puzzle as well

---

7   Jim Sharman, "Director's Introduction", *Big Toys*, (The Old Tote Company, Sydney, 27 July, 1977), theatre program. NIDA Archive.
8   Katharine Brisbane, "Introduction", in *Big Toys* (Sydney: Currency Press 1978), xii; May-Brit Akerholt, *Patrick White* (Amsterdam: Rodopi Press, 1988), 128.
9   Axel Kruse, "Patrick White's 'Big Toys': White and His Critics", *Quadrant* (September 1977): 24–25.

as a game", and a "trick as well as a true confession". This view was not shared by critics. John West on the well-known ABC radio program *Showtime* gave *Big Toys* a bad review proclaiming it "a failure on most counts": it was not funny, Jim Sharman and the actors failed to deliver meaning, and of course the playwright's plot failed.[10] Norman Kessell confined himself to descriptions of character, action and theme, and found the production pleasing for its satirical elegance, its humour, and the performances of the cast. His more left-leaning tolerance for the critique of wealth and power found him sympathetic to the representation of "vulgar elegance".[11] Others such as Frank Harris in *The Daily Mirror* were mesmerised by Kate Fitzpatrick's "luminous performance".[12] Finally, Harry Kippax regrets to say the plot crumbles when the audience is asked to accept that an eminent QC would tamper with a Crown witness, or engage in homoerotic games.[13]

Yet *Big Toys* registers a theatrical world in which homoeroticism plays a crucial role in elite spheres of law and money. The ambiguously queered relations between the men and the lack of intimacy between the heterosexual couple is perhaps one of the most striking advances of this play. It makes unflattering connections between hidden male homosexual desire and access to political and economic privilege. At the cultural level, the burgeoning gay scene in Sydney, followed by the AIDS epidemic, documented by White's photographer and friend William Yang, gave rise to artistic experimentation with identity and masquerade, gender and sexuality, and cruelty and desire, as evident in the play. These embodied practices met with additional criticism from the likes of Kippax because they undermined the moral superiority of white, bourgeois, heteronormative and masculine value systems, in favour of diversity, recognition of its others, and outsider figures, who no longer acceded to colonisation by the dominant culture.

Signal Driver: A Premiere at the Adelaide Festival of Arts.

Signal *Driver* is also set in Sydney but differs in perspective. Harry Kippax referred to it as "a curious, apparently slight play, building from a schematic, laboured beginning to an unexpectedly poignant resolution".[14] Staged five years later, White returns to the theatre of the absurd to explore mundane everyday life in the outskirts of the city. Its scope is however more ambitious, offering an epic view of the growth of the twentieth-century city beginning in 1920 and ending in the early 1980s, the present of the play. As indicated in chapter two, the play consists of variations of a scene played out over three time periods as a married couple live out their lives in an outer suburb of Sydney. There is a symmetry to the dramaturgy

---

10   John West, *Showtime*, aired 31 July, 1977, on ABC Radio. Transcript, NIDA Archives.
11   Norman Kessell, "New White Play Is Event for the Stage", *Daily Telegraph*, 30 July 1977.
12   Frank Harris, "Corruption Is the Theme", *Daily Mirror*, 30 July 1977.
13   Harry Kippax, "Point Piper Calls the Tune in White Play", *Sydney Morning Herald*, 30 July 1977.
14   Harry Kippax, "Patrick White's Curious New Play", *Sydney Morning Herald*, 8 March 1982.

in that each of the three scenes takes place at a public transport shelter early one evening in 1920, 1950 and 1980. Observing the couple are two supernatural Beings, harbingers of the existential danger posed by uranium mining in the Northern Territory and the potential it creates for nuclear war. At the time of its premiere, Patrick White featured in a photograph in *The Sydney Morning Herald* in a raincoat and beanie, at an anti-nuclear march through Sydney, alongside Federal Labor MP, Tom Uren, and Bishop John Reid.[15]

Unlike Ritchie Bosanquet, the play's critique of modernity centres on a melancholic carpenter, Theo Vokes, who is morally and emotionally overwhelmed by the wheels of production. His wife, Ivy, is at first timid but becomes a go-getter, who moves up the social ladder, and acquires a business and a lover, while Theo looks on helplessly. At the end of the play, a willy-willy wind blows as the light from the Aurora Australis floods the sky like a nuclear explosion.

When Jim Sharman was appointed Artistic Director of the 1982 Adelaide Festival of Arts, he asked Patrick White to write a new play and invited Neil Armfield to direct its world premiere at the festival, twenty years after *The Ham Funeral* was rejected by the Board of Governors. In doing so, Sharman effectively passed the directing baton to Armfield, who went on to become White's principle theatre interpreter through the 1980s and 1990s. *Signal Driver* opened the festival in a production by Sharman's Lighthouse Theatre Company with White in attendance. In a further tribute to White's contribution to Australian literary and theatre culture, the festival included the Sydney Symphony Orchestra's preview of composer Richard Meale's adaptation of *Voss* for opera with libretto by David Malouf. Sharman's brilliant festival began with a parade through the city centre with banners, floats and performers in costume. International programming included Sam Shepard's *The Curse of the Starving Class*, a retrospective exhibition of American artist Edward Hopper's city paintings, and three works by Pina Bausch's Wuppertal Dance Theatre.

The governors who had rejected White's early plays were long gone. Sharman's appointment was intent on building a reputation for adventurous programming. John McCallum considered Armfield's production of *Signal Driver* (1982) as indicative of the "way the new Australian theatre in the 1980s was dealing with Australian drama: the shift from representational realism of the tradition to an extraordinarily extended theatrical vocabulary that Armfield, and then Kantor and Andrews were waiting in the wings to produce".[16]

Rehearsals for *Signal Driver* began in February 1982 with Patrick White leading textual read throughs with Armfield, rewriting Act One, attending rehearsals and being moved to tears by Act Three, in which the elderly couple struggle home together

---

15   Richard McGregor "Thousands March in Rain Against Nuclear Weapons" *Sydney Morning Herald*, 5 April, 1982.
16   John McCallum, *Belonging: Australian Playwriting in the 20th Century* (Sydney: Currency Press, 2010), 141–3.

afflicted by age and infirmity.[17] He attended opening night, took a bow with Armfield, gave a short speech and experienced the warmth of the audience's approval.[18] Armfield recalls that for "Patrick it was a triumphant return to the festival after the scandalous rejection of *The Ham Funeral* by its board of governors exactly two decades earlier".[19] But critics continued to be ambivalent about White's plays partly for their philosophical complexity and stylistic plurality while they lauded the creatives involved in staging them. At best there was a mixed response to "an unusual and difficult" play,[20] with a better reception of the Melbourne and Brisbane productions that followed in 1983. This seems odd because the Lighthouse Theatre's Adelaide production had the resources of one of the only ensemble-based theatres at the time with actors such as Peter Cummins, Melissa Jaffer, Kerry Walker and John Wood, who performed in *Signal Driver*. According to David Marr, the Sydney Theatre Company declined to include either *Signal Driver* or *Netherwood* in its repertoire but agreed to a revival of *The Ham Funeral* in 1989 with Neil Armfield directing.[21]

White imagined a sparse minimalist set for *Signal Driver* that features a transport shelter in the 1920s, the 1960s and the 1980s that help track stages in the development of modernity in outer Sydney in the form of urban development. The shelter is at first in an outer suburban area and becomes incorporated in the urban fringe. As a transport shelter, the structure is part of the built set designed by Stephen Curtis with a bench seat, a tiled back wall and a roof, and is a stage within a stage for the drama that unfolds between the Vokes, who arrive and leave without ever hailing the transport. It is therefore a theatrical rather than functional space, liminal like theatre itself in so far as it is neither public nor private, and is the object of the audience's attention. The Vokes make it into a place of dreams and lost opportunities in a materialisation of ideas embedded in the poetry of the play. The set recalls Beckett's *Happy Days*, first performed in 1961, which featured a married couple carrying on with daily life despite being buried up to their waists and then their necks in sand. Beckett's Winnie and Willie are alone on a bare stage, and it seems, in the world, with only an alarm clock to distinguish between night and day. Something has stopped the movement of the sun yet they try to keep busy and have a happy day.[22] *Signal Driver* is similarly interested in the existential question of daily life within the confines of marriage and the family here interlinked with the drive for material prosperity and attachment to earthly possessions.

The presence of two celestial beings – nominated as First Being and Second Being, and designated male and female respectively – offer satirical commentary

---

17 See Anne Pender, "Kerry Walker, Patrick White and the Faces of Australian Modernism", *Coolabah* 9 (2012): 79.
18 Marr, *Patrick White*, 609–10.
19 Neil Armfield, "Patrick White: A Centenary Tribute", *Meanjin* 71, no. 2 (2012).
20 John Ellison, "Extraordinary, Bewildering White", *Melbourne Times*, 28 September 1983. MTC Archive.
21 Marr, *Patrick White*, 640.
22 Samuel Beckett, "Happy Days" *The Complete Dramatic Works* (London: Faber, 1986), 135–168.

on human behaviour and dire warnings about the future. The Beings use the Vokes' transport shelter as a base between missions to various trouble spots around the world, ranging far and wide across space and time. Central to the theatricality of the play is the suspension of disbelief necessary to accept that the Beings are seen and heard by the audience, but not by the Vokes, in a way that splits the play into two modes, one human and the other metaphysical, producing two competing ontologies. The timeless, supernatural Beings represent a commensurate world unbound by time and space, yet co-exist with human time, place and character. They also sing and dance for the human audience. The mixing of ontological worlds such as the everyday and the eternal, the human and extra-human expresses the theatricalist mode of *Signal Driver*, and expands on the austerity of Beckett's modernist masterpiece. Moreover, the Vokes and the Beings are twentieth-century Australian figurations of how modernity impacts on ordinary and celestial lives.

Equally theatricalist as the presence of the visible/invisible Beings, the tram and later the bus never appear and are only ever a sound effect. This absence leaves the audiences to ponder the central questions of the play. Do the drivers continually by-pass the couple and if so why? Do the Vokes ever actually intend to catch the transport? Have they simply not read the sign "Signal Driver"? Do they lack the courage of their convictions? Is the ritual merely theatrical? The text leaves the questions open and ambiguous:

> Act One: [*The invisible tram approaches the shelter bucking and sighing in the accepted way.* THEO *half-raises his arm, then lets it fall impotently and steps back into the shadow of the shelter.*] (67)

> Act Two: [THEO *half raises his hand to signal the driver but lets it fall. The invisible bus charges past.*] (79)

> Act Three: [*As the bus whams towards the shelter,* IVY *makes a little scrabbling gesture in the air. The bus lunges towards the city. She and* THEO *stand looking after it.*] (91)

The text dramatises the failure to raise the arm high enough and with the intention to signal the driver but it is open to interpretation how the scene is played in performance. Critic Leonard Radic is emphatic that the Melbourne production featured the intentional raised arm: "What does not change is that no matter how often they stand there at the shelter, arm upraised, trying to signal the tram or bus driver, he never stops for them".[23] Radic has perhaps not considered that the arm may not have been upraised enough to be seen and the scene is a theatrical ruse

---

23   Leonard Radic, "White's Gentle Look at Partners in Misfortune", *Age*, 15 September 1983, 14.

for other disclosures. It is the place that attracts the Beings with their commentary and prophecy, a space that highlights the sexual or libidinal aspects of liminal space and time, a place to quarrel, to feel desire, and a temporary respite from life. Thematically, Theo and Ivy approach the threshold of mobility but never step over it. The Beings think they lack a "coherent philosophy", taking up the themes set out in "The Prodigal Son", White's essay on the Australian condition:

SECOND BEING: They are without a coherent philosophy.

FIRST BEING: Ideologies haven't touched them.

SECOND BEING: They are minute droplets in a population which will remain largely fluid.

Nor has history, to date, become elastic enough to catapult back ...

SECOND BEING: ... and on their home ground, bloody their little colonial snouts – along with wattle.

FIRST BEING: They're still Lucky Australians, y'now. (69–70)

Here the Beings identify the limitations of Theo and Ivy's efforts to block from consciousness anything that distracts from the here and now of their marriage. This effort necessitates the exclusion of the metaphysical – Theo's artistic aspirations and the remnants of Ivy's lapsed faith – as well as the broader universe of history, philosophy and ideology. The references to "blood", "colonial snouts" and "wattle", however, are further suggestive of that which modern Australia as a whole has blocked from consciousness, that is, the lasting impact of colonialism, and the contested sovereignty of the wattle as a metonym for the nation. The juxtaposition of blood and wattle alludes to several literary, theatrical and historical references to blood on the wattle – from Henry Lawson, D.H. Lawrence, and Leslie Haylen's play *Blood on the Wattle* (1948) to Bruce Elder's *Blood on the Wattle: Massacres and Maltreatment of Aboriginal Australians Since 1788*.[24] Placed at the end of Act One, the Beings' sardonic commentary foreshadows the return of Indigenous sovereignty over the wattle as well as the existential threats facing a distracted or insular nation while uranium mining takes place on Indigenous land in the Northern Territory.

The Beings are represented on stage as a combination of clowns, vaudeville singers, travelling roadshow performers and itinerates. They are ageless, unlike the

---

24 Donna Eileen Coates, "Reality Bites: The Impact of the Second World War on the Australian Home Front in Maria Gardner's 'Blood Stained Wattle' and Robin Sheiner's 'Smile, the War Is Over'" in *Antipodes* 23, 1, (June 2009): n21, 54.

human characters, and are without earthly possessions. Too much time observing human behaviour has led them to the bottle, giving them a character White designated as "*a pair of super deros*" (57). Kerry Walker and Peter Cummins performed the roles for the premiere with Melissa Jaffer as Ivy Vokes and John Wood as Theo. Images of Walker and Cummins' Beings show the character and sets' allusions to Beckett's tramps, Estragon and Vladimir.[24] Curtis' set for Act One in the 1920s features the bus shelter on a bare stage next to a wooden signpost inscribed with the words Signal Driver. There is a single bare tree and mounds of dirt. In one photograph the Beings stand next to each other between the signpost and the tree with a bottle of grog at their feet. They lean in unison looking offstage into the distance waiting for Theo and Ivy to appear. They are dusty, dirty and dishevelled, dressed for outdoors in what would have once been respectable lower middle-class attire. Walker wears a mid-calf length skirt gathered at the waist, a cardigan, scarf and hat; Cummins wears a bowler hat pulled down over his ears, trousers, jacket and shirt. Their shoes are worn out. They represent the theatrical tradition of the vaudeville tramp of the early twentieth-century Anglo-European stage with pale skin and Western dress. Once they speak, however, the allusion to Beckett and Anglo-European theatre remains but is overlaid with the Australian vernacular as spelt out in White's text:

> FIRST BEING: [*stirring, yawning*] Nobody yet. Makes yer fuckun tired waitin' for somethun to happen.
>
> SECOND BEING: [*writhing around*] They'll come though. They're expected.
>
> FIRST BEING: Yair …
>
> [*The* FIRST BEING *takes a swig from a bottle lying beside him. He burps.*] (57)

The long slow Australian "Yair" uttered by Cummins is comic-laconic. Cummins was fifty at the time of the performance and known for his iconic Australian roles as a larrikin ocker figure in New Wave theatre and film including *Stork* and *The Removalists*. His nasal voice captures that which Helen Gilbert and Jacqueline Lo refer to elsewhere as "Australian vernacular language" which acts as a " performative", that is, its utterance brings Australianness into being.[25] Walker is similarly recognised for this quality especially in her localised representation of Alma Lusty in Neil Armfield's revival of *The Ham Funeral* in 1989. This affective

---

[24] David Wilson, photo, *Signal Driver*, Premiere, Adelaide Festival of Arts, (Lighthouse Theatre, 5 March 1983). Patrick White Collection, Series 1477, Barr Smith Library, University of Adelaide.

[25] Helen Gilbert and Jacqueline Lo, *Performance and Cosmopolitics: Cross-Cultural Transactions in Australasia* (London: Palgrave, 2007), 146.

linguistic style captures the Beings' place-based existence in relation to the more Anglo-European tradition of Beckett's tramps. In this premiere production, Armfield and the design crew style the Beings as European but the voices are clearly Australian. The Belvoir production in 1985 utilises an Australian circus aesthetic found in iconoclastic companies such as Circus Oz.

An image of Theo and Ivy Vokes in Act Two shows the middle-aged couple looking prosperous but in different moods. Theo no longer imagines he will escape to the seaside to sleep on a monk's valise and craft wood by day. He sits at the bus stop filled with annoyance, his hands in his pockets looking away from Ivy, who is dressed up in an expensive but simple white dress for a dinner engagement with her business partner and lover Sol. As the Beings remark she now calls herself "Jasmine" and she is happily expectant of a pleasurable evening at "Ro*mah*no's" as she explains to her husband (74–75).

Armfield recast the play for the Queensland Theatre Company Brisbane and Melbourne productions in August and September the same year with design by Mike Bridges. Elizabeth Alexander played Ivy with Errol O'Neill giving Theo, "the kind of urban Australian male quality that is very rarely achieved on the Australian stage … the kind of self-righteous, yet whingeing, strong-willed but malleable, brave but blind sort of bloke that has populated Australian cities for a 150 years".[26] Alexander's Ivy developed "three distinct characterisations while maintaining a chord of continuity".[27] As indicated, George Spartels and Sheila Bradley represent younger, more animated Beings, who "jive, swagger, sing and jest with engaging good humour".[28] John Larkin writes that their Beings "have the time of their eternal lives, lifting us, when needed, as lightly as rainbows".[29] The Company B production at Belvoir in Sydney featured Kerry Walker as Ivy, John Gaden as Theo and Richard Healey and Val Levkowicz as the Beings. Armfield recalls:

> It was the first play produced from the ground up by Belvoir. We'd bought the theatre the year before (with ten shares, Patrick was the greatest shareholder) in an amazing rush of energy and idealism. We rehearsed in a freezing garage across the road from Belvoir Street (it was destined to become the Green Room at the Opera Centre). At Patrick's request, Kerry (for whom Patrick had written the female Chorus figure) was this time playing Ivy, to John 'Yummy' Gaden's Theo. I sat next to Patrick on opening night. 'I haven't had time to iron my shirt,' I confessed. He laughed as the houselights went down and said, 'Your body heat will press it for you.' It was strange and a bit sexy and more than anything complicit in the daring fun of making theatre.[30]

---

26 *National Times*, 30 September, 1983, 36.
27 Ellison, "Extraordinary, Bewildering White".
28 Radic, "White's Gentle Look", 14.
29 John Larkin, "Tramlines of Time and Life", *Sunday Press*, 15 October 1983. MTC Archive.
30 Neil Armfield, "Patrick White: A Centenary Tribute", *Meanjin*, Vol. 71, No. 2 (2012), 24–25.

Photographs of the production design by Curtis show he has modified his original design for the Adelaide premiere using only a long wooden bench painted green.[31] The stage is bare save for shiny dark surfaces, black for the stage floor and bare stage walls that are receptive to lighting effects such as the stars at night and the red sky of the Aurora Australis at the end of the play. The bare look is more contemporary as is the increased role of lighting to create atmosphere. As indicated, Walker and Gaden play Ivy and Theo. In Act One, they are young and photographs show Ivy as a saucy young wife that Theo finds irresistible as the circus troupe Beings look on laughing. The image shows a lighter, less formally arranged stage allowing humour and warmth to enter the play. In Act Two, Ivy and Theo are more formally dressed and posed. Ivy appears over-dressed. Her white dress is now full-skirted, tight waisted and low cut, with a three-stringed pearl necklace, above the elbow white gloves and a tea hat that sits jauntily on her dark curly hair. Gaden's Theo is in a pinstriped suit, shirt and tie, and looks earnestly at Ivy. In Act Three, they are old and sad. Ivy's black coiffed hair is frizzy and white, her face sallow and intense. She sits on the bench far away from Theo with her legs apart and a look of bewildered, defensive attention. Theo's face has collapsed. His eyes appear to have retreated into dark ringed sockets. He wears a beret, scarf, cardigan and loose trousers. The Beings no longer laugh and play but look at their decline with some sympathy but also regret that a couple like the Vokes never woke up to the world around them.

The Belvoir production gave Armfield the opportunity "to dig further into" *Signal Driver* to appreciate the autobiographical elements in Act Three when both Theo and Ivy are old, left behind and bewildered by modern Australia.[32] In this sense he saw the play as an expression of the elderly Patrick White at Centennial Park "seeing the world become more and more alien, and more and more driven by an obvious and shallow materialism".[33] This insight tempers the representation of Theo and Ivy adding depth to Walker and Gaden's portrayal of the characters. Rather than sneering at ordinary folk from an elitist perspective, as many of White's critics assert, Act Three sees the Vokes embody vulnerability and acts of kindness. They are not the rich and materialist Bosanquets of the world.

Verity Masters described *Signal Driver* as an "extraordinarily rich play", noting its echoes of Beckett, T.S. Eliot and C.S. Lewis, but was critical of the representation of Ivy as the wife, who stifles her husband's creative aspirations.[34] Elizabeth Alexander, who performed the role in Melbourne and Brisbane, struggled with this gender stereotype, indicating that she tried to "soften White's" textual portrayal of the character by showing her to be a vulnerable woman looking out for home and children.[35] These feminist critiques rightly focus on adverse gender stereotypes

---

31   Photographs used in this section were viewed at the National Library of Australia, Patrick White Archive.
32   Neil Armfield, interviewed by Sandra D'Urso, 9 January 2018.
33   Armfield, interview.
34   Verity Masters, "Driver Makes a Routine Stop to Put Down Women", *Australian*, 7 September 1983.

that take carriage of patriarchal privilege and harbour barely concealed misogyny. The task for the feminist performer, as Alexander indicates, is to subvert, soften or disrupt these monstrous representations of female characters. While not claiming White was free of patriarchal bias, there are also opportunities to show how the female characters in all the plays are anti-realist figurations intended for non-naturalist theatrical presentation. They are in this sense constellations of ideological falsehoods, and in the Brechtian sense, vehicles for defamiliarising the social construction of the role of wife, mother and homemaker. They are female masquerades or, as Armfield saw it, all the characters are marionettes, and propositions for theatricalist expression. This potential for defamiliarisation was realised in Sharman, Armfield, and Benedict Andrews' cross-gender casting that is frequently used to express the gender fluidity that lies close to the surface of White's plays, and to reject gendered binaries. Peter Carroll's Girlie Pogson in Andrews' production of *The Season at Sarsaparilla* in 2007 captures the performativity of gendered roles under patriarchy.

The Belvoir set staged a spectacular Aurora Australis in the final moments of the play but Theo and Ivy are only partially moved. Ivy thinks it's nice but it's cold and she wants to go home to a dinner of Welsh rabbit. Images show the couple in retreat from the world, frail and melancholy. The Beings mock the "Two blind mice" but Theo, unconcerned about the judgement put upon him, offers to rub Ivy's shoulder as they struggle home. The interplay of sentiment and satire, each rational within its own ontology, offers audiences the chance to hold both worlds in view. After their exit, fog and smoke descends onto the stage and out into the auditorium and over the audience, enveloping the space in the spectre of a nuclear future.[36] Patrick White is cited at the time stating, "I try to speak up against nuclear war … I'm for nuclear disarmament. I hope I may be able to write something, not in a propagandist way but obliquely. Let it seep in. But everything's happening so fast."[37] On this view, in *Signal Driver*, Theo and Ivy's story diverts and moves the audience while signalling an oblique view of the immanent and pressing dangers to human existence, here nuclear war, but equally other large-scale manmade threats. This reading frames *Signal Driver* as White's most overtly political work.

***

The arguments for and against uranium mining during this period remediate longer debates about capitalist development and conservation that date back to the Industrial Revolution but which in the postwar period were framed by the mass destruction of civilian populations at Hiroshima and Nagasaki in 1945 and

---

35   Carol Veitch, "Patrick's 'Unfair' to Ivy", *Herald*, 20 September 1983, 32.
36   See Harry Kippax, "Patrick White's Curious New Play" and Gus Worby, "Signal Driver", *Theatre Australia*, May, 1982, 33.
37   Alan Roberts, "Patrick White: The Inner Struggle", *Advertiser – Saturday Review*, 13 February, 1982.

wider fears of radiation, radioactive poisoning and other non-visible effects of the nuclear and petro-chemical industry. In Australia, the Land Rights Movement led by Aboriginal activists including Charles Perkins, press cuttings of whose involvement are amongst White's papers, challenged the legality of uranium mining on traditional lands.

Big Toys and *Signal Driver* respond from different angles to the growing momentum of anti-uranium politics and demonstrate White's commitment to speaking out on contemporary issues in public forums including the theatre, although politics is not the sole driver of the dramas. Rather the politics deepens the rationale of White's aesthetic revolt against naturalistic theatre in the way that form and politics intersect, often in oblique ways. The critique of the Great Acceleration, now careering towards nuclear power and arms, is broad-based but coherent in that White consistently questions that which Chantal Mouffe has described elsewhere as the underlying universalism that "postulates the rational and moral superiority of Western modernity".[38] While speaking in public at rallies and meetings, the dramaturgy of White's later drama continues the practice of the early plays in which the dominance of realism and rationality on the Australian stage is called into question and destabilised with increasingly satiric, absurdist, gender fluid, and metaphysical theatricality.

---

38 Chantal Mouffe, *Agonistics: Thinking the World Politically* (London: Verso, 2013), xv.

8
Enchantment and Critique: *Shepherd on the Rocks*

Shepherd on the Rocks was first performed at the Playhouse, Adelaide Festival Centre, in 1987. The premiere season was presented by the State Theatre Company and directed by Neil Armfield, who had by then developed a deep knowledge of White's theatrical sensibilities and an appreciation of the plays' radical aesthetics. The creative team included Brian Thomson, whose scenographic solutions to the complexities of White's expansive scenic imagination had contributed to spectacular stagings of the plays since the 1970s. Composer Carl Vine, who had worked on *Signal Driver* and lighting designer John Comeadow, who had worked on Armfield's 1984 production of *The Season at Sarsaparilla*, were also important members of the creative team. By the late 1980s, a network of theatre artists had accumulated knowledge and experience of Patrick White's modernist oeuvre, its blend of theatrical enchantment and social critique. This embodied knowledge extended to actors with previous experience of White's theatre: John Gaden as the Reverend Daniel Shepherd, Kerry Walker as Queenie, the Kings Cross prostitute, Geoffrey Rush as Archbishop Wilfred Bigge, and Jacquy Phillips as Lily Thripp, the Kings Cross madam, the Pink Lady of Budgiwank, and Tilda Strutt, the do-gooder of Tiddler's Bay. Where it is not possible to compare productions of *Shepherd on the Rocks* over time, this chapter considers the play in terms of its realisation by Armfield's team, and then draws out key features of the theatricalist aesthetic in White's last published and performed work.

Gaden, Walker and Rush had leading roles with most of the cast, including Rush, playing multiple parts. Henri Szeps performed the roles of Dean Bartholomew (Bat) Shute, a "short and meanly evangelical" cleric, to Rush's "cadaverous and unctuous"[1] Archbishop, as well as Ern, the Budgiwank newsagent and hardware store owner, and Nat Wormald, the circus proprietor. Cast members filled the many carnivalesque roles of worshippers, Kings Cross prostitutes, touts and drug dealers, circus performers and spruikers, private detectives and newspaper reporters. In this later

---

1   Peter Ward, "White Weaves a Cloth of Faith and More", *Australian*, 11 May 1987, 6.

play, the sacred and the profane, the visionary and the comic are distributed among actors playing many contrasting roles, variously subverting or upholding prevailing norms about sexuality, metaphysics and religion.

The staging was integral to the complex scenic panorama of the performance presenting many visual and mechanical challenges for the design team and operating crew. White's stage directions list the following scenic locations with more detail provided throughout the text:

> SETTING
> The action of the play takes place in DANNY SHEPHERD's bedroom-study, upstairs at the rectory; at LILY THRIPP's Kings Cross establishment (with bedrooms upstairs); the Archbishop's library-study; the Ned Kelly Arms; the Glitz Palace theatre; Tiddler's Bay on the south coast and the Show at Jerusalem, New South Wales.
> Patrick White envisaged all these areas represented onstage, with the Archbishop's study and the bar at the Ned Kelly Arms to be trucked onstage as required.[2] [It is interesting to note the unusual reference to the author here, indicating an editorial addition not elsewhere seen.]

Several moving parts included platforms, rooms moved on and off stage, staircases on wheels, changing cycloramas and hundreds of props. Performers changed costume and role at pace, and transformed space and objects in dynamic scenes full of interaction with place. One critic described the dynamism, variety and audacity of the performance:

> The bare open stage is a world where prostitutes descend in cages, the sea rises to become a circus tent, and Daniel's fate in the lion's den challenges the conventional scriptures as surely as Daniel Shepherd's conduct confronts the establishment.[3]

With this play, White's theatre takes flight across several locations and orthodoxies. Many of these locations are spaces where the overturning of established norms takes place. These performative acts support the central role of illumination, drawing on suggestions in the extra-dialogic text. As a technology and signifier, light is more than the means whereby the stage is made visible to the audience. It adds aesthetic and intellectual value, playing a key role in highlighting the enchantments of symbolic objects, and adding tone to the discursive elements at play. There are several examples of the illuminating qualities of light across White's

---

2 White, Patrick. *Collected Plays, Volume II*: Big Toys, Signal Driver, Netherwood, Shepherd on the Rocks. Sydney: Currency Press, 1994, 172.
3 Ken Healey, "Clergyman's Kings Cross Odyssey", *Sydney Morning Herald*, 12 May 1987, 16.

theatre. The Young Man in *The Ham Funeral* leaves the dark crumbling house to walk with hope towards a luminous light; a razzle-dazzle lighting effect creates a space for reflection in *The Season at Sarsaparilla*; the rhinestone lights of Sydney are imbued with deception in *Night on Bald Mountain*; and the appearance of the Aurora Australis in *Signal Driver* is a spectacular event that refers audiences to the miracle of the universe, but also uranium mining in the Northern Territory and the threat of nuclear war. Each example is a technology of the stage that creates atmosphere and mood, a poetic image with symbolic resonance beyond the theatrical world, and an illumination in the sense of the co-existence of enchantment and critique. In *Shepherd on the Rocks*, Reverend Daniel Shepherd is first seen illuminated, kneeling in his bedroom-study, suggestive of his religious faith; a flickering light through windows of a train indicates the journey to Sydney; a luminous arrow indicates Kings Cross; a cyclorama conveys changes in natural light at Tiddler's Bay; and a final apocalyptic light blazes as Shepherd enters the lion cage while proclaiming belief in magic.

The extensive use of light by means of theatrical illumination is evocative of the optical effects and illusions of the phantasmagoria, the word coined by Etienne-Gaspard Robert in 1797 to describe the popular magic lantern show. Robert would conjure the ghosts of historic figures out of chemicals, light and smoke to rapturous wonder and applause from showground and exhibition spectators. Derived from the ancient Greek term for a gathering of ghosts, the phantasmagoria became a popular nineteenth-century spectacle, especially in Paris and London.[4] By the twentieth century, cultural critic Walter Benjamin used the term to critically capture the rise of the visual commodity and spectacle in capitalist modernity.[5] This gave rise to a new understanding of the phantasmagoria as a sum of the effects of industrialisation and commodity fetishism, as it materialised in the illusory and seductive character of light on objects in the Paris Arcades. The phantasmagoria described the brilliant displays, illusions, enchantments and captive capacities of modernity's goods and wealth. On this view, the Arcades were a performative and novel kind of theatre brought to life by the perambulating movement and reception of Parisian crowds.

Benjamin developed the concept of "critical illumination" as a mode of resisting modernity's persuasive power and thrall. This critical view of the Arcades as phantasmagoria was in constant danger of being undermined by the sense of one's own seduction and enchantment by these light-filled commercial spaces. It was in this sort of attraction to and distance from the market that modernist aesthetics

---

[4] See Margaret Cohen, "Walter Benjamin's Phantasmagoria", *New German Critique* 48 (Autumn, 1989), 87–107.

[5] Margaret Cohen, "Benjamin's Phantasmagoria: the *Arcades Project*" In *The Cambridge Companion to Walter Benjamin* ed. D. Ferris, (Cambridge: Cambridge University Press, 2004), 207.

pinpointed sites of tension; critique was pitted against seduction under the allure of the theatricality of the phantasmagoria.

A similar pull and push tension marks the aesthetic architecture of White's dramatic texts, which combine critique with the alluring indulgences of desire. From Girlie Pogson trading life on the family farm for white goods in a Sarsaparilla kitchen, and Ernie Boyle's settling for a Mixmaster in place of the homoerotic pleasures of army life, White's theatre indulges and withdraws the magic lantern's appeal. In *Shepherd on the Rocks*, Geoffrey Rush's ascetic whisky-drinking Archbishop and Kerry Walker's elfin and seductive Queenie embody these dualities. Magic, to bring the discussion back to Danny Shepherd and the illuminated Lion's Cage, is momentarily preferable to religion, modernity, science and the ultimate phantasmagoria of nuclear war.

A black and white photographic image captures a moment of such illumination in Scene Five inside Budgiwank's Chapel.[6] The stage is bare and appears epic in scale with the floor coated in a reflective black veneer. The outline of a large circle is painted onto its surface in white paint with a smaller circle in the middle painted in bright neon red. Upstage a full-height curtain hangs at a sweeping angle in front of which a thin white cross is suspended. Danny Shepherd is seen at an elevated pulpit stage right. He is in his white surplice and collar, and stands as if preaching with his arms reaching out. Parishioners stand around the circumference of the painted circle and Queenie is visible in the centre on her knees in a miniskirt with a gold bag over her shoulder. She is described as a classic "bump-and-grind hooker, all glitzed over" but images of Walker show a young woman with elfin style short dark hair as a counterpoint to the stereotype, and indicative of a search for greater meaning.[7] Shepherd commences his sermon by calling the flock together, "as lovers in the spirit" (195), but Queenie's belief in the church's offerings is faltering: "Oh God, is it true? Or are you false – like the lovers I have had in many one–hour stands? To pay the rent and buy the smack" (195). Shepherd's sermon becomes one in which he tries to distinguish between the rhetoric coined by "authors of injustice and hypocrisy" and something more authentic than magic lanterns depicting God in heaven (195). From the pulpit and in clerical robes, he launches into a litany of self-doubt:

> As one of these I hope for the forgiveness of God the Father, which he does not withhold from those in need – unless the authors of injustice and hypocrisy. Or am I, without knowing, a hypocrite too? How are we to know? Can we search deep enough in our troubled hearts? Can we survive the shame of what we

---

6   David Wilson, photo, in White, *Collected Plays, Volume II*, 174.
7   Ward, "White Weaves a Cloth". The image of the production accompanying this review shows Gaden and Walker at Budgiwank. They are sitting outdoors on the grass talking. He is in his clerical collar and she is resting on his shoulder.

find? How can we endure the injustices of those who rule our earthly lives? (195)

The sermon gathers momentum as it turns against vain politicians and bureaucrats before wondering if "a holocaust such as history has not experienced ..." (196) will vaporise the world. The stage directions then indicate that Shepherd is whirled out of sight through dry-ice clouds as an unseen choir breaks into lamentations, and Queenie falls to her knees convulsing with fear before a blackout brings darkness and silence. The lights then come up on Queenie and Bee in a peaceful meadow wishing they were back home. Still reeling from Shepherd's sermon Bee asks Queenie, "What's a hollercaust?"; she answers "It's the end of things. It's when the skyscrapers bite the dust" (196).

Within the passing of a few seconds of stage time, the audience has witnessed a theatrical phantasmagoria that begins with light, moves through Shepherd's evocation of the impatient deity that destroys the world and culminates in explosion, darkness and silence before landing in a bucolic scene on a sunny, peaceful morning. The elegance of the composed image of the chapel, dismantled and blown apart before reassembling on a grassy knoll conjures that which Benjamin might have meant by a "profane illumination" that along with its enchantments carries a punchline about nuclear war.[8]

Another image from the archive features a close up of Danny Shepherd in Scene Eleven at The Inquiry into his immoral behaviour. White adds this note to the stage directions:

> *Note: This is not a naturalistic portrayal of a court case, but an impression of the torments suffered by Danny Shepherd and his enemies/friends during investigation of the Budgiwank scandal.*
> *A window is illuminated upper left, framing the rector, who is dressed in conventional clerical gear.* (209)

The close-up shows Shepherd with an expression of amused resignation as he witnesses the hypocrisy on display in the court:

SHEPHERD: ... for the most part the accusations made against me in this case have been conceived in malice by Archbishop Bigge, his satellite Dean Shute, and other luminaries of the Church. (209)

The Archbishop and Shute are to Shepherd as the ghostly figurations of the phantasmagoria were to the showground spectators – spectres of evil and deceit.

---

8   Margaret Cohen, *Profane Illumination: Walter Benjamin and the Paris of Surrealist Revolution* (Berkeley: University of California Press, 1993), 188, 255.

Standing in front of an illuminated upstage window, he holds onto the crossbars of his raised platform. His suit is neat and buttoned but his elevation looks precarious as he holds onto a metal beam above his head and another angled against his body. His frequent interjections are silenced by the court. The scene begins with the statement by Shepherd from on high and is followed by the disembodied Voice of the Law. Lily Thripp, the madam of the strictly-run Kings Cross establishment where Queenie and Bee had rooms, is the first witness, who reveals that Shepherd referred to Queenie as "Queen of my Heart" (210). Elizabeth, his wife, is also called to the witness stand:

> VOICE OF THE LAW: You are the wife of the defendant. How long have you been married to the Reverend Daniel Shepherd?
>
> ELIZABETH: All my life, I'd say.
>
> VOICE OF THE LAW: Now, now, Mrs. Shepherd, much as one appreciates your loyalty, accuracy is expected in a court of law.
>
> ELIZABETH: Love can't be estimated all that accurately. I can only say I loved my husband even before we met, and married, and made five children together. I repeat I've been married to him all my life. (210)

A general blackout allows time for the court to dissolve before Shepherd is again framed in light, still dressed as a cleric, but contemplating a new life:

> SHEPHERD: ... The hard question is: how can a bankrupt without a stipend launch his appeal? Fortunately, God gave Danny Shepherd the talents of a performing artist He earned a modest living in vaudeville before hearing the call. So, he will simply return to the boards with the Lord at his side. All you who believe in Danny Shepherd will, I hope, rally round him and contribute morally and financially to his rehabilitation. His first performance, in song and dance, and humorous recitations, will be at the Glitz Palace, Sydney, on the night of... [Blackout]. (213–14)

An image of John Gaden as Shepherd in the penultimate Scene Thirteen, shows how Tiddler's Bay is created, as suggested in the text, by a cyclorama depicting the sea and the horizon onto which light is projected to show the passing of the time of day. The character stands centre stage in messianic mode, in a long cassock and bare footed.[9] Sand and driftwood cover the stage floor while audio sounds create further effects of water, whales and wavelets. Wendy Harmer's Elizabeth sits behind him in a long white robe, watching as her husband faces the audience with arms raised, palms open outwards and fingers splayed in a gesture of rapture. His head is raised, and he smiles while looking into the distance. His faithful wife might be looking sceptical or worried as the cyclorama shows a darkening sky. The composition shows the performers scenically arranged and getting ready for another phase in the stage life of Daniel Shepherd.

The final scene is set at the Jerusalem Show in a carnivalesque atmosphere at a showground. The scene begins in darkness with a mixture of merry-go-round music, laughter, voices, sideshow spruikers, animal noises, a gunshot and a voice shouting dramatically that an animal has broken its neck and been destroyed. The voice of a protester can be heard shouting "No caged animals". When the lights go up, "*The interior of cage remains amorphous throughout, a tawny glow flaring to a gold blaze at more dramatic moments*" (223) is visible among the booths and rides. Nat Wormald, as well as Queenie and Bee reappear for the grand finale. Shepherd enters dressed as Dick Whittington, carrying a toy cat to amuse the audience with picaresque tales of life as the Lord Mayor of London, and later as a fortune-teller. After a risque song about the habits of the (genderless/desiring/parasitic) mosquito:

> [*The lights fade. A mix of faith music soars through the theatre: Salvo tambourines, whale song, Kol Nidre, 'O for the Wings of A Dove' (Master Lough's version), Hindu, Greek Orthodox Liturgy, 'Alleluia I'm a Bum', 'My Redeemer' ...*] (229)

The song of the mosquito is followed by the sacred in the lead up to Shepherd's key speech foreshadowing his death; a death he welcomes in the face of a materialist world. He has changed out of his Dick Whittington costume into a robe described as a cross between a medieval monk's robe and a contemporary cassock. The final part of the transformation is a thin grey wig, cut like a monks. In this humble mode he delivers his final sermon:

> Are you for magic? I am. Inadmissible when we are taught to believe in science or nothing. Nothing is better. Science may explode in our faces. So, I am for magic. For dream. For love. That pervasive dream which becomes more reality if we have faith in it. If we can resist abusing them, all our dreams can amount to a *world* faith ... (229)

At the end of the speech, delivered in the form of a critical illumination, Shepherd stands for a few minutes with his hands over his face. In a final evocation of the absurd, Tilda Strutt, the do-gooder of the area, enters to say hello to everyone

---

9   David Wilson, photo, "Wendy Harmer and John Gaden in the State Theatre Company of South Australia production (photo)", in Patrick White, *Collected Plays, Volume II*, 173.

including the audience and then exits. This comic and banal intervention changes the mood in the moments before Shepherd as the stage directions indicate: *Turns quietly, unbolts the gate to the lion's cage, disappears inside. An apocalyptic light blazes, accompanied by a roaring of vengeful beasts* (230). Shepherd's screams are heard emanating from the cage and the crowd is in uproar. The women, Elizabeth, Queenie and Bee embrace in solidarity to deliver a choric dialogue, which alludes to the prophetic knowledge of women in the manner of classical figures such as Hecuba, Andromache and Cassandra:

ELIZABETH: [*weeping*] No need to tell …

QUEENIE: No need …

BEE: … we've known …

ELIZABETH: … we knew, we knew how it would end …

QUEENIE: … from the beginning.

ELIZABETH: The women.

BEE: Always the women.

ELIZABETH: … who know …

THE THREE MOURNING WOMEN: The women … (230)

Chaos ensues, the police and ambulance arrive, and the owner of the circus is already trying to assess insurance claims.

Shepherd on the Rocks evokes the allure and intimation of the theatricality of the phantasmagoria from the light that guides Daniel Shepherd's faith in God to the seductive arcades of Kings Cross and the illusions of the circus world. Shepherd's death in the lion's den, where he finally succumbs to the blazing apocalyptic light, is part self-enchantment and part self-annihilation. For the audience the scene offers a critical illumination of the phantasmagoria made visible through the combined elements of belief, vanity, anti-materialism and disavowal of the body. The object of critique is nominally institutional religion embodied in the church, and rampant material culture. But it is complex in so far as the resolution is not a resolution at all for those who are left behind to pick up the pieces. Shepherd resists the persuasive power of the phantasmagoria of the church and market place only to fall victim to the thrall of an ordinary and fantastic modernity.

***

Critics inevitably expressed doubts about the play. Michael Morley, a Brechtian academic and theatre reviewer, found the work to be very odd, even repellent. First, he finds the adaptation of the story of the Anglican vicar to the Australia context in the 1980s incongruent. White's adaptation, he writes, fails to establish a viable motivation for Danny Shepherd's actions or why the story would be of interest to White and his audience. Morley is equally unimpressed by the dramaturgy that he finds to be "a combination of tired expressionist devices" with "forced and infantile" humour and a "patchwork script".[10] As is common for the reviews of White's plays, critic find the plays full of flaws and shortcomings, but praise the beleaguered cast and crew. In this case, Morley has high praise for the "marvellously inventive comic" skills of Geoffrey Rush, noting Henri Szeps showed a wonderfully "smarmy and oleaginous Shute". Wendy Harmer makes a "brave fist" of Elizabeth but Gaden's Shepherd "is an uncomfortable mix of religious convictions, skirt-chaser and adolescent vaudevillian". Then Morley attacks the negative representation of women and claims that the real-life Rector of Stiffkey was dragged from the lion's cage by a young female lion tamer and not the Strongman.

Pamela Zeplin, on the other hand, begins by admitting she was perplexed, even agitated by the play but then sets out to analyse her response. Agreeing the play is awkward and irritating in parts, she also admits to finding it "very funny, disturbing and bleak".[11] She accepts the plot is "profoundly silly" but frames this as "refreshingly implausible" as events based on real-life happenings inevitably turn out to be. Reflecting on the point of the play, she focuses on how Shepherd's final speech about magic and dreams as opposed to science and linearity could be addressed to the condition of contemporary Australian theatre. Here she is critical of expectations that plots must be plausible and that meaning should be "writ large for the audience". She expresses interest in the poetry, the play's savage wit, and the collisions that cause discomfort. Then she turns her critique to the limitations of Australian theatre:

> In this instance, there exists a hiatus between the skilled efforts of this company [State Theatre Company] and the ambitions of White's play; this situation is analogous to the Budgiwank Experiment. Revolutionary ideas require a flexible framework to germinate, or they become academic, occasionally scandal. More often, they are suspended in limbo. [12]

Patrick White claimed he wrote the play "for all of us and everything we stand for".[13] This included the non-naturalist theatre he wrote for actors who were willing to break with convention and experiment with form. By 1987, theatre had moved

---

10   Michael Morley, "White Slips on his Rocks", *Financial Review*, 15 May 1987, 11–12.
11   Pamela Zeplin, "Shepherd on the Rocks", *New Theatre Australia* (Sept/October, 1987): 32–33.
12   Zeplin, "Shepherd on the Rocks".
13   David Marr, *Patrick White: A Life*, (Milsons Point: Vintage Books, 1992), 626.

on from being a vehicle for a good story worked out in a tight plot. Postdramatic theatre, as theorised by Hans-Thies Lehmann, offers a descriptive category for the multimodal contemporary forms of performance that cast off the strict adherence to narrative drama, as well as an aesthetic based on rational coherence, heroes, and a fictional dramatic world.[14] This mode of theatre had entered the Australian field towards the end of the 1970s, and flourished in the 1980s yet theatre critics would not tolerate such flagrant experimentation and challenging of convention in a mature novelist such as Patrick White. Only one critic recognised that the ways in which *Shepherd on the Rocks* "had not succeeded" were due to the lack of "an appropriate vehicle – a more experimental theatre".[15]

---

14 Hans-Thies Lehmann, *Postdramatic Theatre*, trans. Karen Jürs-Munby (London: Routledge, 2006).
15 Zeplin, "Shepherd on the Rocks".

Conclusion

This book is the product of archival research, deep analysis and critical evaluation of White's theatre in terms of the modernist, theatricalist innovations of the written texts, their live performances, and the critical debates they generated. It has not sought to determine whether Patrick White is a great Australian playwright; instead the focus has been on what Patrick White's plays *do*, in terms of their dramaturgical composition, and how they have been *done* on stage by theatre artists over sixty years. It has been a study of a corpus of work and its lasting influence. If there are embedded judgements in the vocabulary of aesthetic modernism, innovation and experimentation, then the book owns up to these but in doing so, and by their very nature, a certain amount of failure, difficulty and awkwardness is treated as a given rather than the history of a fatal flaw. Focusing on the history of aesthetic modernism in Australia, the book has tracked the particular ways in which the international or European model of modernist theatre has landed and adapted to the local context. Overall, the book has considered its task as redressing the absence of a comprehensive study of White's theatre and re-positioning his work within international studies of aesthetic modernism.

The book has argued that as a body of work, White's theatre (plays plus staging) opened up an important but under recognised stream of modernist, anti-realist, symbolist drama in Australian theatre that continues to shape the present. The history of White's theatre is deeply entwined with aesthetic modernism beginning in the early 1960s in the form of debates about realism and anti- realism, naturalism and anti-naturalism, iconic representation and aesthetic formalism, and prosaic language versus poetics. Aesthetic modernism challenged conservative values, censorship, and repressive taboos around gender and sexuality with White's plays pilloried in the press for their provocations. From the 1980s, White's second playwriting period, the plays engaged more overtly with public issues concerning the anti-nuclear movement, mental illness, capitalist materialism, and environmental issues. They continued in an anti-realist expressionist/symbolist mode and acquired a more overt playfulness with gender and sexuality.

Marginalised subjects, not quite colonised by the dominant heteronormative culture, began to appear more confidently in the later plays. In terms of theatre history, the later plays and revivals of the early plays were immersed in the shift from text dominated, playwright-driven drama to the rise of the director, as the principle creative behind the theatrical interpretation and realisation of the text. White's theatricalist sensibilities came to life with a greater emphasis on theatricality and performativity. Simultaneously, the craft of set designer, as creator of the background to the presentation of the text on stage, shifted to the concept of scenography and a greater collaborative role for the design team.

White's radical challenge to the normative codes of stage naturalism and realist drama might have been neglected were it not for the support of the universities whose theatre departments presented the first performances of the early plays. Even so, the plays posed major challenges, artistically and financially, and their efforts were often undermined by hostile critics' bitter reviews. Stage naturalism, and the plays written for it by Ray Lawler and Richard Beynon, among others, dominated mid-twentieth-century Australian theatre with the effect that White's plays, which foregrounded poetic language and modern themes, as well as visual and spatial metaphor, appeared odd and difficult. A typical review in 1964 described White's plays as "awkwardly constructed and theatrically unconvincing", "difficult, uncomfortable pieces of work … in subject matter and technique", while acknowledging, sometimes, that they had "new things to say in the theatre".[1] As Jim Sharman quipped on the opening night of the Paris Theatre in Sydney in 1978: "Australian critics are constantly on the lookout for losers".[2] White was generally considered to be a great novelist who should have stayed away from the theatre. The undertone implied he was not one of us, meaning theatre literate people. In reviewing the reviews of White's plays over the first four decades, the degree of hostility directed at the playwright is overwhelmingly driven by the narrow frame of reference of the well-made play, *la pièce bien faite*, the nineteenth-century pre-modernist form attributed to French playwright Eugène Scribe, which sought to tell stories in such a way that the audience is kept expectant from beginning to end with carefully paced effects and resolutions.[3] Four decades of Harry Kippax as theatre critic for the *Sydney Morning Herald* did not prevent the innovations and experimentation that bring about change and renewal in the arts, but his reviews set up and defended a culture of judgement and disapproval that ultimately deprived the public of open-minded debate. The language of awkwardness and stylistic plurality was still being applied to White's last play, *Shepherd on the Rocks* in 1987. But by then a new generation of theatre artists including Michael Kantor

---

1   R.F Brissenden, "The Plays of Patrick White", *Meanjin Quarterly* 23, no. 3 (September 1964): 243–56.
2   Katharine Brisbane, *Not Wrong – Just Different: Observations on the Rise of Contemporary Australian Theatre* (Sydney: Currency Press, 2005), 282.
3   John Russell Taylor, *The Rise and Fall of the Well-Made Play* (Oxford: Routledge, 2014), 12.

and Benedict Andrews were about to take the plays into the next century and to commit to the hard work of staging productions of the plays, against the grain of Australian theatre's preference for naturalism and realism. Similar commitments were made by those who created the early scenographies, Desmond Digby, Brian Thomson, and Stephen Curtis, and the performers, especially Robyn Nevin, who inhabited difficult and eccentric, and anti-heroic characters for the first time.

In concluding, the history of White's plays in production exposes the dialectic of modernism in Australian theatre and provides a rich vantage point for the story of aesthetic modernism outside the northern hemisphere, where transformations in aesthetics are continually renewed, for better or worse. These transformations do not take place in an orderly fashion, but in dramatic, theatricalised and performative ways that are as unreliable as the history of one playwright's theatre, but readable for the discontinuity, dissonance and contradictions in a body of work over time. The stage does more than merely reflect cultural change; its dramatic, theatrical and performative qualities stage old, new and emerging ideas in forms and shapes that challenge audiences to think and see in new ways. This is how on a long view, theatre contributes to cultural change by aesthetic means. In Patrick White's plays, the fully-rounded integrated dramatic characters of an older nineteenth century-in-origin realism are stylised and abstracted as embodiments of so many tendencies, colloquialisms, satirical reflections, provocations and attitudes. The book contends that the various productions of the plays over time provide indicative and prophetic images that illuminate transformations in Australian society as processes of modernisation and modernity disrupt a predominantly conservative culture and its theatre.

Works Cited

Adler, Thomas P. "Repetition and regression in *Curse of the Starving Class* and *Buried Child*". In *The Cambridge Companion to Sam Shepard*, edited by M. Roudané, 111–22, Cambridge: Cambridge University Press, 2002.
Akerholt, May-Brit. *Patrick White*. Amsterdam: Rodopi Press, 1988.
Akerholt, May-Brit. "Story into Play: The Two Versions of Patrick White's *A Cheery Soul*". *Southerly* 40, no. 4 (1980): 460–72.
Appia, Adolphe. "From a New Art-Material (c.1902)". In *Twentieth Century Theatre: A Sourcebook*, edited by Richard Drain, 14–15. London: Routledge, 2005.
Armfield, Neil. "Patrick White: A Centenary Tribute". *Meanjin*, 71, no. 2 (2012), 18–28.
Armstrong, Madeleine. "The Professor's Tragedy". *Bulletin*, 28 March 1964.
Artaud, Antonin. "Theatre of Cruelty: First Manifesto (1938)". In *The Routledge Drama Anthology: From Modernism to Contemporary Performance*, edited by Maggie B. Gale and John F. Deeney, 296–301. London: Routledge, 2016.
Artaud, Antonin. *The Theatre and Its Double*. Translated by Mary Caroline Richards. New York: Grove Press, 1958.
Aston, Elaine, and George Savona. *Theatre as a Sign-System*. London: Routledge, 1991.
Australian. "Patrick White Names the Men Who Matter". 26 January 1974.
Australian. "Patrick White Protests to PM". 28 May 1975, 9.
Bache, Byron. "Theatre Review: Night on Bald Mountain, Malthouse Theatre". *Herald Sun*, 12 May 2014.
Baden-Powell, Sue. "Actress Was Rarely Out of Work in Stage and Screen". Obituary, Joan Bruce (1928–2014). *Sydney Morning Herald*, 20 June 2014.
Bailes, Sara Jane. *Performance Theatre and the Poetics of Failure*. London: Routledge, 2010.
Bailey, John. "Malthouse: Vision and Delirium". *RealTime Arts* 67 (June–July 2005): 29.
Balme, Christopher. *The Cambridge Introduction to Theatre Studies*. Cambridge: Cambridge University Press, 2008.
Barbour, Judith. "Cheery Souls and Lost Souls: The Outsiders in Patrick White's Plays". *Southerly* 42, no. 2 (1982): 137–48.
Barnett, David. *Brecht in Practice: Theatre, Theory and Performance*. London: Bloomsbury, 2015.
Barthes, Roland. *Critical Essays*. Translated by Richard Howard. Evanston, IL: Northwestern University Press, 1972.
Baugh, Christopher. *Theatre, Performance and Technology: The Development and Transformation of Scenography*. Basingstoke: Palgrave, 2013.
Bauman, Zygmunt. *Liquid Times: Living in an Age of Uncertainty*. London: Scribe, 2007.

Beckett, Samuel. *The Complete Dramatic Works*. London: Faber, 1986.
Benjamin, Walter. *Understanding Brecht*. Translated by Anna Bostock. London: Verso, 1998.
Bentley, Eric. *The Brecht Commentaries 1943–1986*. New York: Grove Press, 1981.
Blake, Jason. "Tamed by Age, Patrick's First is still in the Pink". *Sydney Morning Herald*, May 22 2017, 26.
Bradby, David, and David Williams. *Directors' Theatre*. New York: St Martin's Press, 1988.
Bray, J. J. "The Ham Funeral". *Meanjin Quarterly* 21, no. 1 (1962): 32–34.
Brecht, Bertolt. "From the Mother Courage Model". In *Brecht on Theatre: The Development of an Aesthetic*, edited and translated by John Willett, 215–222. (1964) London: Methuen, 1984.
Brecht, Bertolt. "The Literarization of the Theatre". In *Brecht on Theatre: The Development of an Aesthetic*. Edited and translated by John Willett, 43–47. (1964) London: Methuen, 1984.
Brejzek, Thea. "The Scenographic (Re-)Turn: Figures of Surface, Space and Spectator in Theatre and Architecture Theory 1680–1980". *Theatre & Performance Design* 1, nos. 1–2 (2015): 17–30.
Brek [Harry Kippax]. "Razzle-Dazzle Over Dog Pack". *Nation*, 22 September 1962, 15–17.
Breton, André. "*First Surrealist Manifesto* (1924) and *Second Surrealist Manifesto* (1929)". In *The Routledge Drama Anthology: From Modernism to Contemporary Performance*, edited by Maggie B. Gale and John F. Deeney, 302–309. London: Routledge, 2016.
Brisbane, Katharine. "Introduction". In *Big Toys*, by Patrick White. Sydney: Currency Press, 1978.
Brisbane, Katharine. *Not Wrong – Just Different: Observations on the Rise of Contemporary Australian Theatre*. Sydney: Currency Press, 2005.
Brissenden, R.F. "The Plays of Patrick White". *Meanjin Quarterly* 23, no. 3 (September 1964): 243–256.
Carlson, Marvin. "Performance Studies and the Enhancement of Theatre Studies". In *The Rise of Performance Studies: Rethinking Richard Schechner's Broad Spectrum*, edited by J. M. Harding and Cindy Rosenthal, 13–22. London: Palgrave Macmillan, 2011.
Carroll, Dennis. "Stage Convention in the Plays of Patrick White". *Modern Drama* 19, no 1 (1976): 11–24.
Coates, Donna Eileen. "Reality Bites: The Impact of the Second World War on the Australian Home Front in Maria Gardner's 'Blood Stained Wattle' and Robin Sheiner's 'Smile, the War Is Over'" in *Antipodes* 23, 1, (June 2009): 48–54.
Cohen, Margaret. "Benjamin's Phantasmagoria: the *Arcades Project*" In *The Cambridge Companion to Walter Benjamin* edited by D. Ferris, 199–220. Cambridge: Cambridge University Press, 2004.
Cohen, Margaret. *Profane Illumination: Walter Benjamin and the Paris of Surrealist Revolution*. Berkeley: University of California Press, 1993.
Cohen, Margaret. "Walter Benjamin's Phantasmagoria". *New German Critique* 48 (Autumn 1989): 87–107.
Covell, Roger. "Patrick White's Plays". *Quadrant* 8, no. 1 (April–May 1964): 7–12.
Covell, Roger. "White Play Opens in Melbourne". *Sydney Morning Herald*, 20 November 1963, 14.
Covell, Roger. "Second Play by Patrick White". *Sydney Morning Herald*, 17 September 1962.
Croggon, Alison. "Night on Bald Mountain Review – Scathing Satire and Sensual Tragedy". *Guardian*, 9 May 2014. https://www.theguardian.com/stage/australia-culture-blog/2014/may/09/night-on-bald-mountain-review-scathing-satire-and-sensual-tragedy
Croggon, Alison. "In which TN Discourses at Length". *Theatre Notes* (blog), 29 December 2010. http://theatrenotes.blogspot.com/2010/12/in-which-ms-tn-discourses-at-length.html
Croggon, Alison. "Review: The Season at Sarsaparilla". *Theatre Notes* (blog), 26 March 2007. http://theatrenotes.blogspot.com/2007/03/review-season-at-sarsaparilla.html
Croggon, Alison. "The Ham Funeral/Journal of a Plague Year". *Theatre Notes* (blog), 19 April 2005. http://theatrenotes.blogspot.com/2005/04/ham-funeraljournal-of-plague-year.html
Cullen, Patricia, Geraldine Vaughan, Zhuoyang Li, Jenna Price, Denis Yu and Elizabeth Sullivan. "Counting Dead Women in Australia: An In-Depth Case Review of Femicide". *Journal of Family Violence* 34 (2019): 1–8. https://doi.org/10.1007/s10896-018-9963-6

Works Cited

Davison, Graeme. *City Dreamers: The Urban Imagination in Australia*. Sydney: New South Press, 2016.

Delgado, Maria M., and Dan Rebellato. "Introduction". In *Contemporary European Theatre Directors: A Companion*, edited by Maria M. Delgado and Dan Rebellato, 1–11. New York: Routledge, 2010.

Diamond, Elin. "Modern Drama/Modernity's Drama". *Modern Drama* 44, no.1 (Spring 2001): 3–15.

Diamond, Elin. *Unmaking Mimesi: Essays on Feminism and Theater*. New York: Routledge, 1997.

Dixon, Steve. *Digital Performance: A History of New Media in Theater, Dance, Performance Art, and Installation*. Cambridge: MIT Press, 2007.

Dow, Steve. "STC's A Cheery Soul". *Saturday Paper*, 17 November 2018.

During, Simon. *Patrick White*. Melbourne: Oxford University Press, 1996.

Dutton, Geoffrey. "Ham Funeral in Adelaide". *Bulletin*, 25 November 1961, 31.

Dyce, J.R. *Patrick White as Playwright*. St Lucia: University of Queensland Press, 1974.

Eastaugh, Kenneth. "This Voice Should Have Stayed at Home". *Daily Mirror*, 28 April 1966.

Eckersall, Peter, Helena Grehan and Edward Scheer, *New Media Dramaturgy: Performance, Media and New Materialism*. London: Palgrave Macmillan, 2017.

Edge, John. "New Growth on Bald Mountain". *Bulletin*, 25 June 1996, 84.

Ellison, John. "Extraordinary, Bewildering White". *Melbourne Times*, 28 September 1983.

Esslin, Martin. "The Theatre of the Absurd". *Tulane Drama Review* 4, no. 4 (May 1960): 3–15.

Euripides, *Electra, Phoenician Women, Bacchae, Iphigenia at Aulis*. Translated by Cecelia Eaton Luschnig and Paul Woodruff. Indianapolis: Hackett Pub., Co., 2011.

Farfan, Penny. "Editorial Comment: 'Modernism'". *Theatre Journal* 65, no. 4 (December 2013): x–xiii.

Fensham, Rachel, and Denise Varney. *The Dolls' Revolution: Australian Theatre and the Cultural Imagination*. Melbourne: Australian Scholarly Publishing, 2005.

Fensham, Rachel. "Modernity and the White Imaginary in Australian Feminist Theatre". *Hecate* 29, no. 1 (2003): 7–18.

Fischer-Lichte, Erika. *The Routledge Introduction to Theatre and Performance Studies*. Edited by Minou Arjomand and Ramona Mosse, translated by Minou Arjomand. Oxford: Routledge, 2014.

Fischer-Lichte, Erika. *The Transformative Power of Performance*. Translated by Saskya Jain. New York: Routledge, 2008.

Fitzpatrick, Kate. *Name Dropping: The Life and Loves of Kate Fitzpatrick*. Sydney: Harper Collins, 2004.

Fitzpatrick, Peter. *After 'The Doll': Australian Drama Since 1955*. Melbourne: Edward Arnold, 1979.

Franklin, Adrian. "A Lonely Society? Loneliness and Liquid Modernity in Australia". *Australian Journal of Social Issues* 47, no.1 (2012): 11–28.

Friedman, Susan Stanford. *Planetary Modernisms: Provocations of Modernity Across Time*. New York: Columbia Press, 2015.

Frow, John. *Genre*. London: Routledge, 2005.

Frykberg, Ian. "Patrick White Sees 'Sinister' Overtones". *Sydney Morning Herald*, 29 November 1975.

Fuchs, Elinor. "Clown Shows: Anti-Theatricalist Theatricalism in Four Twentieth-Century Plays". *Modern Drama* 44, no. 3 (Fall 2001): 337–54.

Fuchs, Elinor, and Una Chaudhuri, eds. *Land/Scape/Theater*. Ann Arbor: University of Michigan Press, 2002.

Fuhrmann, Andrew. "Making Room for Modernism: The 1979 Sydney Theatre Company Production of Patrick White's *A Cheery Soul*", in "Patrick White and Australian Theatrical Modernism," ed. Denise Varney and Sandra D'Urso, special issue, *Australasian Drama Studies: Special Issue*, 71, (2017): 89–111.

Gale, Maggie B. "The Historical Avant-Garde: Performance and Innovation". In *The Routledge Drama Anthology: From Modernism to Contemporary Performance*, edited by Maggie B. Gale and John F. Deeney, 165–188. London: Routledge, 2016.

Gallasch, Keith. "Keith Gallasch in the Worlds of Patrick White and Ronnie Burkett". *RealTime* 78 (April–May 2007). http://www.realtimearts.net/article/78/8519
Gilbert, Helen, and Jacqueline Lo. *Performance and Cosmopolitics: Cross-Cultural Transactions in Australasia*. London: Palgrave, 2007.
Gilbert, Helen, and Joanne Tompkins. *Post-Colonial Drama: Theory, Practice, Politics*. London: Routledge, 1996.
Ginters, Laura. "Before The Ham Funeral: 'The Young Man Appears' – John Tasker Returns Home," in "Patrick White and Australian Theatrical Modernism," ed. Denise Varney and Sandra D'Urso, special issue, *Australasian Drama Studies* 71 (October 2017): 13–41.
Gobert, R. Darren. "The Field of Modern Drama, or Arcadia". *Modern Drama* 58, no. 3 (2015): 299. https://doi.org/10.3138/md.0761.
Gough, Sue. "Driving Miss Docker". *Bulletin*, 23 June 1992, 103–4.
Groeneveld, Leanne. "Modernist Medievalism and the Expressionist Morality Play: Georg Kaiser's *From Morning to Midnight*". *Film and Media Studies* 16 (2019): 81–101. Doi: https://doi.org/10.2478/ausfm-2019-0005
Hallett, Bryce. "Out of the Darkness, A Pioneering Play". *Sydney Morning Herald*, 4 August 2000, 18.
Hallett, Bryce. "A Cheery Soul". *Australian*, 10 May 1996.
Harris, Frank. "Corruption is the Theme". *Daily Mirror*, 30 July 1977.
Harris, Frank. "It's a Good Season – At Last". *Daily Mirror*, 10 November 1976.
Harris, Max. "The Ham Funeral". *Theatregoer* 2, nos. 2/3 (December–January 1961/62): 14–15.
Healey, Ken. "Clergyman's Kings Cross Odyssey". *Sydney Morning Herald*, 12 May 1987, 16.
Hernandez, Alex Eric. *The Making of British Bourgeois Tragedy: Modernity and the Art of Ordinary Suffering*. Oxford: Oxford University Press, 2019.
Hoffmann, Beth. "Bloody Mess Review". *Theatre Journal* 58, no. 4 (December 2006): 701–03.
Hutton, Geoffrey. "Bitter Satire of A Cheery Soul". *Age*, 21 November 1963, 5.
Hutton, Geoffrey. "Patrick White is a Born Playwright". *Age*, 17 October 1962.
Jameson, Fredric. *A Singular Modernity*. London: Verso, 2002.
Jones, Brian. "Whitlam and the Stars Draw 11,000 to Opera House Rally". *Sydney Morning Herald*, 14 May 1974, 1.
Jürs-Munby, Karen. "Introduction". In *Postdramatic Theatre* by Hans-Thies Lehmann, translated by Karen Jürs-Munby, 1–15. London: Routledge, 2006.
Kablean, Carrie. "Goats, Bells and All". *Sunday Telegraph*, 14 July 1996, 156.
Kay, Paul. "Australia's Uranium Mines: Past and Present". Science, Technology, Environment and Resource Group, Parliamentary Library, Parliament of Australia. https://www.aph.gov.au/Parliamentary_Business/Committees/Senate/Former_Committees/uranium/rerepo/c07
Kelly, Veronica. "Spatialising the Ghosts of Anzac in the Plays of Sydney Tomholt: The Absent Soldier and the War Memorial". *Australian Literary Studies* 23, no. 1 (2007): 18–35.
Kessell, Norman. "New White Play is Event for the Stage". *Daily Telegraph*, 30 July 1977.
Kessell, Norman. "Could This Really Be Us?". *Sun*, 15 May 1963.
Kiernan, Brian. "From *The Ham Funeral* to *Signal Driver*: Patrick White on Stage", *Sydney Morning Herald*, 6 March 1982, 46.
Kiernander, Adrian. "Chain-Saw Voice Rips into Society". *Australian*, 8 June 1992.
Kippax, Harry. "White Play Still Disappoints Under Sharman Direction". *Sydney Morning Herald*, 23 January 1984, 10.
Kippax, Harry "Patrick White's Curious New Play", *Sydney Morning Herald*, 8 March 1982.
Kippax, Harry. "A Cheery Soul – To Cheer Us Up". *Sydney Morning Herald*, 19 January 1979.
Kippax, Harry. "Point Piper Calls the Tune in White Play". *Sydney Morning Herald*, 30 July 1977.
Kippax, Harry. "The Novelist as Dramatist". *Sydney Morning Herald*, 23 October 1965.
Kippax, Harry (Brek). "Royal 'Season' – and Beyond". *Nation*, 1 June 1963, 17.
Kruse, Axel. "Patrick White's 'Big Toys': White and his Critics". *Quadrant* (September 1977): 24–25.

Works Cited

Lancaster, Lynne. "Patrick White's Play is Glowingly Brought to Life in This Siren Theatre Co Production for Griffin Theatre". *Arts Hub*, 22 May 2017.
Larkin, John. "Tramlines of Time and Life". *Sunday Press*, 15 October, 1983.
Lehmann, Hans-Thies. *Postdramatic Theatre*. Translated by Karen Jürs-Munby. London: Routledge, 2006.
Luckhurst, Mary. *Dramaturgy: A Revolution*. Cambridge: Cambridge University Press, 2005.
McCallum, John. *Belonging: Australian Playwriting in the Twentieth Century*. Sydney: Currency Press, 2009.
McCallum, John. "Night Chillingly Excites". *Australian*, 13 July 1996.
McCann, Andrew. "Decomposing Suburbia: Patrick White's Perversity". *Australian Literary Studies* 18, no. 4 (1998): 56–71.
Macartney, Keith. "Patrick White's Four Plays". *Meanjin Quarterly* 24, no. 4 (December 1965): 528–30.
Macartney, Keith. "Patrick White's 'A Cheery Soul'". *Meanjin Quarterly* 23, no. 1 (March 1964): 93–95.
McGillick, Paul. "The Image as Performance". *Australian Financial Review, Weekend Review*. 25 November 1989, 11.
McGregor, Richard "Thousands March in Rain Against Nuclear Weapons" *Sydney Morning Herald*, 5 April, 1982.
McKinney, Joslin. "Scenographic Materialism, Affordance and Extended Cognition in Kris Verdonck's ACTOR #1". *Theatre and Performance Design* 1, nos. 1–2 (2015): 79–93.
McNamara, Staunton. "Two Seasons of 'Sarsaparilla'". *Theatregoer* 2, no. 12, (December 1962): 20–21.
McPherson, Angus. "A Cheery Soul". *Limelight*, 10 November 2018. https://www.limelightmagazine.com.au/reviews/a-cheery-soul-sydney-theatre-company/
Mao, Douglas, and Rebecca L. Walkowitz. "The New Modernist Studies". *PMLA* 123, no. 3 (2008): 737–48.
Marr, David. "White's London". In *Patrick White Beyond the Grave*, edited by Ian Henderson and Anouk Lang, 68–80. London: Anthem Press, 2015.
Marr, David. *Patrick White Letters*. Chicago: University of Chicago Press, 1996.
Marr, David. "Quite a Night on Bald Mountain". *Sydney Morning Herald*, 9 July 1996, 14.
Marr, David. *Patrick White: A Life*. Milsons Point: Vintage Books, 1992.
Marshall, Jonathan. "Michael Kantor's New Malthouse Brew". *Realtime* 65. http://www.realtimearts.net/article/65/7751.
Masters, Verity. "Driver Makes a Routine Stop to Put Down Women". *Australian*, 7 September 1983.
Menzies, Robert. "The Forgotten People" [Speech], 1942. http://www.liberals.net/theforgottenpeople.htm
Meyrick, Julian. *Australian Theatre After the New Wave*. Leiden: Brill Rodopi, 2018.
Meyrick, Julian. "Modernist Drama Decried: Patrick White, Spoiled Identity". *Australasian Drama Studies* 71 (October 2017): 42–67.
Mildenhall, Kelly. "The Ham Funeral". *Adelaide Theatre Guild*. 4 March 2012.
Milne, Geoffrey. *Theatre Australia (Un)limited: Australian Theatre Since the 1950s*. Amsterdam: Rodopi, 2004.
Morley, Michael. "White Slips on His Rocks". *Australian Financial Review*, 15 May 1987, 11–12.
Morton, Timothy. *Hyperobjects: Philosophy and Ecology after the End of the World*. Minneapolis: University of Minnesota, 2013.
Moses, John. "Ship of Fools Becalmed by Odd Lack of Mystery". *Australian*, 23 January 1984, 8.
Mouffe, Chantal. *Agonistics: Thinking the World Politically*. London: Verso, 2013.
Müller, Heiner. *A Heiner Müller Reader*. Edited and translated by Carl Weber. Baltimore, MD: Johns Hopkins University Press, 2001.
Murphet, Julian. "Introduction: On the Market and Uneven Development". *Affirmations of the Modern* 1, no. 1 (2013): 1–20.

Murphet, Richard. *Acts of Resistance in Late Modernist Theatre: Writing and Directing in Contemporary Theatre Practice*. Amsterdam: Brill, 2019.

Neher, Casper. "Drawing for *The Caucasian Chalk Circle*". In *Bertolt Brecht 1898–1956: Zeit, Leben, Werk: eine Bildmappe*. By Bertolt Brecht, Werner Hecht and Karl-Heinz Drescher. Berlin: Henschelverlag Kunst und Gessellschaft, 1978.

Neill, Rosemary. "Sex and Alma Lusty, the Landlady of a Dangerous Age". *Australian*, 24 February 2012, 17.

Neill, Rosemary. "Drama Falters in House of Words". *Australian*, 16 November 1989, 12.

Neutze, Ben. "The Ham Funeral Review (Griffin Theatre, Sydney)". *Daily Review*, 22 May 2017. https://dailyreview.com.au/ham-funeral-review-griffin-theatre-sydney/

Nunley, John, Cara McCarty, John Emigh and Lesley Ferris. *Masks: Faces of Culture*. New York: Harry N. Abrams, 1999.

O'Donnell, David. "Staging Modernity in the 'New Oceania': Modernism in Australian, New Zealand and Pacific Islands Theatre". In *The Modernist World*, edited by Allana Lindgren and Stephen Ross, 282–90. London: Routledge, 2015.

Packer, Ben. "Night on Bald Mountain (Malthouse Theatre)". *Limelight*, 23 May 2014. https://www.limelightmagazine.com.au/reviews/theatre-review-night-on-bald-mountain-malthouse-theatre/

Palmer, Susan. "Charisma and Abdication: A Study of the Leadership of Bhagwan Shree Rajneesh". *Sociological Analysis* 49, no. 2 (1988): 119–135.

Pender, Anne. "Robyn Nevin, Patrick White and the Art of the Modern in Australian Theatre," in "Patrick White and Australian Theatrical Modernism," ed. Denise Varney and Sandra D'Urso, special issue, *Australasian Drama Studies* 71, (2017): 68–88.

Pender, Anne. "Kerry Walker, Patrick White and the Faces of Australian Modernism". *Coolabah* 9 (2012): 75–87.

Platt, Len. "Popular Theater". In *The Cambridge Companion to Modernist Culture*, edited by Celia Marshik, 221–36. Cambridge: Cambridge University Press, 2014.

Poll, Melissa. *Robert Lepage's Scenographic Dramaturgy: The Aesthetic Signature At Work* London: Palgrave, 2018.

Preston, John. "Disaster Turns into Triumph". *Australian Financial Review, Weekend Review*, 17 May 1996, 15.

Prior, Yoni. "Reclaiming the Middle Ground: The Case of the Malthouse Theatre". *Double Dialogues* 'In/Stead', no. 2 (Winter 2008) http://www.doubledialogues.com.

Radic, Leonard. "White Makes Cheery Return". *Age*, 3 March 1994, 15.

Radic, Leonard. "A Satirical Side of White". *Age*, 1 October 1983.

Radic, Leonard. "White's Gentle Look at Partners in Misfortune". *Age*, 15 September 1983, 14.

Rae, Paul. *Real Theatre: Essays in Experience*. Cambridge: Cambridge University Press, 2019.

Rees, Lesley. *The Making of Australian Drama: A Historical and Critical Survey from the 1830s to the 1970s*. London: Angus and Robertson, 1973.

Reynolds, Malvina. "Malvina Reynolds: Song Lyrics and Poems: Little Boxes [Pete Seeger cover]". Schoder Music Company, 1963. http://people.wku.edu/charles.smith/MALVINA/mr094.htm

Richardson, Owen. "The Ham Funeral". *Age*, 24 April 2005, 32.

Roach, Vicky. "Night on a Precipice". *Daily Telegraph*, 12 July 1996, 45.

Roberts, Alan. "Patrick White: The Inner Struggle", *The Advertiser, Saturday Review*, 13 February, 1982.

Rooney, Brigid. *Suburban Space, the Novel and Australian Modernity*. London: Anthem Press, 2018.

Ross, Stephen, and Allana Lindgren. "Introduction". In *The Modernist World*, edited by Allana Lindgren and Stephen Ross, 1–13. London: Routledge, 2015.

Sartre, Jean Paul. "A Fundamental Idea of Husserl's Phenomenology: Intentionality". In *Critical Essays (Situations I)*, 40–46. Translated by Chris Turner. London: Seagull, 2010.

Saw, Ron. "Everything But the Kitchen Sink". *Daily Mirror*, 23 May 1963.

Works Cited

Schafer, Elizabeth. "A Ham Funeral: Patrick White, Collaboration and Neil Armfield". *Australian Studies* 3 (2011): 1–24.

Scheer, Anna Teresa. *Christos Schlingesief: Staging Chaos, Performing Politics and Theatrical Phantasmagoria*. London: Bloomsbury, 2019.

Shand, John. "A Cheery Soul Review: Surrealism, Anglicanism, Carnal Desire and Satire". *Sydney Morning Herald*, 11 November 2018.

Sharman, Jim. *Blood and Tinsel: A Memoir*. Melbourne: Miegunyah Press, 2008.

Standish, H.A. "'Sarsaparilla' is Challenging". *Herald Sun*, 14 October 1962.

Steffen, Will, Wendy Broadgate and Lisa Deutsch. "The Trajectory of the Anthropocene: The Great Acceleration". *Anthropocene Review* 2, no. 1 (2015): 81–98.

Sunday Mail. "Drama Has Force". 18 November 1961.

Sydney Morning Herald. "No Knights for Patrick White". 23 June 1976, 24.

Sydney Morning Herald. "White Declines Honour". 30 November 1963.

Tasker, John. "Review: 'The Season at Sarsaparilla'". *Theatre-Australia* (Nov–Dec 1976), 17.

Tasker, John. "Notes on 'The Ham Funeral'". *Meanjin Quarterly* 23, no. 3 (September 1964): 299–303.

Taylor, Andrew. "Audacious Director Benedict Andrews Stamps His Style on a Literary Giant". *Sydney Morning Herald*, 27 February 2007.

Taylor, John Russell. *The Rise and Fall of the Well-Made Play*. Oxford: Routledge, 2014.

Thomson, Helen. "Rare Level of Quality". *Age*, 9 May 1996, 17.

Tidermann, Harold. "A Dobell Canvas Comes to Life". *Advertiser*, 16 November 1961.

Times (London). "Putting the Theatre Across in Australia". 15 July 1963.

Tompkins, Joanne. *Unsettling Space: Contestations in Contemporary Australian Theatre*. London: Palgrave Macmillan, 2006.

Tongue, Cassie. "A Cheery Soul Review". *Time Out*, 11 November 2018.

Tongue, Cassie. "The Ham Funeral". *Time Out*, 22 May 2017.

Turnbull, Sue. "Mapping the Vast Suburban Tundra: Australian Comedy from Dame Edna to Kath and Kim". *International Journal of Cultural Studies* 11, no. 1 (2008): 15–32.

Varney, Denise. "Australian Modernists in London: William Dobell's *The Dead Landlord* and Patrick White's *The Ham Funeral*". *Humanities* 5, no. 76 (2016): 1–10.

Varney, Denise. *Radical Visions 1968–2008: The Impact of the Sixties on Australian Drama*. Amsterdam: Rodopi, 2011.

Varney, Denise, and Sandra D'Urso, eds. "Patrick White and Australian Theatrical Modernism". Special issue, *Australasian Drama Studies* 71, (2017).

Varney, Denise, and Sandra D'Urso. *Australian Theatre, Modernism and Patrick White: Governing Culture*. London: Anthem Books, 2018.

Veitch, Carol. "Patrick's 'Unfair' to Ivy". *Herald*, 20 September 1983, 32.

Waites, James. "Armfield Glows with White Magic". *Sydney Morning Herald*, 12 July 1996, 12.

Ward, Peter. "No Human Grandeur in White's Bleak Night". *Australian*, 11 June 1996, 12.

Ward, Peter. "White Weaves a Cloth of Faith and More". *Australian*, 11 May 1987, 6.

Ward, Peter. "White's Suburban Rituals Withstand Time". *Australian*, 26 November 1984.

Ward, Peter. "Netherwood is White Magic". *Australian*, 13 June 1983, 8.

Warden, Claire Altree. "The Shadows and the Rush of Light: Ewan MacColl and Expressionist Drama". *New Theatre Quarterly* 23, no. 4 (November 2007), 317–25. https://doi.org/10.1017/S0266464X07000231

White, Patrick. *Collected Plays Volume I: The Ham Funeral, The Season at Sarsaparilla, A Cheery Soul, Night on Bald Mountain*. Sydney: Currency Press, 1985.

White, Patrick. *Collected Plays, Volume II: Big Toys, Signal Driver, Netherwood, Shepherd on the Rocks*. Sydney: Currency Press, 1994.

White, Patrick. *Flaws in the Glass: A Self-Portrait*. (1981) London: Vintage, 1998.

White, Patrick. *Patrick White Speaks*. (1958) Sydney: Primavera Press, 1989.

White, Patrick. *The Vivisector*. London: Vintage, 1994.

Witkiewicz, Stanislas Ignacy. "From On a New Type of Play (1920)". In *Twentieth-Century Theatre: A Sourcebook*, edited by Richard Drain, 35–37. London: Routledge, 1995.
Woodhead, Cameron. "It's Been a Golden Year on the Stage: The Year in Theatre". *Age*, 27 December 2010, 12.
Woolf, Virginia. *A Room of One's Own*. (1945) London: Penguin, 2000.
Worby, Gus. "Signal Driver", *Theatre Australia*, May, 1982, 33.
Zeplin, Pamela. "Shepherd on the Rocks". *New Theatre Australia*, (Sept/October, 1987): 32–33.

Primary Sources

Annotations in Kerry Walker's *Ham Funeral* script. Kerry Walker Papers, 1979–2004, Mitchell Library, MLMSS 7566 1 (2).
Big Toys. The Old Tote Company, Sydney, Photographs by Brett Hilder, 1977. Theatre program. NIDA Archive.
Sharman, Jim. "Director's Introduction". *Big Toys*. The Old Tote Company, Sydney, 27 July, 1977. Theatre program. NIDA Archive.
Shepherd on the Rocks, The State Theatre Company of South Australia. Adelaide, 1987. Theatre program, Patrick White Collection, National Library of Australia.
Sumner, John. "About the Play". *A Cheery Soul*. Union Theatre Repertory Company, Union Theatre, Melbourne University, 19 November 1963. Theatre program. MTC Archive, University of Melbourne Library.
Tasker, John. "Director's Script, Adelaide University Theatre Guild". John Tasker Collection 1961/2, Adelaide Festival Performing Arts Collection Archive.
West, John. *Showtime*. Aired 31 July 1977, on ABC Radio. Transcript NIDA Archives.
White, Patrick. "Author's Note on THE HAM FUNERAL". World Premiere Season at Union Hall, Adelaide University Theatre Guild, 15–25 November 1961. Theatre program. Patrick White Collection, Series 1477, Barr Smith Library Adelaide, The University of Adelaide.
White, Patrick and Australian National University. "Role of the Australian Citizen in a Nuclear War". Centre for Continuing Education, 1983. Manuscript. Patrick White Papers MS9982, National Library of Australia.

Letters

Hutchison, Neil to Charles Wicks. 15 April 1961. State Records of South Australia 1962. Adelaide Festival Correspondence 1959–62, GRG 153/ 36/ 1.
Medlin, Harry to Patrick White, 30 September 1962. Theatre Guild Collection, Barr Smith Library, University of Adelaide.
Medlin, Harry to Patrick White. 27 July 1963. Patrick White Collection, Series 1477, Barr Smith Library, The University of Adelaide
Tasker, John to George Mayo, Deputy Chairman Guild Theatre, 16 April 1964. Patrick White Collection, Series 1477, Barr Smith Library, The University of Adelaide
White, Patrick to Beryl Sheasby. 10 February 1964. Patrick White Collection, Series 1477, Barr Smith Library, The University of Adelaide.
White, Patrick to Beryl Sheasby. 19 October 1962. Patrick White Collection, Series 1477, Barr Smith Library, University of Adelaide.
White, Patrick to Desmond Digby. 15 August 1963. MS 10056/1, National Library of Australia.
White, Patrick to Desmond Digby. 2 June 1963. Papers of Desmond Digby, MS 10056/1/1, National Library of Australia.
White, Patrick to Desmond Digby. 15 March 1963. Patrick White Collection, Series 1477, Barr Smith Library, University of Adelaide.
White, Patrick to Desmond Digby. 8 March 1963. MS 9982/1.1/12, National Library of Australia.

Works Cited

White, Patrick to Harry Medlin. 10 August 1963. Patrick White Collection, Series 1477, Barr Smith Library, University of Adelaide.
White, Patrick to Harry Medlin. 17 July 1963. Patrick White Collection, Series 1477, Barr Smith Library, University of Adelaide.
White, Patrick to Harry Medlin. 3 October 1962. Patrick White Collection, Series 1477, Barr Smith Library, University of Adelaide.

Photos

Wilson, David, *Signal Driver* Premiere, Adelaide Festival of Arts, Lighthouse Theatre, 5 March, 1983. Patrick White Collection, Series 1477, Barr Smith Library, University of Adelaide.
Cullin, Hedley. Folios Series 662, Box 5, 1477, Patrick White Collection, Series 1477, Barr Smith Library, University of Adelaide.
Photos, Adelaide Theatre Guild. Patrick White Collection, Series 1477, Barr Smith Library, University of Adelaide.
Miss Quodling's Shack and Goatyards, photo. *Night on Bald Mountain*. Union Building, University of Adelaide, 9 March, 1964. Barr Smith Library, University of Adelaide. Photographer: Sheridan Photography.
Nita Pannell as Miss Quodling, photo. *Night on Bald Mountain*. Union Theatre, University of Adelaide, 9 March, 1964. Barr Smith Library, University of Adelaide. Photographer: Sheridan Photography. Archive
Interior, Photo. *Night on Bald Mountain*. Union Theatre, University of Adelaide, 9 March, 1964. Barr Smith Library, University of Adelaide. Photographer: Sheridan Photograph. Archive

Interviews

Armfield, Neil. Interviewed by Sandra D'Urso. Sydney, 9 January 2018.
Fitzpatrick, Kate. Interviewed by Sandra D'Urso. Sydney, 23 August, 2018.
Gaul, Kate. Interview by Denise Varney by phone from Melbourne, 26 September 2019.
Marr, David. Interviewed by Sandra D'Urso. Sydney, 25 October 2017.
Sharman, Jim. Interviewed by Hazel de Berg. 19 February 1976. NLA.obj.192631976. Tape 3, National Library of Australia.
Thomson, Brian. Interviewed by Sandra D'Urso. Sydney, 18 May 2018.

Index

Aboriginal Australians *see* identity: Indigenous Australians
abuse 43, 62
  sexual 43, 139, 145, 150
Adelaide Festival 3, 31, 48, 55, 60, 75, 76, 81, 90, 104, 127, 138, 165, 166
aesthetics 8, 11, 115, 175, 177, 187
Andrews, Benedict 16, 17, 19, 98, 100, 111, 112, 114, 115, 116, 137, 144, 166, 173, 187
anti-nuclear movement 19, 71, 159, 166, 185
Armfield, Neil 2, 16, 19, 55, 67, 82–85, 87, 106, 108–110, 115, 120, 126–127, 130, 135, 137, 142–145, 152, 166, 170–173
Artaud, Antonin 11, 38, 45, 108, 122, 156
Aurora Australis 15, 37, 58, 166, 172, 173, 177
Australian Elizabethan Theatre Trust 2, 21, 48, 99
authoritarianism 8, 19, 31

Beckett, Samuel 5, 10, 27, 141, 167, 168, 170–172
Belvoir St Theatre 19, 75, 86, 87–90, 130, 135, 137, 142, 171, 172–173
Benjamin, Walter 15, 33, 177
Beynon, Richard 2, 186
Big Toys 1, 15, 19, 27, 44, 51–54, 152, 160–165, 174
Borghesi, Anna 19, 137
bourgeois values 125, 157, 165
Boyd, Robin 110
Brecht, Bertholt 5, 15, 23, 31, 33, 34, 47, 53, 78, 81, 108, 120, 121, 122, 125, 126, 157
Brek *see* Kippax, Harry
Bruce, Joan 77, 81, 140, 141
Buzo, Alex 16, 49, 104

Caldwell, Zoe 17, 82, 99, 100, 102, 113
capitalism 8, 54, 157, 173, 185
carnivalesque 59, 60, 67, 175, 181
Carroll, Dennis 26, 46–47
Carroll, Peter 19, 98, 112–113, 124, 144, 146, 148, 173
censorship 22, 31, 50, 83, 185
Cheery Soul, A 3, 16, 19, 27, 28–29, 34–39, 115, 117–120, 121–125, 126–135, 159
Chekhov, Anton 61, 154
childlessness 84, 114
circus 67–71, 90, 171, 172, 175, 182
class 2, 9, 15, 28, 39, 40, 49, 53, 54, 80, 84, 100, 104, 150, 156, 160, 162
clowns 17, 78, 93, 125, 133, 169
colonialism 11, 22, 58, 65, 169
Comeadow, John 20, 175
comedy 6, 55, 78, 89, 102, 118–119, 123, 139, 144
Company B *see* Belvoir St Theatre
consciousness 6, 7, 9, 25, 57, 60, 77, 86, 157, 169
  existential 97
Cook, Adam 75, 86, 90
corruption 29, 43, 49, 53, 163
Cousins, Robert 111, 114
Covell, Roger 5, 46, 102, 117–120
Cramphorn, Rex 105, 153
cross-gender 65, 112, 138, 144, 173
cruelty 26, 38, 45, 98, 108, 122, 142, 150, 156–158, 165
Cullen, Hedley 77–78, 80, 100, 102
Cullen, Max 84, 105, 107, 161
Curtis, Stephen 109, 167, 170, 172, 187

Dead Landlord, The (painting) 23
desire 28, 40, 54, 63, 111, 165, 169
dialogic 1, 8, 11, 25, 33, 52, 69, 115, 176
Dickson, Wendy 3, 82, 104, 106, 108, 109, 139–141, 146
Digby, Desmond 37, 99–101, 108, 115, 117–118, 121, 135, 187
directors 16, 18, 77, 79, 115, 153
  collaboration 19, 105, 137, 143, 152
  rise of 105, 153, 186
disability 62, 138
Dobell, William 23
Docker, Miss 4, 7, 34–39, 47, 87, 117–125, 127–130, 131–135
do-gooder 2, 117, 175, 181
Doll school 2, 3
domesticity 34, 43, 81, 109, 114–115, 137
  drag 57, 163; *see also* cross-gender
    dramaturgy 5, 13–15, 24, 38, 46, 52, 53, 65, 78, 121, 126, 135, 143, 146, 155, 165, 174, 183

economy 28
  matrimonial 56
embodiment 25, 29, 53, 98, 150, 165, 187
empathy 58, 70, 119, 150
enchantment 20, 112, 145, 175, 176–177
environment, natural 41, 50, 56, 82, 137, 161, 185
Esson, Louis and Hilda 9
ethics 19, 41, 55
Everage, Dame Edna 28, 97–98, 108
everyday 5, 7, 11, 16, 23, 32, 36, 88–90, 97, 127, 159, 164, 168
  objects 53
Everyman/Everywoman 55, 56, 59
exile 158
expressionism 5, 7, 22, 27, 76, 85, 86, 88, 90, 118, 120, 183

family 6, 22, 30, 31–34, 39, 43, 52, 60–61, 89–92, 99, 104, 106, 139, 154, 163, 167, 178
Farfan, Penny 12
Ferguson, Dale 19, 127, 130, 135, 137, 146
Flaws in the Glass 49, 59
Forsyth, Julie 87–90, 128, 146, 148, 149, 151
fourth wall 30, 76, 77, 93
Freud, Sigmund 63

Gaden, John 112, 171–172, 175, 180, 183
Gaul, Kate 75, 80, 86, 93–95, 115
gender 15, 39, 53, 62, 80, 93, 101, 172, 185

ambiguity 63
fluidity 19, 20, 54, 112, 144, 173
roles 103, 173
gestus 15, 34, 53, 64, 81, 101, 125
goodness 34, 38, 43, 128, 133, 148; *see also* do-gooder
great acceleration 49, 174
grotesque, the 9, 37, 38, 60, 98, 125, 133

Ham Funeral, The 3, 7, 10, 18, 21, 22–28, 31, 54, 76–81, 82–85, 86–89, 90–92, 93–95, 115, 129, 139, 156, 167
homoeroticism 63, 107, 164, 165
Huebsch, Ben 2
humanity and human relationships 8, 20, 25, 40, 41, 59, 78, 97, 110, 129, 156, 164, 173
Humphries, Barry 50, 97, 108, 110; *see also* Everage, Dame Edna
Hutchison, Neil 2, 17
hysteria 45, 63, 132

idealism 42, 47, 70, 156
identity 16, 57, 61, 63, 73, 108, 112, 125, 154, 162, 164, 165
  illumination 17, 20, 30, 83, 93, 124, 176–178, 182
  Indigenous Australians 12, 22, 58, 66, 71, 169
institutionalisation 62, 83, 137
interiority 9, 38, 41, 85, 121

Jung, Karl 25, 85

Kantor, Michael 16, 75, 79, 86–87, 89, 93, 115, 153, 166, 186
Kemp, Jenny 10, 127, 128, 153
Kippax, Harry 2, 17, 38, 45, 47–48, 65, 68, 82, 101–102, 121, 142, 143, 155–158, 165, 186

land rights 22, 49, 174; *see also* identity: Indigenous Australians
Landlady, the 24, 25–26, 77, 80–82, 84–85; *see also* Lusty, Alma
landscape 8, 17, 41, 45
Lascaris, Manoly 6, 28
Lawler, Ray 2, 186; *see also Doll* school
  Summer of the Seventeenth Doll 2
Lehmann, Hans-Thies 13, 153, 184
light 17, 20, 29, 37, 58, 76, 87, 93, 101, 118, 131, 140, 172, 176–177; *see also* identity: illumination
Lighthouse Company *see* Lighthouse Theatre

Index

Lighthouse Theatre 19, 55, 108, 128, 137, 152, 166, 167
loneliness 34, 108, 114, 117, 123, 129, 135
loss 25, 61, 97, 142, 151
Lovejoy, Amanda 109
Lusty, Alma 7, 15, 24, 25, 26, 27, 47, 54, 72, 77, 78–81, 84, 87–90, 91, 93, 103, 129, 170
Lusty, Will 24–26, 54, 77, 80–81, 85, 89, 92, 93
Lutton, Matthew 19, 137, 146–151, 152

MacColl, Ewan 7
magic 5, 14, 67, 71, 177, 181, 183
Malthouse Theatre 19, 75, 79, 86–90, 137, 153
Marr, David 2, 6–7, 22, 51, 68, 106, 145, 155, 167
marriage 25, 43, 51, 54, 56, 80, 137, 142, 150, 167
masculinity 33, 109, 112, 115, 165
masquerade 61, 63–65, 144, 154, 157, 173
materialism 8, 32, 59, 98, 172, 185
mayhem 35, 45, 65
melodrama 11, 26, 30, 45, 78, 102, 141, 144, 156
memory 34, 37, 57, 111, 118, 119, 131
mental health 132, 138, 154, 157
metaphysics 5, 7, 10, 36, 59, 105, 168, 176
metatheatrical 14, 23, 24, 27, 86, 121, 153
mimicry 63, 64
mining 11, 50, 52–54, 114–116; *see also* uranium mining
misogyny 62, 173
modernism 1, 3, 5, 8–13, 17–18, 22, 26, 38, 46, 48, 49, 55, 73, 78, 79, 95, 97, 104, 116, 121–122, 128, 137, 144, 168, 175, 177, 185–187
modernity 8, 10, 11, 19, 22, 23, 34, 48, 51, 59, 71, 72, 73, 101, 110–112, 123, 137, 166, 174, 177, 182, 187
morality 19, 43, 51, 55, 67, 69, 151
morality play 55, 59, 60
Müller, Heiner 153
Murphet, Julian 12
Murphet, Richard 10, 153
Mussorgsky, Modest 11, 20, 45, 67, 143

naturalism 3, 9, 46, 86, 102, 119–123, 135, 185, 186
 anti-naturalism 2, 4, 9
Netherwood 7, 15, 19, 60–67, 114, 128, 137, 152–158
Nevin, Robyn 3, 39, 84, 85, 98, 105, 108, 115, 120, 121–125, 127, 128–130, 135, 187
New Wave 11, 16, 46–47, 49, 105, 108, 128, 133, 170

Newton, Helmut 119
Night on Bald Mountain 3, 11, 19–20, 21, 40–45, 47, 54, 59, 65, 67, 78, 104, 138–141, 142–145, 146–152, 158; *see also* Quodling, Miss
non-conformists *see* outsiders
nuclear power 37, 44, 59, 159, 173; *see also* uranium mining
nuclear war 44, 60, 159, 166, 173, 177

objects 14, 32, 37, 53, 63, 91, 93, 101, 111, 115, 140, 154, 164, 176
Old Tote Theatre Company 16, 20, 104, 160
ordinary, the 29, 55, 67, 98–99, 112, 159, 168
Ostoja-Kotkowski, J. L. 76–77, 79, 91
outsiders 39, 59, 67, 137, 141, 154, 156, 158

Pannell, Nita 117, 119–120, 138, 139, 141
Paterson, Ailsa 90, 91
patriarchy 10
Peirse, Sarah 39, 132–133, 136
performative, the 7, 11, 15–17, 29, 70, 73, 98, 118, 125, 153, 170, 173, 186
phantasmagoria 177–178, 182
Phillips, Jacquy 90, 109, 113, 158, 175
play text 15, 21, 105, 122, 135, 145, 153
Playhouse Adelaide Festival Centre 19, 108, 155, 175
poetics 17, 57, 93, 185
postcolonialism 11
privilege 41, 43, 49, 85, 94, 141, 162, 165, 173
protest 54
psyche 5, 7, 9, 25, 61, 88, 127
psychoanalysis 61

Quodling, Miss 40–42, 43–44, 128, 139–141, 144–145, 148–151

Rabe, Pamela 84, 85, 113
rationality 14, 34, 73, 153, 174
razzle-dazzle 29–31, 101, 103, 111, 177
realism 2, 3, 9, 14, 30, 40, 45, 49, 61, 64, 98, 116, 137, 144, 155, 157, 164, 174, 185, 187
 anti-realism 2, 143, 185
realist 10, 30, 53, 111, 145
Relatives, The 25, 79, 82, 83, 88–89, 92, 91
religion 20, 38, 43, 59, 67, 71, 73, 118, 145, 176, 178, 182
Rimsky-Korsakov, Nikolai 20
rurality 28, 61, 67, 73
Rush, Geoffrey 138, 158, 175, 178, 183

sacrifice 40, 60
sanity/insanity 154, 155
Sarsaparilla 8, 19, 28, 114
satire 2, 6, 14, 29–30, 54, 98, 102, 123, 129, 139, 161, 165, 167, 173
Scavenger Ladies 23, 26, 59, 83, 86, 89, 90
scenography 1, 100, 105, 116, 126, 129, 131, 140, 142, 143, 146, 175, 186
Schubert, Franz 20, 67
Scribe, Eugène 186
Season at Sarsaparilla, The 4, 16, 19, 28–34, 51, 97–103, 104–108, 108–116, 152, 160, 177
self-deception 65
set design 76, 80, 91, 93, 146, 167, 186
sexuality 31, 54, 104, 163, 164, 176, 185
Seymour, Alan 2
Sharman, Jim 2, 3, 4, 7, 16, 19, 51, 53, 55, 64, 87, 98, 100, 104–108, 115, 120, 121–125, 126, 127, 128, 135, 137, 144, 152–156, 160, 164, 166, 173, 186
Shepherd on the Rocks 7, 17, 20, 67–73
Signal Driver 16, 19, 37, 55–60, 165–174
soul 5, 34, 39, 54, 67, 158
sovereignty 61, 69, 164, 169
  Indigenous 66, 169
space 8, 17, 24, 29, 31, 52, 59, 61, 76, 88, 93, 100, 111, 115, 118, 129, 131, 140, 158, 160, 169, 176
  urban 8, 28, 56, 111
spatiality 37
spirituality 10, 41, 69
staging *see* set design
Strindberg, August 7, 28, 137
subjectivity 7, 27, 75, 113
surburbia 8, 19, 28, 33, 97, 99, 103, 114, 123
surrealism 10, 23, 25, 65, 128, 129
surveillance 101, 112
Sydney Opera House 16, 19, 22, 50, 51, 104, 111, 121, 125, 130, 135, 160, 162
Sydney Theatre Company 16, 17, 19, 82, 111, 117, 130, 167

Tasker, John 17, 19, 23, 75–81, 87, 99–104, 105, 106, 108, 137, 138–139, 141
Theatre Guild (University of Adelaide) 3
theatre 1, 6, 8, 9, 12, 13, 21–22, 23, 33, 47, 53, 73, 86, 90, 104, 105, 116, 128, 145, 151, 152, 167, 183, 185

practice 1, 15, 143
technologies 1, 17, 99, 130, 160, 177
theatricality 1, 8, 11, 26, 38, 46, 48, 53, 61, 67, 84, 86, 93, 106, 108, 115, 120, 122, 126, 135, 140, 153, 161, 168, 178, 182, 186
  modern 7
  radical 20
Thomson, Brian 3, 20, 83, 121, 125, 135, 160, 162, 175, 187
time and temporality 5, 12, 14, 24, 38, 85, 89, 111, 118, 129, 147, 152, 162, 168
Tregloan, Anna 87

unconscious, the 23, 79, 127, 130
Union Hall (University of Adelaide) 19, 75, 137, 138
Union Theatre Repertory Company 3, 19, 117
Union Theatre (University of Melbourne) 3, 19
uranium mining 11, 37, 44, 52, 53, 59, 60, 159–160, 166, 173, 177

vaudeville 5, 10, 22, 24, 26–28, 58, 78, 105, 169
vernacular 32, 43, 103, 105
  Australian 32, 108, 130, 170
  dramatic 33
Vine, Carl 84, 143, 148, 175
violence 30, 45, 80, 133
  against women 25, 94, 137
  institutional 60, 154
vitalism 47, 82, 156
vulgarity 23, 26, 36

Walker, Kerry 68, 84–85, 138, 155, 167, 170, 172, 175, 178
White, Patrick 2, 6, 22, 23, 46, 48, 49, 50, 71, 73, 83, 115, 138, 139, 160, 166
  arts criticism 4, 5, 48
  early plays 6, 60
  influences 6, 49
  premieres 3, 16, 55, 67, 75, 81, 117, 138, 152, 166, 175
  rejection 3, 10, 31, 75, 81, 138, 166
whiteness 12, 22, 66, 165
Whitlam, Gough 22, 50
Williamson, David 49, 133

www.ingramcontent.com/pod-product-compliance
Lightning Source LLC
Chambersburg PA
CBHW081826230426
43668CB00017B/2386